HINDUISM AND CHRISTIANITY

Hinduism and Christianity

JOHN BROCKINGTON

St. Martin's Press New York

First published in the United States of America in 1992

Printed in Hong Kong

ISBN 0–312–08404–8

Library of Congress Cataloging-in-Publication Data
Brockington, J. L.
Hinduism and Christianity / J. L. Brockington.
p. cm.
Includes bibliographical references (p.) and index.
ISBN 0–312–08404–8
1. Hinduism—Relations—Christianity. 2. Christianity and other religions—Hinduism. I. Title. II. Series.
BR128.H5B75 1992
261.2'45—dc20 92–9658
CIP

Contents

Series Editor's Preface

A series of monographs on themes in comparative religion might possibly give rise to misgivings in the minds of some readers because of misconceptions concerning the nature of comparative religion. It is often maintained, for example, that comparisons are odious; that religious comparisons are more odious than most; and that those who are concerned with comparative religion are only comparatively religious. The aim and purpose of this series of monographs, however, is not to present a comparatively religious outlook, nor to engage in odious comparisons which could result in one religious tradition being elevated to a position of superiority over others. The intention rather is to look at what might be called 'family resemblances' that pertain in the major religious traditions of the world.

Contributors to the series were asked to examine certain basic themes in the different world religions from an empathetic standpoint – that is, so far as possible, from within the religious traditions concerned and in a way that would meet with the approval of adherents of those religions. Since Christianity is the basic religious tradition of the West it was considered appropriate that the comparative thematic approach adopted by the series should involve Christianity on each occasion, and that religious themes in the different religious traditions of the world should be related to similar themes in the Christian tradition.

An indication of this approach would be the way in which the mystery of divinity takes different forms and finds expression in a variety of ways in different religious traditions. The Tetragrammation or Logos of the Judeo-Christian tradition, for instance, might take the form of the Tao of the Chinese religious tradition, or the Brahman/Atman synthesis of the Hindu way of life, or the Kami of Shinto. A similar comparative approach involving 'family resemblances' would apply to other themes, such as creation and emanation; death and immortality; liberation and salvation; revelation and enlightenment; ethics and morality; the Kingdom of God, moksha and nirvana; and the ritual practices involved in the realisation of ultimate goals.

Naturally the choice of themes for the different monographs in the series, which include a comparison of the relation of Hinduism, Buddhism, Islam, Judaism, Japanese religions, Chinese religions, Sikhism, Zoroastrianism, primitive religions and Humanism with Christianity, would depend to a great extent on the way in which the different contributors to the series approached their subject matter. But the concept of empathy prevails throughout and the odious kinds of comparisons sometimes associated with comparative religion, albeit mistakenly, are excluded.

It is hoped that this open-ended thematic approach to comparative religion will prove helpful to the enquiring mind. In the pluralistic religious situation of today, with its great variety of religious experiences, we ought to be able to escape from the small island of our own culture, and from the ghetto mentality that would confine us to the insights of a single religious tradition. Such a mentality simply isolates us from the richness and diversity of other cultures and from the deep, spiritual insights of other religious traditions.

GLYN RICHARDS

Introduction

This volume contains a selection of themes from the two religions of Hinduism and Christianity and does not claim, therefore, to constitute a full presentation of either. The themes I have selected are intended to do justice to both religions in their central concerns but many more peripheral matters are either omitted entirely or touched on only incidentally. I have also tried to avoid the tendency to apply to other religions simply the categories applicable to Christianity, but to cover topics which are genuinely significant for both religions. The themes have been laid out in the successive chapters in an order which is aimed at revealing their interconnection, as well as involving a broad progression. The main exception is that the final chapter provides a survey of the contacts over the centuries between the two religions by way of a summary; indeed, some readers might prefer to start with this more historically oriented material. As this material demonstrates, the existence of several major religions is not of course anything new, but for most Christians in Europe or America it has not been part of their everyday experience until very recently (and not always now), whereas Hindus have for centuries had to reckon with the fact that people belonged to different communities, worshipped different deities and followed different rituals. Religious pluralism has thus long been a fact of life in India, even if on a local rather than a global scale.

It should also be recognised from the outset that both religions reveal a substantial degree of internal diversity. The style of treatment adopted is intended to illustrate this (so far as is possible within the limits of space available) and to avoid presenting a monolithic view of either. So considerable, indeed, is the diversity within Hinduism that there has been quite a scholarly debate over the last decade or two about whether it should be classified as one religion or as many. Perhaps the best way of giving some notion of what is involved without too gross oversimplification is to invoke the idea of 'family resemblance', for even if the different forms of Hinduism should be treated as separate (as 'individuals') they do have certain characteristics in common (the 'family likeness') which set them apart from other religions. On balance, I would regard Hinduism as one religion, while acknowledging that the opposite argument deserves to be taken seriously. What is perhaps not so immediately obvious is that Christianity too is very varied; it encompasses, over time and regional variations, so wide a range of theological expression, of worship and of organisation that attempts undertaken on a much larger scale than this to provide a single, yet comprehensive definition have proved inadequate.

In part the reason for this lies in the nature of religion in general, in the tension between the traditional and conservative (often rather cynically seen as especially characteristic of the religious temperament) and the radical or prophetic. Recurrently in all religions a teacher or leader has taken a 'prophetic' role and, in reflection on the tradition, has reached a more original perception of its meaning. Often such radical reshaping has led to a breakaway from the older, 'orthodox' grouping, with the emergence of a new sect, which may over a longer or shorter period develop into an entirely separate tradition. The real question is: when is such a new movement a sect within an existing tradition and when is it a separate religion? Christianity is clearly distinct from Judaism but the issue was not settled overnight and there are still contexts in which it makes most sense to talk of the Judeo-Christian tradition. How, though, do we define the results of the Reformation? Luther was after all excommunicated in 1521 and to this day the Roman Catholic Church does not in some respects recognise the Protestant Churches as churches, denying the validity of their orders and excluding their members from the Eucharist. Yet, the general consensus would surely be that Roman Catholic, Protestant and, let us not forget, Orthodox alike are all Christians. Within Hinduism, too, there have occurred movements of dissent, including a number of such 'prophetic' character which have nonetheless remained or been reabsorbed within the wider tradition. Here, one of the most extreme examples is that of the Liṅgāyat or Vīraśaiva movement, emerging in the twelfth century, which rejected the supremacy of brāhmans and the authority of the Vedas in a movement of radical social protest, but which has now become a distinct community or caste (depending on one's viewpoint) within the total Hindu social structure.

There is, however, a cluster of beliefs or doctrines which serve to give Christianity a definable core, while the same cannot really be said for Hinduism. Indeed it is possible to be a Hindu and an atheist, for belief in the existence of a deity is not an essential component of religion for all Hindus. What is far more difficult is to reject the various practices typifying different Hindu communities and yet to remain accepted as a Hindu. On the other hand, the absence in many forms of Hinduism of a centralised authority, such as is typical of much of Christianity, makes any categoric statements dubious. This is not to say that different types of religious leaders and centres of religious authority are non-existent but that their influence is not universal. Temples are significant foci and in some of the major ones their priests cater for worshippers and pilgrims from a wide area, providing rituals of some complexity, while in many local shrines the *pūjāri,* who is more of a shrine attendant than a priest and often belongs to a lower caste, has only modest ritual functions and little standing in the community. Others with religious authority include renouncers, the leaders of religious communities and more particularly the ritual specialists who conduct the life-cycle rituals. This diversity of religious authority is in part a reflection of the fact that the individual's religious duties, his *dharma,* are centred on his caste and his family and thus Hinduism is as much a way of life as a belief system and not infrequently more so. In addition, the sheer size of India and the diversity of its regions are important features. Each region or state has a distinct historical experience and consequently a religious composition that is peculiar to itself.

The selection of themes to be treated is also intended to provide a reasonable balance between doctrine and practice. Many studies of Christianity tend to concentrate on the doctrinal side and conversely there is a tendency for much that is written on Hinduism to focus mainly on the area of practice. This has led on occasion to rather unbalanced comparisons between the two, usually to the detriment of Hinduism. There is a real need to compare like with like, at all levels, not only by greater care in discriminating between theory and practice but also by greater awareness of the context, whether social or historical, in every case.

Since the treatment is thematic and only to a limited extent chronological within a given theme, dates have been included so far as practicable to provide a reminder to the reader of the process of historical development which is so important for a complete understanding of any religion. These dates are not necessarily always based on very firm evidence and the reader is asked to accept them, despite any lack of precision, as a useful pointer to the period and thus to the stage of development to which the individual or movement concerned belongs. Where there is an inherent improbability about some aspect of the dates given (most often in the lifespan of an individual) this has generally been signalled by adding some such word as 'traditionally'. Unless otherwise indicated, dates are in years of the Christian era and dates originally expressed in one or another of the several eras used at various periods in India have been converted to that (but minor discrepancies due to the fact that the year usually begins with the month corresponding to March-April have been ignored).

It is assumed that the reader will already have at least some acquaintance with the basic features of both religions, such as could be gained by reading a general introduction to either (and a certain number of these are included in the Bibliography). It is not expected, however, that this acquaintance will be such that a great deal of detail is actively in the reader's memory and so a fair amount of incidental or supporting information is included. On the assumption that in most cases the reader will be rather less familiar with Hinduism, description of related material is somewhat fuller for that religion and treatment of the themes normally begins with it, although there is also quite an intermingling of the material as part of the process of comparison.

A certain number of technical terms in both Sanskrit and Greek have been retained but a definition of their meaning has been provided on their first occurrence (and subsequently, if appropriate); there is therefore no separate glossary, since these definitions are accessible through the Index. For such terms, and names, in Hinduism I have adopted the standard transliteration for Sanskrit, the language from which most come (and are then taken over virtually unchanged into the modern Indian languages). Although this may appear slightly complex at first, it means that each sound has only one representation and so the pronounciation is certain (it will also be found in almost any other scholarly treatment of Hinduism to which the reader may turn). Long vowels are distinguished from short by the macron (ā), except that *e*, *ai*, *o* and *au* are regularly long, being diphthongs in origin; *ṛ* represents vocalic r (a sort of purring sound). The letter *h* always indicates aspiration even in such combinations as *th* and *ph* (pronounced roughly as in *coathook* and *uphill*), and *c* is always pronounced as in the Italian *cinquecento* (or like the *ch* in English *church*, but in Sanskrit *ch* is the aspirated form of *c*). A dot below the letter distinguishes retroflex consonants, pronounced with the tongue far back in the mouth, from the dentals (*t, th, d, dh, n*) made with the tongue against the teeth. Of the three sibilants, *s* is pronounced as in English *sit*, while *ś* and *ṣ* represent slightly differing sounds, both close to *sh*. In Hindi and other North Indian languages a final short *a* at the end of a word here given in its original Sanskrit form is not in fact pronounced, and so, for example, Rāma is now said in these languages as Rām and *āśrama* as *āśram*.

It remains, in conclusion, for me to make various acknowledgements. I should like to express my appreciation to Glyn Richards for inviting me to contribute this volume to the series. I am also indebted to Macmillan's reader and to Professor J. P. Mackey for helpful comments, which I should no doubt have taken into account more fully than I have done. In particular, I am indebted to my wife, Mary, who once again has compiled the Index, as well as having contributed immensely to the volume in many other ways.

JOHN BROCKINGTON

1

The Nature of the Divine

There are two basic ways in which the ultimate reality which is the goal of religion may be viewed. One is the concept of a deity, of God, in which this ultimate reality is seen as personal; the other is the concept of the Absolute, in which it is seen as impersonal. It is often thought that these two different ways of thinking are the Christian and the Hindu views respectively, but this is to paint too simple a picture. Not only are there occasional trends within Christian thought which make use of the idea of the Godhead as transcending the personality of the Trinity, but the concept of Brahman, though widely current in more intellectual forms of Hinduism, is by no means as important at the more popular level as the concept of Īśvara, the supreme deity conceived personally and so as an object of devotion.

In addition, within the context of worship, there is the tendency to view Christianity as monotheistic and Hinduism as polytheistic. This results in effect from the application of a double standard, whereby Christianity is judged at the level of its doctrinal formulations and Hinduism is judged by its day-to-day practice. If both were judged at the same level, the distinction would not seem nearly as clear-cut. Even at the level of doctrine, the notion of the Trinity is often seen by non-Christians as incompatible with monotheism; this is particularly true, of course, of Muslims but it is a view that occurs among Hindu apologists as well. If we define the deity as the highest or deepest principle of existence, the ultimate reality, then most Hindus are monotheists, since in this sense they believe in only one absolute or one deity. But if we understand the deity as whatever is venerated through invocation, prayer or offering, then the cult of the saints which is general in Roman Catholic and Orthodox communities would make of many Christians as much polytheists as those Hindus who worship the many minor powers (distinguished as *devas* from the one supreme deity as *īśvara*) that operate at a comparatively mundane level. At a rather deeper level, again, there are the issues of the relationship of transcendence and immanence in the nature of the divine, of the nature and purpose of creation, of monistic and dualistic views (and of their precise definition) and so on, in all of which the lines of demarcation are drawn as much within the two religions as between them.

Let us begin with the understanding of the divine in terms of an impersonal absolute. This emerges within Hinduism by the end of the Vedic period as the culmination of trends away from the plurality of deities praised in the hymns of the Vedas and towards greater emphasis on the power of the ritual. However, even in the earliest levels of the Vedic hymns (from perhaps 1200 B.C. onwards) we may note the significance of the principle of *ṛta,* which Varuṇa superintends. As the guardian of *ṛta,* the principle of order in the cosmos in both its natural and its moral aspects, Varuṇa is the sovereign ruler of gods and men and the punisher of sin. This cosmic order, *ṛta,* with which men's actions here on earth should be in accord, is nevertheless not fully known to men, who may therefore offend Varuṇa unwittingly, but even so it constitutes a principle felt in some sense to underlie the power of the gods themselves. There is, though, a clear shift of attitudes by the end of the period of the Vedic hymns.

On the one hand, dissatisfaction with the existing pantheon led to a search for some underlying principle or power operating through it, or in some of the speculative hymns of the relatively late tenth book of the *Ṛgveda* and of the *Atharvaveda* more specifically to attempts at establishing the origin of the cosmos in terms of a first cause. On the other hand, the emphasis on the efficacy of ritual action characteristic of the Brāhmaṇas (the next stage of the Vedic literature following the hymns, belonging to the first half of the first millennium B.C.) leads to exaltation of the sacred power, *brahman,* as somehow operative universally. Already in the *Atharvaveda* the term *brahman* is used both to denote the incantations contained in that Veda and to name the universal principle, the ultimate cosmic power, thereby invoked. In the Brāhmaṇas, which constitute the next stage of the Vedic literature and which, as their very name suggests, deal with and expound *brahman,* the sacred power above all now manifested in the sacrificial ritual, the sacrifice in effect takes over from the gods as the centre of the religion. Even earlier, there had been a notion that the world was not just due to a chance encounter of elements but was governed by an objective order, intrinsic to the cosmos, of which the gods were only the guardians. In the Brāhmaṇas, these fundamental laws of the universe came increasingly to be identified with the laws of sacrifice and so, since the sacrifice was considered to maintain the world in existence, the sacred power residing in the sacrificial ritual comes to be regarded as the power underlying the universe. In the Upaniṣads (perhaps eighth to third centuries B.C.), which complete but also supersede the Brāhmaṇas in their conceptualisations, speculation then centred on the nature and identity of this sacred power, Brahman. This speculation, which is in origin ritually based, then leads to the understanding that the world has Brahman as its inner essence and emanates from Brahman, which is therefore the underlying reality behind everything.

Such an understanding is clearly much more than that of a first cause (which does, however, continue to be one component in an understanding of Brahman) but it could be seen in basically material or mechanical terms, and there are traces of such an attitude in some of the early speculations in the Upaniṣads, which identify Brahman either as food or as breath or as both. However, the thinkers whose ideas are recorded for us in the Upaniṣads were also in greater or lesser measure dissatisfied with the externals of the ritually-centred religion of the Brāhmaṇas and so looked inwards to explore the concept of the *ātman*, the permanent self or soul within, which also could be equated with the breath. Systems of correspondence had been a central aspect of the way in which the Brāhmaṇas had sought to extend mankind's control through the sacrifice over the whole of the cosmos. It is thus natural and indeed a logical outcome of the older ways of thinking that Upaniṣadic thinkers now identify the basic principle in man, the *ātman*, with the basic principle of the cosmos, Brahman. Yet such an identification has profound implications for the nature of both, which the Upaniṣads themselves only begin to explore. It means, for one thing, that Brahman can no longer be seen as in any sense material and, for another, that Brahman is impersonal not in the sense of being devoid of personality or neuter but in the sense of being supra-personal or perhaps, to use Paul Tillich's term, transpersonal (although the equation of Brahman with *ātman* is a complex issue on which more will be said at other points).

Virtually all of the major elements in the understanding of Brahman can be found in the Upaniṣads but, before we survey some of them, it is as well to remember that there are many speculations put forward in the Upaniṣads and that they certainly do not put forward the single coherent viewpoint which later Hinduism –

and especially the Vedānta system – sees in them. In the sixth chapter of the *Chāndogya Upaniṣad* (perhaps eighth century B.C.), the great sage Uddālaka instructs his son Śvetaketu in the identity of *ātman* and Brahman. He first declares through many examples that individual objects are only the matter of which they are made and that only formless matter is real. He then challenges one of the hymns of the *Ṛgveda* (10.72), which had asserted the priority of non-being over being, by declaring that originally there was being, *sat*, alone and denying on the grounds of logic that existence could come out of non-existence (thus ruling out the possibility of creation *ex nihilo*, as is generally the case within Hinduism, which sees the origin of the cosmos rather in the imposing of order onto chaos); it is interesting to compare with this the statement by St Thomas Aquinas (c.1225–1274) that 'being' is the most proper name of God, since it is the least limiting of terms, whereas every other name adds some kind of form or limitation. In the next two sections Uddālaka expounds this 'being' or *sat* as the essence of the cosmos, producing the three basic elements (fire, water and earth), and then as the essence of man. The whole of the second half of this chapter is taken up with a series of examples, mostly drawn from the natural world, to illustrate this insight, each of which ends with Uddālaka's claim to his son 'You are that' (*tat tvam asi*); Uddālaka particularly identifies this 'being' with the *ātman* and with truth (*satya*, that which is real or true, since it exists) and he does not actually use the name Brahman, although the Advaita Vedānta later confidently makes the equation. In the *Taittirīya Upaniṣad* (2.1.1) there occurs the definition of Brahman as truth, knowledge and infinity, which is taken up in the Advaita Vedānta system to provide the definition of Brahman as *saccidānanda* (*sat* 'being', *cit* 'consciousness' and *ānanda* 'bliss'). On the other hand, the *Kena Upaniṣad* emphasises the ineffability of the all-pervasive Brahman: 'He who thinks it not thinks it, he who thinks it knows it not; it is not understood by those who know and known by those who do not know' (2.3). Even more emphatically, the older *Bṛhadāraṇyaka Upaniṣad* affirms at several points that Brahman is *neti neti*, 'not thus, not thus'.

It is this emphasis on the ineffability of Brahman that we see most clearly in Śaṅkara (traditionally 788–820), who is generally regarded as the founder of the Advaita ('non-dual', hence monistic) school of the Vedānta, which insists on Brahman as the sole reality and denies any duality. His most important work, a commentary on the *Brahmasūtra* (a synthesising summary of the Upaniṣads), makes use of an exegetical device deriving ultimately from the Madhyamaka school of Buddhism, the theory of the two levels of truth. According to this, on the lower level of conventional reality, the world exists and evolves under the control of Īśvara, the personal deity already recognised in some Upaniṣads, but on the higher level of ultimate reality the whole world is unreal and Brahman alone exists in reality. The plurality and finitude of entities in the phenomenal world are illusory, since everything is essentially identical with Brahman, the Absolute; for this illusion Śaṅkara uses the term *māyā* which originally meant the creative power of the Vedic gods, with perhaps some suggestion that, because it was beyond man's comprehension, it could be deceptive, but neither in the Vedas nor in most of later Hinduism does it indicate the unreality of the world as it does for Advaita Vedānta. This illusion (*māyā*) is sustained by our ignorance (*avidyā*) or more exactly our error in perceiving something other than Brahman in these phenomena. Whenever we perceive something, it is because there is something there but that something is not what we think but only Brahman. Śaṅkara is notably averse to defining the nature of *avidyā* or where it resides, unlike some of his followers, and indeed for him its nature is indescribable, for if it were real Brahman would not then be the sole reality whereas if it were totally unreal we should not be entrapped by it.

Śaṅkara also makes use of this concept of indescribability or inexplicability in relation to causation, where the acceptance of real change would again compromise the sole reality of Brahman. This is entirely consistent with the main thrust of his thinking, which is centred on Brahman as the sole reality, and his refusal to assign any permanent reality to the world should be seen rather as an affirmation of the total and absolute reality of Brahman, with which in its essential nature the *ātman* is identical. Just as the world is a combination of appearance and reality, of *māyā* and Brahman, so too is the individual self, which is real in so far as it is *ātman* and thus Brahman but unreal in so far as it is finite and limited by its individuality. The truly transcendent is experienced in pure selfhood, unlimited by interaction with finite objects, whereas mundane existence is a distorted world of unreality when compared with the experience of the transcendent subject. Thus Śaṅkara begins his *Brahmasūtra* commentary with the declaration that to confuse subjective with objective existence is to confuse darkness with light.

One of Śaṅkara's favourite texts is the Upaniṣadic dictum 'you are that', with which Uddālaka inculcated the identity of being, *sat*, and the *ātman*; he argues that the identity of 'you' and 'that' lies in the removal of the incompatible elements of individuality and transcendence to reveal the pure consciousness which is the ground of both. On the whole, however, Śaṅkara is very hesitant about making any positive statements about Brahman, regarding all definition as limitation and so as being illegitimate. Thus, he avoids, at least in his major works, the well known formulation of later Advaita that Brahman is being, consciousness and bliss (*saccidānanda*). Indeed, when he comments on the passage in the *Taittirīya Upaniṣad* which gave rise to this, he elaborates instead a theory of indication by which such statements point to rather than define Brahman, just as Thomas Aquinas develops his theory of analogy to avoid the danger of suggesting that the unseen reality of the deity is exactly like the symbol. Even when he speaks of Brahman as the 'real of the real' (*satyasya satyam*, cf. the *ens realissimum* of scholastic theology), Śaṅkara harks back to the *Bṛhadāraṇyaka Upaniṣad's* 'not thus, not thus' to support his stress on the undefinability of Brahman. The unqualified (*nirguṇa*) Brahman is precisely that transcendent state of being about which nothing can meaningfully be said. Nevertheless, Brahman is not just some abstract philosophical postulate but rather the goal of all human endeavour, for to realise existentially the identity of oneself with Brahman is to achieve release (*mokṣa*), the supreme aim of developed Hinduism.

While the concept of Brahman as the ultimate reality (though not as the sole reality) is widely accepted in Hinduism even by the theistic strands, which necessarily extensively reinterpret it, in Christianity the idea of God as personal has been so strong that there is very little evidence of the impersonal aspect. Nevertheless, the concept of the Godhead, which sums up and in a sense transcends the three persons of the Trinity, is one which has been found useful by some. Already in the sixth century Dionysius, the pseudo-Areopagite, talks of the 'superessential' Godhead, which surpasses all thought and conjecture, and elaborates three ways of knowing God: the way of affirmation, the way of negation and the way of transcendence. Certain mystics have preferred to use the term Godhead in attempting to give expression to their experience; the most famous example is no doubt the mediæval German Dominican, Meister Eckhart (1260–1328?), who speaks of 'the silent void of the Godhead', but another is his student, Heinrich Suso (c.1295–1366), who talks about the soul plunging into the abyss of the Godhead. It is notable, of course, that this preference is linked with their perception of the mystical experience as unitive, a feature which clearly has analogies with the understanding of the *ātman*-Brahman relationship in Advaita Vedānta, but this is a point that will be taken up in Chapter 5.

The understanding of the ultimate as personal is in fact at least as typical of Hinduism as the impersonal view and indeed in terms of numbers holding it has almost certainly been the predominant view at all periods of the religion. Even in the Upaniṣads, which are so often seen as the champions of the concept of Brahman, we find at a slightly later stage the emergence of the concept of Īśvara, 'the Lord', as a generic term for the supreme deity. This is clearly seen in the *Īśa Upaniṣad*, which takes its name (another form from the same root as Īśvara) from its opening word, 'enveloped by the Lord' (*īśāvāsya*), a programmatic statement of its purpose; in a mere eighteen verses it teaches the essential unity of the deity and the world, while emphasising the union of the contemplative and active sides of life. Similarly, the *Śvetāśvatara Upaniṣad* is concerned to establish the existence and supremacy of the Lord, supporting its claims by quoting and reinterpreting older Vedic texts to show that the many gods (*devas*) of the Vedic hymns are all aspects of this great Lord. It thus proclaims a personal deity as originator of the cosmos and names him as Rudra or Śiva, in so doing giving a particular identity to the general concept. On the relationship between the deity and the cosmos it is less consistent, since some of its images suggest that nature or matter is a part of the deity himself while others suggest a dualistic separation of spirit and matter; there is a long history within Hinduism of controversy over this point. However, it is quite clear that the personal deity transcends both the perishable and the imperishable which together constitute Brahman. Another Upaniṣad, the *Mahānārāyaṇa Upaniṣad*, similarly quotes from older Vedic literature to support its belief in a personal supreme deity (and indeed uses several of the same quotations) but in this text this Īśvara is identified with Nārāyaṇa, one of the names of Viṣṇu.

The mythology and the cults of these two deities, Viṣṇu and Śiva, developed on the whole in more popular milieux over the next several centuries and these early developments are recorded for us, in so far as we can still trace them, in the two great Sanskrit epics, the *Mahābhārata* and the *Rāmāyaṇa*, and in earlier parts of the Purāṇas, the compendia of popular Hinduism produced between the fourth and about the twelfth centuries. In due course, however, definite theological systems evolved, which then address themselves, among other tasks, to analysing the nature of the deity and to defining the relationship between Brahman and Īśvara. In varying degrees all are influenced by Śaṅkara's Advaita, despite being basically opposed to his most fundamental insight. Perhaps the earliest of them is that known as Kashmir Śaivism or the Trika system, which is no later than the beginning of the ninth century, although its origins probably lie considerably further back in time and its peak came at the end of the tenth century in the person of Abhinavagupta. It puts forward a monistic viewpoint with analogies to Advaita Vedānta. Śiva is the *ātman* residing in all beings and objects individually as well as in the universe as a whole, for reality is essentially unitary and has the nature of pure consciousness. Śiva as the supreme reality is the experiencing principle as distinct from what is experienced, whose essence is pure consciousness; he is eternal and immutable in his own nature but underlies the universe as *ātman*, immanent through his creative energy (*śakti*), which is often personified as his consort. Creation is simply the self-projection of consciousness which is essentially free but has the choice both to limit itself by projecting other entities or to reabsorb them. Through error (*māyā*), objects which owe their existence to consciousness appear as distinct from it, thus forfeiting its omniscience, just as the limitation involved removes the omnipotence. The manifestation of the world is thus the expression of Śiva and is not unreal as in Advaita, but only an aspect of the ultimate reality which is Śiva. Although Śiva is eternal and remains unaffected by these appearances, he conceals himself through *māyā* and so the bondage of selves results from ignorance of reality, and continuous recognition of reality – of man's identity with Śiva – brings release.

By contrast with the decided monistic strand in Kashmir Śaivism, the Śaiva Siddhānta system, originating at the opposite end of India in the twelfth century, reveals little influence from Advaita in its understanding of Śiva. For if Śiva is the supreme deity, stainless and pure, although, since he transcends all conceptualisation, he cannot be known except through his grace and cannot be expressed by any image or symbol. Unlike most Hindu traditions, the Śaiva Siddhānta regards Śiva's activity as definitely purposive, with his aspect as Naṭarāja, Lord of the Dance (the rhythm of the cosmos), symbolising his threefold activity in creating, maintaining and ultimately dissolving the cosmos as the means for granting his grace and so enabling his worshippers finally to enter into union with him. The immanence of Śiva is emphasised both in this activity in relation to the cosmos and in the mystical union of the soul with him, but his transcendence is also stressed in the soul's realisation of its total dependence on Śiva. Śiva is immanent as his creative power (*śakti*), through which he is the material cause of the universe, but transcendent as Śiva, the efficient cause; ultimately, however, there is no distinction between Śiva and his *śakti*.

Among the various Vaiṣṇava schools, that of Rāmānuja (traditionally 1017–1137) and his followers is the one most strongly influenced by Advaita Vedānta; indeed, in its theological or philosophical dimension it is termed Viśiṣṭādvaita Vedānta (the qualified non-dual Vedānta), while as a religious community it is known as the Śrīvaiṣṇava movement. Rāmānuja seeks to integrate a Vedānta standpoint (though not a purely Advaita one) with devotion to Īśvara, who for him is Nārāyaṇa or Viṣṇu. He differs from Śaṅkara in ascribing a definite and ultimately valid reality to the world and its two constituents of matter (*prakṛti*) and souls (*ātman*). Rāmānuja gives clear expression to this in his doctrine that the deity stands to the world of *ātman* and *prakṛti* in the relationship of a soul to the body which forms its attribute, arguing that Īśvara is real and independent but that souls are also real though wholly dependent on Īśvara. Inevitably, to render this workable, Rāmānuja has to adopt a broad definition of a body as anything that can be controlled by and is subordinate to a conscious *ātman*. As the body of Īśvara, the world is his instrument and also part of his self-expression; equally, just as the soul controls its own body, so Īśvara is the inner controller of individual souls. This designation as the inner controller had been used in the Upaniṣads to describe Brahman in relation to *ātman*, and its use here by Rāmānuja is part of his claim that Īśvara is the full and complete expression of the impersonal absolute, Brahman, which is basically just a philosophical abstraction and as such falls far short of the fullness of the deity.

The self-body analogy as a whole also serves to differentiate

Īśvara from his dependent bodily parts and to explain how *ātman* and *prakṛti,* since they constitute the body of Īśvara, function to promote the realisation of Brahman or Īśvara. It highlights the inseparable and organic relationship between Īśvara and the world by stressing the total dependence of the world on the will of the deity. Rāmānuja also uses the analogy to elucidate the all-inclusive nature of the deity, affirming both the reality of the world and of individual selves and its subordination to the divine purpose which, in common with most Vaiṣṇavas, Rāmānuja defines in terms of *līlā,* which literally means 'play' or 'sport' but here denotes rather the deity's self-expression, for he is unconstrained by anything outside his own spontaneously creative nature. This model to express the deity's freedom from any constraints to his activity has also been employed in the Christian context by the contemporary theologian Jürgen Moltmann (b. 1926), who has characterised God's relationship to his creation as a game played out of 'delight', and not either from necessity or on a whim.

Were it not that Rāmānuja sees this relationship in at least quasi-physical terms, there would also be some analogy with St Paul's use of the image of the Church as the Body of Christ, when he talks of Christians as being incorporated in Christ and envisages the Christian community as a harmoniously co-ordinated organism, even regarding Christ as the living body of which Christians are the limbs. One area of agreement, though, is that this image or analogy points to the deity as an inclusive personality, personal certainly but transcending our ordinary categories. Most strikingly, however, Moltmann regards the crucifixion as God opening his being to include within himself the whole of human history; all of human history is thus taken up into this 'history of God' so that he may become 'all in all' in an eschatological 'panentheism',[1] for the term 'panentheism' is perhaps the simplest definition of the implications of Rāmānuja's soul-body analogy.

Far from defining the deity in purely negative terms, Rāmānuja emphasises the fullness of the deity's perfections. Though beyond mankind's reach in the fullness of his divinity, Viṣṇu is full of grace and love for his creation. He has therefore made himself accessible to his devotees by descending into the world in a form like theirs (the doctrine of *avatāra*) and his six beautiful qualities of knowledge, strength, sovereignty, immutability, power and splendour, which reflect his transcendence, are balanced by another group of his auspicious qualities of compassion, graciousness, forgiveness and generosity, reflecting his accessibility to his worshippers. The statement that Brahman is *nirguṇa* means for Rāmānuja that the deity is devoid of any kind of imperfection, not that he is essentially beyond any qualification; it is to acknowledge that even scriptural descriptions do not exhaust the deity's perfections, while accepting that they are reliable so far as they go. In his absolute form Viṣṇu is knowledge and bliss, antagonistic to all evil and comprising all that is good. Indeed, it it notable how vigorously Rāmānuja seeks to distance the deity from all evil, including suffering, by emphasising that it is only the divine body, not the highest self, that is qualified by the world.

In his more philosophical works Rāmānuja concentrates entirely on Īśvara, who for him is of course Viṣṇu or Nārāyaṇa, but in his more devotional works he also has a place for Śrī, Viṣṇu's consort, who had earlier been an important figure for the Pāñcarātra school (an older Vaiṣṇava movement already attested in the *Mahābhārata* and prominent between the fifth and tenth centuries). One of its texts propounds a cosmogony in which Lakṣmī (= Śrī) as Viṣṇu's energy projects the world, which is therefore part not of Viṣṇu but of Lakṣmī, who is both identical with him and yet distinct. The paradox is left unresolved within the Pāñcarātra system but the Śrīvaiṣṇava movement established by Rāmānuja, which inherited many of its ideas, does address the issue (and indeed it was one of the issues leading to the subsequent split into two subschools). In both, though, the role of Śrī is to mediate between the worshipper and Viṣṇu through her intimacy with him. The relational aspect which this introduces into thinking about the deity is obviously particularly important in the *bhakti* or devotional context, although in fact it is a standard notion for Hindu deities to be provided with consorts (part of the more anthropomorphic attitude to the deities generally apparent); the husband-wife model produces certain differences of attitude on the part of the worshipper compared with the father-son relational model found in the Christian Trinity. Within the Judeo-Christian tradition the female element was deliberately excluded to avoid any hint of goddess-worship; yet it could not be kept out entirely and so resurfaced in Judaism in the personifying of Wisdom and in Christianity in the honour accorded to Mary as the chaste mother (not wife) of God.

For Madhva (probably 1198–1278), however, even Rāmānuja's position is suspect as too closely involving the deity with the world, while he regards the Advaita Vedānta with abhorrence; he propounds a Dvaita ('dualist') Vedānta. He claims that the Vedas describe Brahman, that is the deity, as full of infinite perfections and so he dismisses as purely figurative any monistic passages in the Upaniṣads. Equally, he considers that Viṣṇu, individual souls and matter (*prakṛti*) are eternally and entirely distinct. He thus emphatically rejects any suggestion that the world is a mere illusion or emanation of the deity and propounds an absolute dualism, in which he insists on a total distinction between inert matter and conscious spirit. The motive for Madhva's attitude is clearly revealed in his claim that the Advaita view destroys the purpose of the Vedas by propounding a goal in which everything vanishes and that a deity who must be surpassed is no deity.

Later figures in the Vaiṣṇava tradition tend to revert to a position closer to that of Rāmānuja, though not generally argued with such sophistication. Within the movement centred on the charismatic figure of Caitanya (1486–1533), for instance, Jīva Gosvāmin (c.1523–1618) declares simply that there are three aspects of ultimate reality: Brahman, the Supreme Self (*paramātman*) and Bhagavat. Brahman as the unqualified, undifferentiated absolute of the philosophers is the least significant and is only an incomplete manifestation of the infinitely qualified Bhagavat, who is the fullest, personal expression of the divine, while the Supreme Self is an intermediate aspect of the deity, entering into relationship with individual selves and with nature. The movement founded by Vallabha (1479–1531) attempts somewhat naïvely on its doctrinal side to outdo Śaṅkara by claiming the title Śuddhādvaita ('pure non-dualism') on the grounds that Śaṅkara's Advaita is flawed by its acceptance of *māyā* as a second to Brahman. Vallabha asserts instead that the whole world is real and is Brahman (which for him is another name for Kṛṣṇa), with individual souls and matter having no separate existence from Brahman. Being, consciousness and bliss (*saccidānanda*) are not just qualities of but actually are Brahman; when Brahman conceals part of himself by his power of *māyā* to produce the world, only the being aspect of Brahman is present, and similarly individual selves manifest only the being and consciousness aspects, with the bliss aspect still concealed. The real heart of both these movements lay in their fervent emotional devotion to the deity Kṛṣṇa, a form of Viṣṇu, and in their belief that surrender to him would prompt his grace (*prasāda*). Partly in reaction to such attitudes typical of Vaiṣṇava *bhakti* there also emerged in North India the *sant* tradition, also called *nirguṇa bhakti* – a name which clearly expresses its difference of emphasis, since it stresses direct worship of the supreme deity in his unqualified (*nirguṇa*) form as well as the demanding and strenuous nature of the path of spiritual progress. With such emphasis on the directness of the relationship to the deity there is also apparent, especially in the figure of Kabīr (traditionally 1398–1518 but probably in the first half of the fifteenth century), an uncompromising – one might almost say a Puritan – rejection of the use of images and of anything that is external or mechanical in religion, in favour of a purely inner experience, when the deity may reveal himself by his grace within the individual soul. Although Kabīr describes the goal as union in monistic terms originating from Advaita, his overall position is monotheistic, though highly abstract.

Within Christianity the monotheistic rather than the monistic emphasis has, of course, been dominant, although recognition of divine transcendence has led to the same kinds of statement about God being beyond definition recurring throughout the history of the church. The combination of this insight with the revelation of God's nature in Christ is encapsulated in the words: 'No one has ever seen God; God's only Son, he who is nearest to the Father's heart, has made him known' (John 1.18). Among the Greek Fathers, Clement of Alexandria (Titus Flavius Clemens, c.150–215) declares: 'The deity is without form and nameless. Although we ascribe names, they are not to be taken in their strict meaning; when we call him one, good, mind, existence, Father, God, Creator or Lord, we are not conferring a name on him. Being unable to do more, we use these appellations of honour in order that our thought may have something to rest on' (*Stromata* 5.12). St Thomas Aquinas, in the thirteenth century, talks in his great *Summa Theologiae* of God as absolutely without duality, without composition of any sort, whether of matter and form, or substance and attribute, or even essence and existence, since there is nothing that can limit or qualify him (1.3.1–8).

Nevertheless, God is conceived of in personal terms, though not properly speaking in anthropomorphic terms (unlike the frequently anthropomorphic treatment of Viṣṇu or Śiva in Hinduism). His definition as personal implies that values which we attach to the personal at a human level have a correlate in the divine nature. Since the belief in a personal God is at the heart of traditional Christian doctrine, it is both surprising and revealing that a recent survey found that two-fifths of the population in Britain conceive of God as some sort of spirit or life force, under one-third believe in a personal God, one-fifth are unsure, and a further 10 per cent profess no belief in either.[2] In particular, by referring to God the Father, Christians assert that relationships matter ultimately, that God the Father relates to the Son through the love personified in the Holy Spirit. Yet there is no question of there being three gods; this is the internal self-differentiation of the one deity. There is a unity of essence but this one essence is shared equally by three persons, and the three are joined in a total harmony of will and being, which goes far beyond the unity between individuals that we can observe at the human level. The Trinity has therefore emerged as the orthodox formulation of the nature of God in the fullness of his being.

Probably the clearest evidence for the doctrine of the Trinity within the New Testament is found in St John's Gospel. In its opening verse there is expressed, in the terminology of God and the Word (Λόγος), what orthodox Christian thought has always understood as the eternal relationship between Father and Son, while towards the end Jesus tells his disciples 'I will ask the Father, and he will give you another to be your advocate, who will be with you for ever – the Spirit of truth' (14:16–17, cf. 14:26) and 'When the advocate has come, whom I shall send you from the Father – the Spirit of truth that issues from the Father – he will bear witness to me' (15:26). There are, of course, other passages that may be pointed to. The account of the baptism of Jesus is a particularly obvious one, involving as it does the presence and activity of all three persons of the Trinity, though without any attempt to explain their precise relationship (Matthew 4:13–17, Mark 1:9–11, Luke 3:21–2, cf. John 1:32–4).[3] On the other hand, there are other passages which tend to minimise the distinctions and suggest that the three persons are merely different aspects of the divine activity. For St Paul in particular there is a functional identity between the Spirit and the risen Lord Jesus in his own experience and that of other Christians and at times he seems almost to equate the Spirit and Christ in a way that could be interpreted as meaning that the Spirit is simply another manifestation of the Son.[4] The emphasis in the Synoptic Gospels on the role of the Spirit in Jesus's life and ministry clearly puts a rather different slant on the relationship. While it is fair enough to say that Christology is at the centre of New Testament ideas, the connection between Jesus and the Spirit is significant enough to require its being taken into account.

Nevertheless, much of the early doctrinal controversy within the church centred inevitably on the Incarnation and the precise nature of the relationship between Father and Son. Some of these issues will therefore be outlined in the next chapter but they also have implications for the doctrine of the Trinity, as various scholars realised. Origen (c.185–254), for example, has important points to make. He recognised the centrality of the issue of the internal relations of the persons of the Trinity, which must be eternal; thus, the Incarnation must re-enact within time a generation of the Son which lay beyond the temporal. He also focused attention on the question of how the person and the work of the three persons of the Godhead were connected, in effect whether the generation of the Son and the procession of the Spirit were logically cause or effect of their redemptive function.

After the recognition of the church by the Eastern Roman Empire in the fourth century, the creed first formulated at the first Ecumenical Council of Nicaea in 325 was further worked over and an agreed text was adopted at the second Ecumenical Council at Constantinople in 381; this creed, reaffirmed at the third and fourth councils (at Ephesus and Chalcedon in 431 and 451) and usually known as the Nicene Creed, became the official creed of the church, being accepted in both East and West.[5] Nevertheless, it was to become a major doctrinal issue in the split between the Orthodox and the Roman Catholic churches, with the controversy centring on the Filioque ('and from the son') clause, which the Western bishops insisted should be (indeed claimed had always been) part of the creed to express the belief that the Holy Spirit proceeded from the Father and the Son, whereas the Eastern bishops (taking their stand on John 15:26) denied that it was part of the agreed creed. There was not in fact a basic disagreement on the doctrine; both sides recognised that in God there are three persons or hypostases but a single essence or nature, but, while the East characteristically emphasised the distinctiveness of the three persons, the West stressed the oneness of the shared divine nature.

In more modern times the doctrine of the Trinity has often been rather put to one side, especially in more popular religious belief. There is a sense in which an emphasis on the Son at the expense of the other two persons, which has perhaps been the main trend, tends towards a kind of Christian humanism, whereas an overemphasis on the Father, more apparent at certain earlier periods, can lead to a legalistic morality by stressing God's justice and wrath, and overemphasis on the Spirit can lead to a breakdown of the church structure (conversely underemphasis on the Spirit can lead to the church becoming mechanical and bureaucratic). Already by the beginning of the nineteenth century Friedrich Schleiermacher (1768–1834) in his major work, *Der christliche Glaube* (1821–2), was presenting a liberal view of Christianity and practically ignoring the doctrine of the Trinity, which he treats as an incidental rationalisation of the Christian experience of God. By contrast, Karl Barth (1886–1968) opens his massive work, *Die kirchliche Dogmatik* (1932–67), with his treatment of the Trinity and clearly regards it as fundamental to the Christian faith.

God is also centrally affirmed as the Creator. Creation is the work of the whole Trinity; the Credo calls the Father 'creator of heaven and earth', the Son 'he through whom all things were made' and the Holy Spirit 'the creator of life.' According to St Basil the Great (c.330–79), the Father is the primordial cause of all that is created, the Son is the operative cause and the Spirit is the perfecting cause. Recognition that the self-sufficiency of God within himself is affirmed by the doctrine of the Trinity helps to explain how creation, though involving all three persons of the Trinity, was not necessary for God's own existence or happiness (this contrasts, we may note, with Rāmānuja's view that as the body of Īśvara the world is a part of his self-expression). Greek philosophy saw creation, or the formation of the cosmos, as the imposition of order on some kind of pre-existing chaos or unformed matter; this view is quite similar to the usual Hindu idea, for κόσμος literally means 'order', and we have noted above the importance of *ṛta* in the Vedas.

Partly at least to counter the Greek position, Christian theology developed an understanding of the creative act expressed in the doctrine of creation *ex nihilo*: here, though, there is no pre-existent matter of any sort and the world derives totally from God, to whom it owes everything including its existence. This is not wholly reconcilable with the understanding of the goodness of God which would exclude anything evil as being opposed to him, traditionally personified as the Devil or Satan; the powers of goodness are with God and evil is linked with the Devil. If God is truly creator, then he must be responsible for every facet of the world's existence. The orthodox response to this, right from the start of the Judeo-Christian tradition, has been to ascribe the origin of evil to a rebellion against God, expressed both mythologically in the story of Adam and Eve and in the fall of Lucifer and theologically in the doctrine of original sin. This hypostatising of evil in a wholly malignant being opposed to God has at times degenerated almost into an ethical dualism.[6] Yet there is also a strand of thought, found in the Bible more often in the Old Testament (as, for example, when Isaiah sees the ravages of the Assyrian as the rod of God's anger) but also permeating the Book of Revelation, which sees God turning even the forces of destruction to his own purposes and thus asserts his personal control over the whole of history. This approach is closer to the general Hindu view, in which there is only the world with its own inbuilt rhythm, harmony with which is basically the good, while the evils of life result from failure to conform to this rhythm or pattern; even in the theistic forms of Hinduism this ethical neutrality of the world is often maintained. However, if God is ultimate, then by definition he must transcend all categories and attributes that our contingent human understanding can arrive at. Nevertheless, the more humanist interests of European society since the Renaissance led to a tendency to exclude God from active participation in his creation, which saw its popular manifestation in what has been dubbed the 'god of the gaps' mentality and its more intellectual side in a steadily increasing secularism of all forms of thought. This had, indeed, been prefigured to a limited extent in the emergence of the concept of the 'supernatural' in Western theology in the ninth century and in Thomas Aquinas's definition of a miracle as something that surpassed the capabilities of nature, which could be seen to imply that ordinarily nature alone operated and only in the miraculous were both God and nature necessary. The appearance of evolutionary theory in the second half of the nineteenth century, however, forced the recognition by more reflective Christians that God was either nowhere in creation or he was everywhere; although the immediate effects of the controversy over Darwin's views and particularly the stance adopted by some prominent clerics were damaging, the long-term result was probably beneficial. Whereas Bishop Samuel Wilberforce in challenging Darwin's views gained a certain notoriety for his acrimonious exchanges with T. H. Huxley at the 1860 British Association meeting, by 1884 Frederick Temple (who was to become Archbishop of Canterbury in 1896) could assume evolution as axiomatic in his Bampton lectures on *The Relations between Religion and Science*.

One early result of the Hellenising tendency carried to extremes was the appearance in the second and third centuries of the heresy called Gnosticism (from γνῶσις, meaning 'knowledge', and implying possession of a superior wisdom), a syncretising movement seeking to integrate with the Gospel concepts current Hellenistic ideas about the cosmos as a divine emanation. Although there were in fact considerable variations in the views of Gnostic teachers (such as Basilides, Valentinus and Marcion), they generally agreed that the world was created by a demiurge, an inferior deity, who was responsible for the mixing within man of the pure spirit and defiling matter. Many Gnostics thought that the God of the Old Testament was this demiurge in contrast to the supreme deity whom Jesus called his Father.

The orthodox Christian view, however, raises in an acute form the problem of theodicy, because of the difficulty in defending the justice and righteousness of God in the light of the existence of suffering and evil. In its over-simplified version, this has been put in the form of a dilemma – if God is wholly loving, then he would surely act to remove suffering, and, if he were omnipotent, he would have eliminated it – from which it is concluded that God must be deficient in love or power or, especially in the modern world, that he simply does not exist. Essentially, the answer given in the New Testament is to point to Christ's own suffering as an earnest of God's real involvement with the suffering of mankind, rather than to elaborate theoretical explanations. Christ's redemptive activity was directed at remedying sin as the state of separation from God through his sacrificial offering of himself, seen in more personal terms as his victory over the forces of evil. The idea of original sin is essentially an assertion that the fall of Adam, the original rebellion of man against God, has tainted the whole human race. The development of the concept was quite gradual and in its earlier forms original sin was seen more as an inherited tendency than an absolute condition; thus, although the doctrine can be seen in an incipient form in Tertullian and Cyprian in the third century, it is not until St Augustine of Hippo (354–430) that it reaches its full rigour. He argues that evil is not a self-subsistent principle but an absence of good, since it is the consequence of the misuse of freewill, which God foresaw and permitted, because it was preferable to bring good out of evil than to exclude the possibility of evil. An alternative view, first expressed in any detail by Irenaeus (c.130–200), who was a major opponent of Gnosticism, is that man is naturally imperfect and has to undergo moral development until finally he reaches the perfection that God intended; thus, the fall of Adam is not some catastrophic reverse to God's plan, but rather an example of this immaturity from which he is gradually leading mankind, and Christ's life recapitulates, as it were, this evolution of humanity in his growth from the baby to full manhood.

To return to the affirmation of the deity as creator, we see this affirmed in Christianity both on the basis of scripture and on philosophical grounds in the various theistic proofs developed in the scholastic tradition and commonly designated as natural theology. From the way that these have been discussed in modern times they might be supposed to form a relatively neutral forum for the demonstration of the existence of a deity. In fact, when we look at the way that they were used in their heyday, whether in the Christian tradition or elsewhere, it is clear that, despite significant similarities on particular points, their overall use is normally specific to the tradition within which they are being used. Such proofs are already involved in a particular doctrinal scheme and their specific meaning is shaped by it, even in those instances when they may have been borrowed from elsewhere. When Thomas Aquinas propounded his 'five ways', he was selecting from the numerous arguments then in circulation those that fitted best with his theological position, although he does indicate that rational proofs were needed in persuading Muslims to follow Christianity and presumably was in this instance envisaging them as a common basis from which to start such persuasion.[7] The various arguments for God's existence can be correlated with different types of religious experience and thus of worship; for example, the ontological argument as propounded by Anselm (c.1033–1109) attests a deep sense of awe in the presence of God and is consonant with a contemplative approach, while the argument from design, so widely found in different religions, seems naturally to be associated with devotional worship. Use of natural theology has within Christianity been more characteristic of the Roman Catholic Church and many Protestant churches have questioned its propriety, seeing it as implying a form of salvation by works in allowing that human reason can find a way to God. Right at the beginning of the Reformation, Jean Calvin (1509–64) argued in his *Institutes of the Christian Religion* that, even though some knowledge of God is implanted naturally, it merely serves to condemn men for failing to respond to God as manifest in our intellects and in his works, while in this century abhorrence of natural theology is particularly strongly expressed by Karl Barth.

Both the argument from design and the cosmological argument are common within Hinduism, and Anselm's approximate contemporary, Udayana (who flourished in the first half of the eleventh century), puts forward aspects of the ontological argument in his debates with the Buddhists and propounds in total over twenty different arguments for the existence of the deity; for example, he argues from the fact that the world is an effect to the necessity of a cause, from the need for a conscious agent to direct the universe, and from the authority of the Vedas to an infallible author (this last elaborately argued on linguistic details which presuppose a certain common ground with his opponents – here the Mīmāṃsā school[8] – but would seem unusual in another tradition). The main work in which he does this however, the *Nyāyakusumāñjali*, reveals the link between worship of the deity and philosophical argument, since its name designates it as a garland consisting of flowers of logic, intended (as the opening verse makes clear) to be offered at the feet of Śiva, and this image or metaphor is carried through the whole of the text. This text, the first systematic account of Nyāya theism, was clearly intended by Udayana to defend his own Śaiva beliefs against the Buddhist and Mīmāṃsā attacks and not as some general or philosophically neutral examination of the topic, and thus his proofs are constructed around the nature of Īśvara as upheld in the Nyāya-Vaiśeṣika theological scheme and controlled by its specific teachings.[9]

Equally though, in the Hindu tradition, there is expressed strong opposition to rational proofs for broadly similar reasons. Most obviously and at much the same period as Udayana, Rāmānuja inveighs against all possible theistic proofs as being both religiously dangerous and philosophically unsound (*Śrībhāṣya* 1.1.3), developing arguments that anticipate – from different motives – those of David Hume (1711–76). His motives were in fact much closer to those of Karl Barth, since his stress on the deity's grace and the devotee's utter dependence similarly excluded intellectual arguments for his existence as illicit attempts to establish rationally what can be known through scripture alone.

One grouping within Hinduism which has sometimes erroneously been likened to the Trinity in Christianity is that termed the Trimūrti, literally 'three forms', which is in fact a rather arbitrary linkage of the three deities Brahmā, Viṣṇu and Śiva. It may reflect a transition phase between Vedic religion and classical Hinduism (seen to some extent in the two Sanskrit epics) when Brahmā was for a time a major figure alongside the other two deities who eventually were to oust him from supremacy. In this grouping, as it is rather mechanically retained in later Hinduism and attested in the Purāṇas, Brahmā is conventionally regarded as the creator of the world, Viṣṇu as the preserver and Śiva as the destroyer. Despite the name given to it, the grouping does not suggest that the deities are in any real sense aspects of one whole, for even systems of thought such as the Advaita Vedānta, which regard everything as emanating from the one Absolute but allow some role for a personal deity as Īśvara, operate at that conventional level in terms of one Īśvara. Its only real purpose is to function as another mechanism for the acceptance of essentially competing sects worshipping different deities within the one umbrella of Hinduism. The only point of similarity to the Trinity is the trivial one of the common occurrence of three in the formulation.

Interestingly, Indian Christian theologians, when they have endeavoured to express the doctrine of the Trinity in indigenous terms, have turned to the classic formulation of the nature of Brahman as *saccidānanda*, 'being, consciousness and bliss', as the most helpful model, not merely for presenting Christ to Hindus but also for deepening the meaning of the Trinity for Christians.[10] In this they had been anticipated by the noted Hindu reformer, Keshab Chandra Sen (1838–84), for whom Christianity had a great fascination. He suggested that the Father, the Creator, is the True and *sat*, the Son is Wisdom, the Good and *cit*, and the Holy Spirit, the Sanctifier, is Holiness, the Beautiful and *ānanda*. According to Sen, the Trinity can also be envisaged as an equilateral triangle at the top of which is the Father, while one side represents the descent of the Son to earth, the base represents Christ at work for the regeneration of mankind, and the other side represents the Holy Spirit taking regenerate mankind up to the Father; however, in Sen's view Christ, like the rest of mankind, is human nature in which divinity dwells and so not unique, for 'fragments of Christ-life' can be found widely scattered. While continuing this identification of the Father with *sat*, the Son with *cit* and the Holy Spirit with *ānanda*, well expressed in the hymn to the Trinity as *saccidānanda* by Brahmabandhab Upadhyaya (1861–1907), Indian Christians also applied to the nature of God the idea that Brahman is both without qualities (*nirguṇa*) and qualified (*saguṇa*). As *nirguṇa* he cannot truly be known, since he transcends the phenomenal world, whereas as *saguṇa* he appears in a qualified form as the personal God (Īśvara). There is the obvious danger here that in the Advaita system such a formulation is linked with the view that Brahman is impersonal and that Īśvara is of secondary importance. On the other hand, the concept of *nirguṇa* Brahman is helpful in emphasising the transcendence of God and in emphasising that he cannot be reduced to the level of anthropomorphism and to merely human analogies, while the *saguṇa* aspect helps to affirm the immanence and accessibility of God as Christ (who as the Λόγος is readily identifiable with *cit*). Another approach is associated with Raimundo Panikkar, who is unusually well placed to attempt such rapprochement, being himself born of a Hindu father and a Spanish Roman Catholic mother and having become a Roman Catholic priest; this has been to link the Trinity with the three ways of action, knowledge and devotion (*karma*, *jñāna* and *bhakti*) first propounded in the *Bhagavadgītā*;[11] these three ways are seen as related, though not identical, and the spirituality depending on *karma* (seen as service to God, especially through ritual – an interesting reversion to the meaning of ritual action found in the Brāhmaṇas) relates to God the Father, that depending on *jñāna* (essentially inward realisation) to God the Holy Spirit, and that depending on *bhakti* (one's personal love for God) to God the Son.

Thus, even in turning to the most monistic aspects of Hinduism for their comparisons, Indian Christians have preserved the emphasis on the personal, which is at the core of Christianity. Equally, they have been anxious to stress the aspect of the interaction of God with mankind in the person of Jesus Christ. The Incarnation is above all for Christians the focus of God's interaction with mankind, whereas for Hindus there is not only the concept of the *avatāra* but also a number of other ways in which they envisage divine interaction with the world. A purely transcendent deity would have no connection with and thus no relevance to human affairs, remaining merely theoretical; all religions in one way or another attest that the transcendent is somehow revealed to or experienced by man in the world. It is to this topic of the ways in which the deity approaches man, and especially to the similarities and differences between *avatāra* and Incarnation, that we turn next.

2

Divine Interaction with Mankind

In its orthodox form, as laid down at the Councils of Nicaea and Chalcedon, the Christian doctrine of the Incarnation states that Jesus was God incarnate, the Second Person of the Triune God living a human life. It is axiomatic that there cannot be another divine Incarnation, for in all respects Christ is unique. This uniqueness of Christ has traditionally been seen as justifying Christianity's claims to exclusiveness, but the way in which it is formulated needs to be carefully defined in the light of the Hindu *avatāra* doctrine; as classically expounded this states that Viṣṇu makes a series of ten descents into the world to punish evil for the benefit of his worshippers. This contrast between uniqueness and plurality is not found only here; Christianity, in common with Judaism and Islam, tends to regard anything which it holds to be of ultimate importance as for that reason singular, whereas in the Hindu view plurality is more characteristic of this world even in relation to the divine.

Even the statement just made that it is Viṣṇu who manifests himself in ten *avatāras*, though valid as a generalisation, is too narrow, for with Śaivism there is the concept of as many as twenty-eight incarnations of Śiva, among whom one, Lakulīśa, is of some importance as the supposed author of a major text; in general, however, the concept of the *avatāra* has not been theologically significant for Śaiva sects as it has been for Vaiṣṇavas. Equally, the number of such *avatāras* is not fixed in all texts; there seems to be an original nucleus of four but in some later works as many as twenty-four or twenty-nine are listed. Essentially, the concept is that a varying number of animal and human heroes come to be viewed as paradigms of Viṣṇu's benevolent activity in the world and in due course are completely identified with him. The first four *avatāras*, the fish, the tortoise, the boar and the dwarf, adapt cosmogonic myths from the Vedas and Brāhmaṇas (taken over from other deities in the first three cases); as incarnations of Viṣṇu they clearly play a similar cosmogonic role. Paraśurāma, the fifth, and the Buddha, as the ninth, are of only marginal importance. Narasiṃha, the man-lion, conforms to the standard pattern in that he destroys the demon Hiraṇyakaśipu, who has been oppressing his son Prahlāda (a devotee of Viṣṇu), but the ferocity of his methods – disembowelling the demon – are more Śaiva in character. Two *avatāras* in particular are significant: Rāma, the son of Daśaratha and hero of the *Rāmāyaṇa*, and Kṛṣṇa, a major figure in the *Mahābhārata* and the expounder of the *Bhagavadgītā*, his sermon to Arjuna on the eve of the battle, incorporated into the *Mahābhārata*. This is the order in which they are traditionally thought to have appeared as the seventh and eighth *avatāras*, although the cult of Kṛṣṇa is in fact attested much earlier than that of Rāma and was in the past more popular (a situation that seems to be changing quite rapidly nowadays). The list concludes with an *avatāra* yet to come, Kalkin, who is due to appear at the end of the present age to punish the wicked, reward the just and establish a new era symbolising the ultimate triumph of traditional brāhman values. He is thus an apocalyptic and millennial figure, quite possibly deriving ultimately from Zoroastrian ideas of the future Saviour, but having a definitely political and this-worldly aspect in contrast to the spiritual dimensions uppermost in the Christian concept of the Second Coming (except as misunderstood in various fringe groups).

Despite their common background in the Sanskrit epics (which is indicative of their more popular character), Rāma and Kṛṣṇa present a considerable contrast. Rāma is the ideal ruler, promoting justice and the welfare of his subjects, and exemplifying perfect filial obedience, but he is not in any real sense a teacher; he is the model of how to live properly and in consequence is at times a slightly remote figure. It is not Kṛṣṇa's actions, however, which inspire his followers to devotion, but his teaching. In the *Mahābhārata* narrative he acts as adviser to one set of combatants; the advice he offers is not infrequently morally questionable, although it must be admitted that moral issues in the *Mahābhārata* are complex and apparently deliberately so, for that epic is at least in part an exploration of *dharma* (a word with a wide range of meaning: here one's duty in its universal and particular aspects, elsewhere tradition, law and religion).[1] In later texts the aspect which is emphasised is his erotic dalliance with the young women of his tribe. Of much greater importance, though, is his role as the expounder of the *Bhagavadgītā*, in which he elaborates what was at the time an innovatory synthesis of certain views already current and which has in more modern times become one of the favourite texts among Hindus. Kṛṣṇa is the great teacher, or the great lover of his devotee. Within the *Bhagavadgītā* he declares what is generally taken as the rationale for every *avatāra*: 'Whenever there occurs a decay of righteousness (*dharma*) and a springing up of unrighteousness, then I send forth myself. To protect good men and to destroy evil-doers, in order to establish righteousness, I come into being from age to age' (4.7–8).

General beliefs about the major *avatāras* held by most Vaiṣṇavas include their reality, their human birth and their blending of divine and human in their lives, their death, the successive appearance of *avatāras* in the world and the purposiveness of their appearance, and their revelation of a personal deity, who is a god of grace. Their reality and their human birth go together to a large extent, and vary from one *avatāra* to another. Both Kṛṣṇa and Rāma are born to human parents, even though the divine and the miraculous is brought into the accounts of their birth from a very early date; equally there are accounts of how Kṛṣṇa was mortally wounded in the foot by a hunter's arrow and how Rāma, following the summons by the god of death, gives up his life in the river that runs past his capital. The blending of the divine and human, virtually absent from the earliest narrations of the Rāma story and seen most clearly in the developed mythology of Kṛṣṇa, is a general feature of *bhakti* Hinduism. There are also differing views between the various Vaiṣṇava schools about which are full *avatāras* (*pūrṇāvatāra*) and which partial (*aṃśāvatāra*), corresponding basically to the relative importance attached to each in the particular school.

Not only is there a succession of *avatāras*, but some texts go a stage further by linking them with the successive periods, the *yugas*, into which traditional Hindu thought divided the cosmic cycle; these *yugas* mark four successive stages in the steady decline of the world from its original perfection, in a manner similar to the scheme of the four ages in Greek and Roman thought. For instance, in one scheme Narasiṃha is supposed to have appeared at the junction of the first and second *yugas*, and Paraśurāma (earlier known as Rāma son of Jamadagni) at the junction of the second and third, while Kṛṣṇa is assigned to the junction of the third and fourth and Kalkin to the end of the fourth, when he will usher in the first of a new cycle of *yugas*. In another scheme it is Rāma son of Daśaratha who is assigned to the junction of the second and third *yugas* and the less important Rāma son of Jamadagni is relegated to the middle of the second *yuga*. The underlying assumption is clearly that at such times of crisis the intervention of the deity in the form of an *avatāra* is needed to maintain *dharma*. But the regular descent of an *avatāra* to check or reverse the moral decline of the world is not entirely compatible with the process of inexorable degeneration implicit in the theory of the four *yugas*, for the two systems are based on different theoretical premises.[2]

Varying motives, both cosmic and soteriological, are assigned for the *avatāras* in the different Vaiṣṇava texts and schools: to preserve the world from danger and disaster, to sustain the good and punish evil-doers, to reveal Viṣṇu's true nature, to manifest his mode of acting and to give man help in realising this mode and entering into loving union with him. Within the oldest texts the purpose may well be expressed in a victorious conflict with some figure of evil; thus, Rāma defeats Rāvaṇa and Kṛṣṇa kills Kaṃsa (and later a whole series of evil beings in various exploits). It may also, though, be some act of mercy, such as Kṛṣṇa's compassionate acceptance of the hunchback girl, Kubjā. Yet, however divine and merciful Kṛṣṇa is shown as being in the texts and in the theologies derived from them, he is not a redeemer or saviour in the sense of personally taking on himself the responsibility of the human race and saving it from the consequences of sin. His involvement in the human condition never goes as far as Christ's.

The very personality of the *avatāras* is in itself a witness to a personal deity in the way in which the doctrine develops, even though in the *Bhagavadgītā* Kṛṣṇa seems to identify himself with Brahman rather than with Viṣṇu, as in later doctrine. However, already in the *Bhagavadgītā* Kṛṣṇa talks about his devotee being dear to him and urges Arjuna to seek his grace (18.62–66), while Rāmānuja goes so far as to suggest that the deity needs his worshipper, so great is his love for him (*Gītābhāṣya* 7.18). The latter attitude is paralleled almost exactly in the Pope's declaration in the encyclical *Mystici Corporis Christi* (1943) that not only are the members of Christ's mystical body, the Church, in need of Christ as their head, but Christ, surprising as it may seem, is also in need of his members and that this is an awesome mystery (*tremendum sane mysterium*). In a less emphatic form it is implicit in the justification for much of the church's social work that, because

Christ is no longer physically present on earth since the Ascension and can no longer act directly, he 'needs people to be his hands and feet', as it is sometimes put.

Among some Vaiṣṇavas Kṛṣṇa is seen as so supremely important that he is no longer regarded as an *avatāra* of Viṣṇu but rather as the supreme deity himself. A notable example of this occurs in the Caitanya movement, where an additional factor within that group was the popular belief (not formally expressed in their theological texts) that Caitanya himself (1486–1533) was an *avatāra* of Kṛṣṇa or of Kṛṣṇa with Rādhā, his favourite among the young women of his clan, the *gopīs*; successive levels of incarnation may well have been felt undesirable. On the other hand, the great poet Sūrdās (c.1478–1564), who is often but probably incorrectly linked with the contemporary Vallabha movement, can make very effective use of the essential identity of the successive *avatāras*.

The modern Hindu thinker, Aurobindo Ghose (1872–1950), has discussed the issue of the *avatāra* quite extensively in his *Essays on the Gita*. He suggests that the world-process sometimes needs a special form of descent of the Spirit, the *avatāra*, which is distinguished by the fact that it is the descent in human form of the whole of the Divine Personality. The upholding of *dharma* is not the only purpose for the descent of the *avatāra* but rather the main aim is the birth of man into the Godhead: 'For there are two aspects of the divine birth; one is a descent, the birth of God in humanity, the Godhead manifesting itself in the human form and nature, the eternal Avatar; the other is an ascent, the birth of man into the Godhead, man rising into the divine nature and consciousness, *madbhāvam āgatāḥ*; it is the being born anew in a second birth of the soul' (First Series, p. 216). Thus, for Aurobindo the *avatāra* is primarily an example, born in order to show man what he is capable of becoming; he is therefore comparatively unconcerned about the historical character of an *avatāra* but yet he insists that an *avatāra* is a true incarnation, not a mere appearance. He holds that the purpose of the descent of an *avatāra* is to show that human birth, even with its limitations and suffering, can be made a means of the will and that this would not be achieved unless the *avatāra* were real. He accepts Christ as an *avatāra*, mentioning him not infrequently alongside Kṛṣṇa and the Buddha; for him Christ is the Consciousness-Force, the dynamic aspect of the Divine which is manifested as the soul incarnated as man in Jesus.

Much earlier, the Pāñcarātra system had provided an elaborate classification of the ways in which Viṣṇu manifests himself in the world in five different modes, of which the *avatāra* is only one. The first is that of the ultimate personal godhead in his transcendental form. The second is that where this supreme deity Vāsudeva (a patronymic of Kṛṣṇa but identified with Viṣṇu) creates from himself three emanations (*vyūhas*) and the basic elements of the universe in a complex procedure; these emanations, while they are mythologically identified with other members of Kṛṣṇa's family (Saṃkarṣaṇa, Pradyumna and Aniruddha), are regarded in the developed system as not merely aspects of the divine nature but gods in their own right, so that deity is simultaneously one and many. There is no question here of different levels of truth but of an eternal paradox. This theory of the four emanations seems to have emerged early in the Christian era, at much the same time as the *avatāra* doctrine, and gives a cosmological basis to the legends of Vāsudeva Kṛṣṇa by identifying him and his family with cosmic emanations. The third mode, then, is that of the *avatāras* (in fact usually called *vibhavas* within the Pāñcarātra system), which also belong to the level of pure creation but are of less significance here than in other Vaiṣṇava movements. The fourth mode is that of Aniruddha as the inner controller (*antaryāmin*) of all souls and the fifth is that of the *arcā avatāra* (the incarnation for worship in cult images). In the Pāñcarātra literature attention is typically focused mainly on the last mode, the rationale of which is that the deity graciously condescends to be present in this material world in his *arcā* form for image worship.

This specifically Pāñcarātra formulation of the modes of divine interaction with the world nonetheless does give in its fifth mode one of the clearest presentations of the general Hindu view of image worship. Basically the image is there as a channel through which the deity can communicate with the worshipper and through which the worshipper can visualise the deity. This is also very clearly seen in the tantric *nyāsa*, in which the presence of a deity is invoked into an image or into the worshipper's own body as a necessary preliminary to worship. Thus a deity who is in essence beyond space and time comes to dwell in the spatially and temporally defined image. The question of how the divine predicates of omnipresence and eternity can co-exist with the limitations of spatial and temporal particularity has on the whole not been as fully explored in Hinduism as the corresponding issue within Christianity of the Incarnation, whereby Jesus has ascribed to him both divine and human (that is limiting) predicates.

The Purāṇas give the first detailed rules relating to the cult of images, beginning with methods of manufacture, next their installation in the temple and then the ritual practice.[3] Although canons of porportion are given, the concern in these and other texts is not artistic but exclusively iconographic in order to ensure the correct representation of the deity concerned. Nevertheless, the image is properly to be seen simply as a symbol, pointing to the higher reality of the deity himself, for all language and action is at a level that can do no more than point towards that ultimate reality (that is, it is not at the essential level, a distinction which Tillich also held). Sincere Hindus who go to the temple for sight (*darśana*) of the deity, will perceive the image, and the whole temple complex, as an actual embodiment of the sacred; yet most would no doubt also recognise that the fullness of the deity is not confined to such sacred places and sacred embodiments. Indeed, it is only because the deity is perceived as greater than the image that reality can be experienced through the image. Incidentally, many theistic Hindus would take a similar view of the meaningfulness of sacred language as truly pointing to and conveying the reality of the deity, but not exhaustively describing his greatness: in fact, as symbolic.

Images were not recognised in the Vedic ritual, except in its latest forms (and then only in the domestic ritual), although various small statues and figurines from the preceding Indus Valley Civilisation (third to second millennium B.C.) have on rather slender grounds been seen as images of deities and precursors of particular Hindu deities. The Vaikhānasas, a parallel Vaiṣṇava sect to the Pāñcarātras, do in fact claim that their worship of the image not only goes back to the Vedic period but is indeed a transformation of the aniconic Vedic ritual, since Viṣṇu's five aspects represent the five Vedic sacrificial fires; the claim says more about their conservative outlook than about historical realities. Equally, the Śrīvaiṣṇava movement, descending from the Pāñcarātra system, assigns a major place in its daily practice to worship of the image. An important point to be realised is that the elaborate iconography of images (described in great detail in the Purāṇas and other texts) was a way of presenting the theology and the mythology to largely illiterate worshippers. An icon or a relief of Viṣṇu reclining on the cosmic waters supported by the snake

Ananta or as the boar rescuing the Earth from drowning, and the many South Indian bronze images of Śiva as the Lord of the Dance (Naṭarāja) are making the same kind of statements about the cosmic role of each deity. In the same way the murals painted on the walls of mediæval parish churches in Britain or the great carved portals of Chartres Cathedral in France (to take just two examples) present the narratives, the ethics and the eschatology of the Christian message to the illiterate majority; to many in the Middle Ages in Europe such visual representations were their scriptures.

On the other hand, another of the Hindu *bhakti* movements, the Liṅgāyats or Vīraśaivas (which emerged in Karnataka in the twelfth century), emphatically rejects temple worship and thus the general use of images, although each member of the sect at initiation is given an individual *liṅga,* which he wears thereafter round his neck in a kind of amulet. The *liṅga* is the symbol of Śiva and its constant wearing symbolises the fact that no intermediary is required between Śiva and the worshipper. A still more iconoclastic attitude is shown in the fifteenth century by Kabīr, perhaps the most noted figure of the *sant* or *nirguṇa bhakti* tradition, who pours scorn on the preoccupation with the externals of religion by both Hindus and Muslims of his time. It has often been suggested that his iconoclasm derived from the influence of Islam as the religion of the rulers of North India at that time but, while it may be true that this provided a stimulus for the forceful expression of his ideas, the concept is rooted in the *bhakti* tradition. Equally, it is of interest to note that iconoclasm in the Orthodox Church, associated with the Isaurian dynasty (717–867), came at a period when, despite Constantine IV's victory over the Saracens in 678, Islam still posed a serious political threat to the Byzantine Empire and the Isaurian emperors may well have been influenced by its attitudes. Yet such an explanation is obviously inapplicable to Puritan iconoclasm.

Certainly, it is true to say that at the popular level of Hinduism the worship of images has often been in effect the worship of the image itself as the deity. Indeed, some of the prescriptions in the Purāṇas about the ritual of installing an image for worship, in particular 'the opening of the eye' which as it were animates the figure, do suggest this at the textual level as well. It is for this reason that the attitudes of various Hindu reformers towards images have been ambivalent, ranging from condemnation to qualified acceptance. The earliest reform movement, the Brāhmo Samāj (which adopted a deistic type of theism, much affected by European deism and by the Unitarians) under the influence of its founder Rām Mohan Roy (1772–1833) banned any image or other representation of any deity within buildings (as is explicitly laid down in the trust deed of the first building opened in 1830). The founder of the Ārya Samāj, Dayānanda Sarasvatī (1824–83) narrates in his autobiography how, during the first *Śivarātri* (all-night vigil for Śiva) that he attended at the age of fourteen, he alone remained awake long enough to see mice come out and run about over the image in search of food; his father was unable to explain to him why the omnipotent deity could allow himself to be polluted in this way. Certainly, as part of the message that he propounded (which was essentially a return to the purity of the Vedic religion), Dayānanda rightly claimed that the Vedas had nothing to say about image-worship and so rejected that along with many other practices which he regarded as illegitimate accretions, reviving instead a form of Vedic ritual without priests or temples. Dayānanda in fact advocated a rigorous monotheism which rejected all representations of the deity so emphatically that he even regarded belief in *avatāras* or incarnations as idolatrous. On the other hand, Vivekānanda (1863–1902), from the neo-Vedāntic standpoint that he popularised through the Rāmakrishna Mission and in reaction against the Brāhmo Samāj, urged the value of image-worship as a suitable means of approach to the divine for those who needed such external props in order to envisage the deity, though he considered it inferior to other means, to which it could form a preliminary.

Images are, then, nearly universal to Hindu understanding of the mode of the deity's interaction with the world. *Avatāras,* which we were examining earlier in this chapter, are specific to the Vaiṣṇava strand of Hinduism. Other strands of Hinduism also have their own ways of representing the deity's involvement with the world. Within Śaivism the most favoured paradigm is that of Śiva's power or energy, his *śakti,* represented mythologically as his consort Umā or Pārvatī, in which role she domesticates and makes responsive to his devotees the otherwise rather aloof and unresponsive Śiva. On a more abstract level, *śakti* is Śiva's immanent aspect as his creative energy, not independent but manifested in *samsāra,* the cycle of the world's existence. In Kashmir Śaivism, for example, the supreme reality is Śiva as the supreme experiencer, whose essence is pure consciousness but who pervades the universe as *ātman* or spirit. His *śakti* is manifested in five aspects – consciousness, bliss, desire, knowledge and activity – which correspond to his five faces, the five facets of reality. Creation is essentially the self-projection of consciousness which, though free, can choose to limit itself by projecting other entities. The Śaiva Siddhānta system declares that Śiva is transcendent as Śiva and immanent as his *śakti* and that he is the efficient cause of the world as Śiva and the material cause through his *śakti*; ultimately, however, there is no distinction between Śiva and his *śakti*. More mythologically, in various Śaiva texts, this is expressed in the statement that Śiva and his consort are reborn on earth in every man and every woman. Iconographically, just as Śiva is represented by the phallic symbol of the *liṅga*, so his consort is represented by the *yoni*, a representation of the female genitalia; the most frequent image in Śaiva temples is indeed the *liṅga* in the *yoni*, symbolising the union of Śiva with his *śakti* as the supreme expression of creative power. This deity-consort model, most characteristic of Śaivism but found also in Vaiṣṇavism (especially in some Kṛṣṇa cults) utilises explicitly the imagery of the love-life involved in the husband-wife relationship; this, of course, has no real parallel within the Judeo-Christian tradition, where, apart from the isolated example of the pseudepigraphical *Odes of Solomon* (end of first century A.D.), the nearest that could be cited are the Song of Songs and the image of the church as the Bride of Christ (prefigured in Hosea using his own marriage as an analogy for the Lord's love for Israel). It is often stressed that *śakti* is the active partner in the cosmic act of procreation, while Śiva remains purely passive (and according to some texts could not even move without her impulse). Pārvatī, who is inseparable from her husband when he is benevolent, prevails on Śiva to be benign, reducing him as it were to human terms as the indulgent father. Indeed, a favoured method in Śaivism (comparable to the use in Vaiṣṇavism of the *avatāra* concept) for bringing within the ambit of its mythology and cultus the many local manifestations of deity that are so common in India is to turn them into members of Śiva's family circle.

The goddess is also significant as another major focus of worship alongside Viṣṇu and Śiva, independent of either male god; the cults associated with her in her independent form, usually called Śākta or tantric (after the Tantras, which are the main texts on this system), are nevertheless not always easy to separate from some aspects of Śaivism. Both Śaiva and Śākta Tantras are usually presented as dialogues between Śiva and his *śakti* as teacher and pupil. The goddess is often seen in the more theologically oriented texts not strictly as independent but rather as the *śakti* of the Absolute but this means that for all practical purposes attention is directed exclusively towards her. She is identified with the primary cause of the world (*prakṛti*, 'matter' or 'nature') and appears as the creatress of the worlds (analogous but not identical to the role of Īśvara in Advaita Vedānta) through her sportive or playful activity (*līlā*); to her are applied all the titles of a supreme deity, such as the Supreme Lady, the Mother, or the Great Goddess. The world is not only permeated by her but also a manifestation of her as *prakṛti* and so identical with her – a more materialistic pantheism than in Advaita Vedānta. Besides the textually based worship of the goddess at this more abstract level, there is also a widespread cult of village goddesses – local manifestations of divine power and fertility, often seen in ambivalent terms – who are frequently worshipped with the sort of bloody animal sacrifice which would be anathema in other forms of Hinduism.

The system of the deities' mounts (*vāhanas*) represents another mechanism, alongside the growing number of Viṣṇu's *avatāras* and Śiva's ever enlarging family circle, by which the Purāṇas and traditional Hinduism have endeavoured to assimilate the multiplicity of local cults into the framework of the developed religion. This system brings into relationship with each of the major deities an appropriate animal symbol of his particular nature or activity. For example, Viṣṇu rides on Garuḍa, the bird-like figure who in the Vedic literature is an independent deity, or reclines on the cosmic serpent Ananta or Śeṣa (literally 'infinite' and 'remainder'), while Śiva rides on his bull, Nandin. These figures may then act as intermediaries between the worshipper and the major deity; the placing of shrines to Nandin in front of the main temple to Śiva with the bull looking in towards the sanctum illustrates visually his implicit identification with the worshipper coming to the temple. These different mechanisms may also be combined, as in the case of Śiva's elephant-headed son Gaṇeśa (strictly, according to most texts, he is the son of Pārvatī without Śiva's participation, except that the elephant head is owed to his decapitation by Śiva); he too is furnished with a mount, the superficially incongruous rat, which in fact symbolises another aspect of Gaṇeśa's nature as 'Lord of obstacles' (Vighneśa), able both to produce and to remove them.

The sonship of Christ is used in the New Testament, especially in the Gospel of John, to designate not so much an absolute status but a relationship, for in traditional Jewish thought to be a son was to have the character of and to act like the father, whether Abraham or God; for example, Jesus says: 'If my deeds are not the deeds of my Father, do not believe me' (John 10:37). Jesus was uniquely open to the working of God through him and so most perfectly reflected the nature of the Father. This is fully compatible with his humanity as well as with his divinity, a tension which finds expression in orthodox Christian theology's doctrine of the Virgin Birth of Jesus, conceived by Mary through the power of the Holy Spirit (Matthew 1:18–25, Luke 1:26–38), a doctrine which in reality is a consequence of belief in the Incarnation rather than a precondition for it. Over the last century or so the doctrine of the Virgin Birth has been challenged by various liberal theologians on several grounds, including its lack of attestation and indeed its implicit denial elsewhere in the New Testament. The function of the doctrine is clearly to give expression to the belief that this man of otherwise most obscure origin was indeed God's son, not in any literalist sense but as having his humanity uniquely inspired by God in a way that necessitated belief in his divinity.

The divinity of Jesus Christ is implied or accepted quite often in the New Testament itself. He has unique knowledge of the Father (Matthew 11:27, Luke 10:22), he is the equal of the Father (John 5:17–27), to know the Son is to know the Father (John 14:7–11), and Christ is identified with God (John 20:28, Titus 2:13, Hebrews 1:1–9, 2 Peter 1:1, 1 John 5:20); further examples could easily be given, although the precise significance of many has been the subject of much scholarly debate over whether Jesus is explicitly called God. His role as saviour is implicit in his name (Jesus is the Greek form of Joshuah, 'Yahweh is salvation'), as is indeed recognised: 'She will bear a son; and you shall give him the name Jesus, for he will save his people from their sins' (Matthew 1:21).

The crucifixion is clearly central to any understanding of the nature of Christ and also of the Trinity; it dominates the writings of St Paul, the first great propagandist for Christianity, and in John's Gospel the death of Jesus is his 'hour', in which the Father will glorify his name (12:23–33 and 17.1–5). Equally, within the life of the church the Communion proclaims the death of the Lord (1 Cor. 11.26), and baptism is 'into his death' (Romans 6:3). Yet, the manner of his death was a stumbling-block to preaching the risen Christ to Jews, the first audience of the early church, even more than to other people. The passion narratives accordingly make heavy use of allusions to the Old Testament to show how it is foretold there.[4] The redemptive activity of God in Christ is centred on the fact that the one who offered himself as a ransom for many was God himself, that in the person of Jesus Christ, God himself endured the burden of men's sin and thereby offered himself for man's redemption. Thus, God is not a deity who inflicts suffering from outside but himself suffers on mankind's behalf. The cross is the point at which the love between the Father and the Son overcomes even the gulf which separates sinners from God. By this event believers have been redeemed from the bondages of their lives and freed for a new relationship with God; alienation has given way to reconciliation.

The crucifixion cannot, however, be separated from the resurrection which was just as basic to early Christian preaching as Christ's death on the cross; as St Paul bluntly puts it: 'If there is no resurrection, then Christ was not raised; and if Christ was not raised, then our gospel is nul and void, and so too is your faith' (1 Cor. 15.12–13). For Paul with his Pharisaic background belief in resurrection was not new; what was new was the experience of Jesus as Lord in his life. The other apostles were convinced that they had seen Jesus alive after his crucifixion, the same individual whose life they had shared before his death on the cross, a fact expressed in the references to the everyday activities of seeing, hearing, touching and eating with the risen Christ. The whole New Testament witness is that the resurrection means the experience of Jesus as a power in their lives, an experience at once so clearly of the same Jesus as before and so vividly alive that the writers naturally used such images.

The first major schism over the nature of Christ is that associated with the name of Arius (a priest teaching in Alexandria, d. 336), who interpreted the Incarnation in terms of contemporary Hellenistic philosophy and taught that, if the Father had begotten the Son, then there must have been a time when the Son did not exist. Thus, though recognising Jesus Christ as the Saviour, he subordinated the Son to the Father (quoting, for example, in support of his views Mark 13:32 and John 14:28).[5] Arianism thus contradicted the orthodox belief that the redemption of the world was achieved by God himself and not by some messenger sent from above or some holy man rising from the human condition; it also involved a technically idolatrous position, if the Christ whom Christians worship is other than God. The official response to this heresy was formulated at the Council of Nicaea in 325 in terms of a begetting of the Son from eternity and is associated with the name of Athanasius (293–373); the Nicene creed defined more exactly the equality of the Father and the Son and introduced the concept of the Son being of the same substance (ὁμοουσιος), despite its association with the heretical views of Paul of Samosata (d. c.270); it is the creed still used by the Roman Catholic Church in the liturgy of the Mass. It was further developed by the inclusion of several Christological propositions, including some added by the councils of the fourth and fifth centuries.

The creed finally agreed at Chalcedon in 451 defined the nature of Christ as follows:

> We proclaim in unanimity that one must confess a single and only Son, our Lord Jesus Christ, perfect in divinity and perfect in humanity, true God and true man consubstantial with the Father by divinity and consubstantial with us by humanity, similar to us in everything, except sin, born of the Father before all ages according to divinity, born in these last times of Mary the Virgin, Mother of God, according to humanity, for us and for our salvation; a single and only Christ, Son, Lord, the Only-Begotten makes Himself known in two natures without mixture, without change, indivisibly, inseparably, in such a way that the union does not destroy the difference of the two natures, but on the contrary the properties of each only remain more firm when they are united in a single person or hypostasis which does not separate nor divide into two persons, being the same and single person of the Son, Only-Begotten, God and Word, Lord Jesus Christ.

For all the complexity of wording involved, this creed represents the main achievement of the Council of Chalcedon and serves to stress the full and undiluted humanity of Jesus alongside his divinity; essentially it is declaring that just as in Jesus believers encounter God, so too they encounter a fully human being.

Nevertheless, it did so in terms of the doctrine of the two natures already propounded by Nestorius.

Nestorianism, developing from the school of Antioch with its emphasis on the historical side of the scriptures and thus on Christ's humanity, divided Christ into two different persons. Nestorius (who became Patriarch of Constantinople in 427) himself carefully distinguished between the two natures of Christ. The traditional belief was that Christ was both true God and real man, yet also one person, not two beings operating in one body. Nestorius' views seemed reasonably orthodox until he denied the title of Mother of God (Θεοτόκος) to Mary and tried to replace it with Mother of Christ. He now conceived the person in terms of nature and so opposed the person of the Word to that of Jesus, linking them by the concept of an election that made Jesus the receptacle of the Word. For Nestorius, only the human person of Christ was born from Mary and the two sons, of God and of man, were united but not one in Christ. However, the implication of this is that, if Christ has no unity of person, our nature was not genuinely assumed by God and the Incarnation loses its full meaning.

This heresy in turn led to an opposite one when its opponents, to defend the unity of Christ, expressed it in terms of nature and specifically of divine nature. St Cyril of Alexandria (412–444), in opposition to Nestorius, insisted that one and the same being was simultaneously the eternal Word of God and had been born of the Virgin Mary, although this one being had two natures in that he was both divine and human. Some of St Cyril's followers took this further to the doctrine of a single nature in Christ, his divinity, thus producing the Monophysite heresy, which, while not actually denying the humanity of Christ as such, so subordinated it to his consubstantiality with the Father as effectively to do so. This position was not far then from the earlier heresy of Docetism (which declared that the body of Jesus was just an appearance and thus that the Son of God did not truly become man or suffer on the cross); it also, incidentally, became linked in Egypt with resistance to foreign rule and so developed distinct nationalist overtones. Docetist tendencies have surfaced from time to time throughout the history of Christianity but have not usually had much influence at the doctrinal level; already in the second century the Gnostic Marcion (d. c.160) put forward the view that the body of Christ was pure appearance but even his followers drew back from that to the extent of saying that it was a real body, though composed from cosmic elements.

Inseparable from any understanding of the Incarnation is the doctrine of Christ's emptying of himself (κένωσις), perhaps most fully expressed within the New Testament in the Letter to the Philippians 2:5–11. The Son of God descends into the human condition, abandoning his divine glory to identify himself fully with mankind. This emptying is thus the Incarnation in its aspect of humility and mortality, of Christ becoming mortal in order to conquer death. As St Gregory of Nazianzus (330–389) affirmed, only because one of the Trinity became a real man, can men ascend to union with God; the Incarnate Word, being both God and man, retained the characteristics of his two natures and at the same time remained one person, thus showing that man can be united with God without losing his personality.

The doctrine of κένωσις assumed a new degree of relevance with the challenge that modern science began to pose to traditional religious views; for various reasons this challenge focused on the theory of evolution (the Darwinian controversy) but had much wider ramifications. A particular instance was the problem of how to reconcile Jesus's world-view, which was obviously that of his own time and so pre-Darwinian, with omniscience. This could be answered by a Christology based on this concept of emptying: Jesus chose not to know more than his contemporaries.

With the application of biblical criticism and historical scholarship to the New Testament in the nineteenth century, there emerged the 'quest for the historical Jesus', which had a number of implications. Whereas Christ as defined in the traditional creeds was safely controlled by the churches, the figure that appeared when the gospels were treated in this new way tended to be drawn rather differently. He was often portrayed as the preacher of a universal religion, implicitly regarded as larger than institutional Christianity, and so belonging to all mankind and not just to the Church, while his message was cast, not in terms of his relationship to the Father, but in terms of conscience and of eternal moral values. The extent to which this liberal trend shook the religious establishment of the time can be seen in the massive scale of Victorian religious reaction.

It is interesting to note the analogies with the views on Christian belief in Christ expressed by the noted Indian philosopher, Sarvepalli Radhakrishnan (1888–1975). He argues that the difference between the Eastern and the Western attitudes to religion is revealed by comparing the life and teaching of Jesus, as recorded in the Gospels, with the Nicene Creed: his non-dogmatic tolerance and universalist ethics show Jesus himself to be a typical Eastern seer, whereas the emphasis on definite creeds, intolerance and exclusiveness are the typical features of Western Christianity.[6]

The Incarnation is in many ways the most difficult part of Christian doctrine for Hindus to come to terms with, but equally it is the hardest for Christian theologians to present in a manner which is not offensive to those of other faiths. The general issue of dialogue between the two religions will be examined in the last chapter but a few remarks on the attitudes to *avatāra* and Incarnation are appropriate here. From the Hindu side, the biggest problem is in understanding the Christian insistence on the uniqueness of Christ against the background of Hindu acceptance of the repeatability of the *avatāra* (indeed the need for the repeated intervention of Viṣṇu in this way, according to many schools of thought).[7] From the Christian side, the uniqueness of Christ has always been part of traditional belief and this can be attested within the New Testament in the assertion that Christ 'has appeared once for all at the climax of history to abolish sin by the sacrifice of himself' (Hebrews 9:26).

It is necessary, however, to define with some care just what is meant by the uniqueness of Christ and to guard against implicit assumptions that uniqueness is valuable in itself or somehow a guarantee of truth. At one extreme, after all, we are all unique in that we are separate individuals, while at the other so much stress can be laid on Christ's distinctiveness as to undermine the truth of the Incarnation by making him some kind of anomalous exception, who enters but is not really part of the human scene. There is a sense in which Christ is unique in being truly man, in living the kind of life that God intended man to live and so in embodying the relationship with God for which man was created. Yet, according to orthodox trinitarian theology, this is not enough and, from the perspective of comparative religion, on this basis Christ becomes one inspired man among others. There is no longer the living Saviour, by incorporation into whose body Christians become part of God's purpose. This is in effect the point that the Indian Christian writer V. Chakkarai is making in his *Jesus the Avatār*, published in 1930, where he stresses that Rāma and Kṛṣṇa were temporary and, after they had done their task, left this world, whereas 'the Spirit of Jesus is incarnated again and again in human hearts'. However, on the one hand it scarcely does justice to the direct personal experience of the deity by, for example, the Śrīvaiṣṇavas, and on the other it is liable to reduce the significance of Christ to that of a series of appearances.

Much earlier, the Jesuit missionary, Roberto de Nobili (1577–1656),[8] carefully distinguished the Christian doctrine of Incarnation as *mānuṣa avatāra*, 'human descent', from the Hindu concept of *avatāras* as *deva avatāra*, 'divine descent', on the basis that according to the Christian view God assumes human nature, which is body and soul together as one reality, whereas in the Hindu view Viṣṇu assumes only the human body (and, in de Nobili's opinion, such an *avatāra* cannot be said to be human incarnation). De Nobili also rejected the idea of many *avatāras*, saying that one Incarnation is sufficient, just as the one sun is enough for illumination, and that more would imply both change and limitation in God. He also criticises the Hindu view of *avatāra* as being brought about through the power of *māyā* or *līlā*, arguing that this would make the real union of human with divine nature a mere appearance. Incidentally, another Hindu term that de Nobili adopts for Christ is that of *guru*, 'teacher' (and especially *sadguru*, 'true teacher'), perhaps not only because of its intrinsic appropriateness but also because its use to denote Śiva (especially in the Śaiva Siddhānta, which as a South Indian movement, would be familiar to de Nobili) would balance the linking of *avatāra* with Viṣṇu.

Claims for the uniqueness of Christ are also based on the concept that he came in the 'fullness of time' and to inaugurate the 'last time', phrases that tend not only to suggest Christ's centrality to the historical process but also to link this 'last time' with the eschatological expectation of the Second Coming. From the Christian perspective such ideas are clearly valid but they are scarcely an adequate basis for claims to uniqueness. The way in which the successive *avatāras* of Viṣṇu are linked to the *yugas* is sufficient evidence for the Hindu recognition of the opportune time, while the inclusion in the scheme of Kalkin – a distinctly apocalyptic figure in much popular mythology – as the future *avatāra* has distinct analogies with the doctrine of the Second Coming, as has already been noted.

Rudolf Otto (1869–1937), the Protestant theologian who was

also a significant writer on Hinduism, addresses the comparison between Incarnation and *avatāra* in several of his works. He sees the basic difference as lying, not in the fact that Christ was a mediator (since Kṛṣṇa and Rāma were mediators too), not in the doctrine of incarnation as such (refusing to recognise any fundamental difference here and denying, for instance, the docetic interpretation of *Bhagavadgītā* 4.6[9]), but in the fact that Christ was the propitiator and, according to Otto, that all doctrines about his person derive their special meaning and their validity from that fact. Propitiation clearly implies the concepts of human sinfulness and divine grace and Otto fully acknowledged the presence of the doctrine of grace in *bhakti* Hinduism, noting the similarities of the internal split within the Śrīvaiṣṇavas with Protestant controversies on this topic. Nevertheless, the underlying point that the crucifixion and resurrection are pivotal to any understanding of the uniqueness of Christ is significant.

The Indian Christian theologian M. M. Thomas (b. 1916), writing from a perspective much influenced by Karl Barth's distinction between religion and revelation, speaks about recognising the possibility of a transcendent Christ reshaping other religions from within; for if Christ is seen as transcending Christianity as a religion, then one may conceive of his transcendence being extended to include other religions to transform them. The uniqueness of God's revelation in Christ is central to this understanding, which excludes a syncretistic blurring of the issues but attempts to take Hinduism seriously, although such a Christo-centric approach does still imply a form of exclusivism.

An essentially relativist approach is found in the writings of John Hick who, in response to the fact of religious plurality, has developed a theology which he has termed 'Copernican', in that it is centred on God, rather than 'Ptolemaic' or centred on one's own religion.[10] He sees the exclusive soteriological claims made for the uniqueness of Christ's person and work as the main obstacle to positive Christian acceptance of religious pluralism. Accordingly he reinterprets the doctrine of the Incarnation and suggests that Christ should be regarded as a human being and not as the second person of the Trinity. Traditional language about the Incarnation should be understood as mythological, expressing the fact that God has been encountered through Jesus in the activity of loving. In response to the question whether such a mythological interpretation of the Incarnation supports the traditional exclusivism of

Christianity, Hick uses the analogy of human relations, where we do not consider our own love or loyalty to be exclusive or more authentic than that of others, to make clear that we should not expect the same exclusiveness in man's experience of God. It is reasonable, therefore, to accept that God has revealed himself in different ways and we can apply this same mythological interpretation to claims to divinity made about figures in other religions.

A contrast is sometimes drawn between the importance of history in the Judeo-Christian tradition and the supposed absence of any historical sense in the Hindu tradition. There may be a limited measure of truth in this but it completely ignores the fact that for the average Hindu the narratives about Rāma and Kṛṣṇa are far more real – are viewed, that is, as having actually occurred and in that sense being historical – than any of the history of India that has been compiled over the last couple of centuries or so. In any case, the linear idea of history implicit in this contrast is a comparatively modern development in the West and its unstated corollary that the direction of change is towards progress cannot be regarded as proven. Hinduism certainly places much more emphasis on the cyclical aspects of human existence (not unnaturally in a country where life is so dominated by the seasonal cycle). But it is relevant to note that Kṛṣṇa, in many ways the most significant of the *avatāras*, is the expounder of the *Bhagavadgītā*, transmitted as part of the *Mahābhārata*, and takes a leading, though non-combatant, role in the great battle which is the core of the *Mahābhārata* ('Great <war> of the Bharatas'), for not only has that text become a virtual encyclopaedia of Hinduism but that battle is seen as the focus of Hindu identity; it is no coincidence that the modern Republic of India also calls itself Bhārat. The noted Bengali novelist, Bankim Chandra Chatterjee (1838–94), who is best known for the poem 'Bande Mātaram' included in one of his novels, which became in effect the anthem of the Indian nationalist movement, also wrote a work, *Kṛṣṇacaritra*, in which he attempts to reconstruct the original life of Kṛṣṇa, trying to demonstrate his historicity and to present him as an exemplar of human moral perfection. That this endeavour, obviously modelled on the nineteenth-century 'quest for the historical Jesus' and suffering the same reductionist tendencies, ran into severe criticism not only from Christian missionaries but also from contemporary Hindus is scarcely surprising.

Bankim Chandra Chatterjee's attempt was indeed basically misconceived, for the stories of the two epics, the *Mahābhārata* and the *Rāmāyaṇa*, and even more the narratives about Kṛṣṇa in later texts, though regarded as real by most Hindus, do contain a strong supernatural element in the direct participation in events of various deities, fabulous animals and so on. In this respect there is a genuine contrast with the New Testament narrative, which does operate in a basically historical and so naturalistic framework, and has come to be seen increasingly from such a standpoint as the rationalistic impulse in Western culture has grown stronger. Nevertheless, the contrast should not be overplayed, for the account of Jesus's life includes a number of miracles and the intellectual climate of that time certainly envisaged outstanding individuals being able to achieve extraordinary acts. Jesus himself warns about impostors who will produce signs and wonders (Mark 13:22) and there is the man named Simon who 'had captivated the Samaritans with his magical arts' (Acts 8:9), to take just two examples from the New Testament, while a contemporary neo-Pythagorean, Apollonius of Tyana (who apparently reached Northwest India at much the same period as that of Jesus's ministry), was widely known as a wonder-worker, being reputed to have raised people from the dead and healed many who were sick.

The miracle stories in the New Testament in many cases function in the same way as such stories in other religious literatures: they narrate various wonders performed by their subject not in order to prove something but basically as a means of drawing attention to his greatness (the Greek terms usually translated by the Latin-derived word miracle mean 'marvel', 'power' and 'sign' and do not carry the implication of an event contrary to what is known of the laws of nature already found in St Augustine). A considerable number can also be understood as symbolising the conflict between the forces of life and the forces of death and thus as anticipating the message of Christ's death and resurrection. A number, and arguably the most central ones, reflect what was undoubtedly a major aspect of Jesus's teaching in terms of the wholeness of human life and the healings recorded give every appearance of being its practical outworking; indeed, Matthew sums it up thus: 'He travelled throughout Galilee, teaching in the synagogues, proclaiming the good news of the kingdom, and healing every kind of illness and infirmity among the people'

(4.23, cf. 9.34, preceding and following the Sermon on the Mount respectively). They are the practical expression of that power which resides in the gospel itself.

Nor were miracles thought to have ceased after the time of Jesus and his direct disciples in the traditional view, which is still held by the Roman Catholic and Orthodox Churches, that the mark of a saint was the ability to perform miracles. By contrast, the Protestant outlook normally restricts the miraculous to those events recorded in the Bible, except perhaps among some charismatic groups. However, folk belief in such supernatural powers is not easily suppressed, and can be transformed into a belief in the power of witches, who employ evil forces to achieve their ends, whether good or bad; the Salem witch-trials in colonial America furnish a notorious example of the persistence of this belief in a community otherwise dominated by Protestant values.[11]

In the context of the Incarnation's significance for personal salvation the description of Jesus as the Son of God naturally predominates, as it has done in this chapter, but in the cosmic context the designation of Christ as Λόγος ('word' but also 'reason'), such as we see at the start of John's Gospel, also has its place and serves too to remind us that Christ is understood within Christianity as revealing the nature of the Father. Already in the second century Tatian and Athenagoras stress the role of God's word in creation and Justin Martyr, seeking to reconcile the claims of faith and reason, affirms that the Word of God, begotten before creation and inseparable from God in power, became man as Jesus Christ; before the end of that century Theophilus propounds his view of a God who communes with his own Word or Reason, utters his Word in order to create, sends his Word through the prophets and finally makes his Word incarnate in the person of Jesus. The nature of revelation – and the role of reason in relation to it – is indeed of great importance in both Hinduism and Christianity and forms the main subject of the next chapter.

3

Authority and Mediation

Christian use of the term Λόγος for Christ did not, of course, spring out of nowhere. It had its precursors within the Jewish tradition as well as in the use of the term in Greek thought. In the works of the Jewish philosopher Philo (probably a part contemporary of Jesus) the term Λόγος broadly replaces the divine Wisdom (σοφία) which Hellenistic Judaism stresses, and he even refers to this Word as the first-begotten son of the uncreated Father and the 'second God'. Already in the Old Testament Wisdom was seen as having a special role in God's scheme of creation as 'formed in earliest times, at the beginning, before earth itself' (Proverbs 8:23; compare the whole of Proverbs 8–9). Hellenistic Jews would further be familiar through their Greek scriptures (Proverbs, *Qoheloth* and the apocryphal Wisdom of Solomon) with the personification of Wisdom as an intermediary between God and the world. Later rabbinic speculation identified Wisdom and Law.

There is a striking analogy in the *Ṛgveda*, where the experience of the power of the word is mainly personified in the form of the goddess Vāc (whose femininity links her with σοφία, while her name is the equivalent of Λόγος). She is the precursor in some respects of the notion of Brahman, the Absolute, for the terms which later designate the Absolute (*brahman, akṣara*) first signified sacred formulae or speech. *Vāc*, 'speech', is pronounced at the beginning of time and is often personified as a creative and powerful force, an energy (*śakti*) which is both cosmic and human; man can harness it by means of sacred formulae in which it is expressed and is therefore on a level with the gods or the first creative principle. Vāc as a goddess seems to have been popular only in a limited priestly circle, in which she represented the ultimate power of the words or *mantras* used in ritual.

The place of scripture within both Hinduism and Christianity is very significant but has different nuances within different branches of each. In one sense both are scriptural in that appeal to the authority of the Bible would be acknowledged by all

Christians, even if not accepted as the prime authority, and acceptance of the authority of the Vedas has long been one of the main criteria for being counted a Hindu. There are also some significant convergences in patterns of thinking about scriptural authority to be found but equally it must be acknowledged that there are profound differences as well.

According to orthodox thinking the Vedas are the sole revelation within Hinduism and this is attested by two of the terms by which they are most frequently designated: *śruti*, meaning literally 'hearing' and thus denoting the aspect of reception from an outside source, and *śabda*, meaning literally 'word' (like the Greek Λόγος) and thus denoting rather the active revealing agent. Of the two, *śruti* is more commonly applied directly to the Vedas themselves, while *śabda* tends to be reserved for Brahman as identical with the Vedas or in certain other more specific contexts; *śruti* is then frequently contrasted with all other religious texts, which are ranked as *smṛti*, literally 'remembering' but meaning rather 'tradition'. Acceptance of the authority of the Vedas, of *śruti*, is then possibly the most widely endorsed criterion for being regarded as a Hindu but only because it has so little content and so amounts to little more than a declaration that someone claims to be a Hindu. Admittedly certain Vedic hymns are still recited at weddings and funerals (and every strict brāhman should recite one verse as part of his first morning worship) but these have become pure formalities. Even though study of the Vedas was made obligatory for men of the three higher *varṇas* (broadly classes, there being four *varṇas* in this early scheme of social organisation), in actual fact accurate knowledge of them was lost at a fairly early period and we find considerable evidence of incomplete understanding in the works of mediæval commentators. Already in the Vedic period itself, the chief use to which the Vedic hymns were put in the Brāhmaṇas was the provision of suitable texts to accompany the sacrificial rituals; although originally they were chosen for their relevance, soon it was their exact pronunciation and not their meaning that was vital, and so originated the Hindu use of *mantras*. Those schools which claimed to study the Vedas did so from an extremely limited point of view. The Mīmāṃsā system concentrates on the ritual commands found mostly in the Brāhmaṇas, ignoring the older hymns as well as the Upaniṣads, and the Vedānta system concerns itself almost exclusively with the Upaniṣads, while the other philosophical systems have only a perfunctory attachment to the Vedas. Even acceptance of the authority of the Vedas is by no means universal, for many of the devotional trends in Hinduism tend to be critical of it, while some groups, most notably the Liṅgāyats, have definitely rejected it.

Although the Vedas are regarded as the revealed scriptures of Hinduism, they are not in fact read by the vast majority of Hindus, most of whom – the lower castes and all women – were in due course forbidden to read them. Nor do the Vedas have a canon in the sense of the Bible, and two basic concepts of the Vedic exegetical tradition rule out even the possibility of delimiting the Vedic corpus. The first is the doctrine according to which all texts of all Vedic schools have equal authority in matters of *dharma* (which in this context means primarily one's duties, especially the obligation to perform the ritual). Historically most of the Vedic texts were created or at least edited into their present form within the Vedic schools whose origin can often be traced to disputes regarding the canon of the respective hymn collections. The second doctrine concerns the Vedic basis of all *smṛti* commands, which gave rise to the theory of the lost or scattered Vedas, for this held that, if all *smṛti* injunctions must correspond to Vedic injunctions, then those *smṛti* texts for which we cannot find a Vedic basis in the extant Vedic texts must be based on Vedic texts that are either lost or are found only in some remote location in India (as the seventh-century Mīmāṃsā scholar Kumārila argues in his subcommentary on *Mīmāṃsāsūtra* 1.3.1). Since many *smṛti* injunctions lack Vedic counterparts, this doctrine makes it theologically impossible to determine the extent of the Vedas. They are more extensive than the sum of their available parts; consequently the Vedas have no canon and cannot have a canon.

This assumption that there is a corresponding Vedic text to authenticate a *smṛti* text is just one of the steps by which the Mīmāṃsā system enlarges the scope of authority, while carefully subordinating other categories of authority to *śruti*. Next, the customary practices of those who regularly perform Vedic sacrifice are to be regarded as authoritative, unless they can be shown to be motivated by self-interest, since again the inference is that there must be or have been Vedic texts to support them. In addition, in the absence of any direct mandate from these, people can follow their consciences.

On the other hand, the Nyāya system presents quite a different list of the four sources of valid knowledge, which are in descending order of validity: perception, inference, analogy and *śabda*. The last (literally 'word') was a recognition that we accept many things outside our own direct experience on the authority of others; the fact that it is reckoned as the weakest of these means of knowledge clearly reveals the Nyāya system's original interest simply in epistemological issues. Subsequently, however, as Nyāya was absorbed into the orthodox synthesis, *śabda* came to cover the authority of scripture (*śruti*), which, according to the conservative Mīmāṃsā system, should have been placed first. It is interesting to note that it was the Nyāya view on the sources of knowledge, with its rationalist approach, that the other philosophical systems broadly adopted, rather than the Mīmāṃsā view, with its appeal primarily to scriptural authority. It should also be noted that a corollary of this view is that revelation applies only to what is beyond the range of the senses, the metaphysical, and thus the material world is left open to investigation by scientific procedures independently of religion. It is this that underlies the claims by many proponents of neo-Hinduism from Vivekānanda onwards that Hinduism is a 'scientific' religion.

There are essentially three sources of authority that are recognised in one or another branch of Christianity: the Bible, the Church and individual experience. The emphasis on the authority of the Church is characteristic of the Roman Catholic position which sees the Church as the divinely commissioned vehicle and guarantee of the truth of the Gospel, with the corollary that there is no salvation outside the Church. The emphasis on the sole authority of the scriptures, the Bible, is a characteristically Protestant position, which typically affirms that everything necessary for faith is to be found in or can be deduced from the Word of God, the Bible. The emphasis on the importance of the individual's experience is found quite widely as a buttress or a qualification to the other two in various branches of Christianity but forms the principal authority most obviously in the Society of Friends, who would place the divine inward revelation above anything else; it is, however, on the whole too individual and private to be susceptible of treatment here. These three basic sources of authority are, of course, combined in various ways, for example in the way that the Roman Catholic Church regards itself as the sole authentic interpreter of the Bible.

Within the Christian tradition, fundamentalism as a distinct position can be dated to the appearance from 1911 onwards of a series of pamphlets called *The Fundamentals: A Testimony to the Truth*; their main emphasis was on the infallibility of the Bible but they also condemned a range of other 'Christian deviations', such as Roman Catholicism and liberalism, by which was meant especially the application of higher criticism to the study of the Bible. As the process of secularisation within the Protestant churches continued, the growth of fundamentalism has been broadly commensurate, appealing for a return to traditional and absolute values and asserting the need for total acceptance of an absolute religious authority vested in the scriptures. The central feature of Protestant fundamentalism is this assertion of the inerrancy of the Bible, which in itself becomes a test of faith and is the key to the whole ideological system. There is often a concurrent desire to return to the golden age of early Christian beliefs and practices, together with a condemnation of the sin and wickedness of the contemporary world, but in an individualistic manner which leaves no room for social concerns.

The term fundamentalism can perhaps be broadened to refer not just to a specific school of thought within Protestant Christianity but to a rigid adherence to any precisely defined, usually scriptural, tradition. What is most obvious here is the sense of a need for objectivity expressed in the attempt to make clear that the centre of authority lies outside the scope of human subjectivity; for fundamentalist Christians there is an objective reality but this objectivity is not located in Christ as a person but in the Bible. Objectivity is held to be outside the personal, for individuals cannot be relied on (neither the writers of the books of the Bible, seen as simply the instruments of divine inspiration, nor even Christ himself, except as witnessed to by an inerrant scripture), and so the Bible is in effect reified by being turned into an objective reality that stands over against human thoughts and ideas. In this sense fundamentalism may be held to emerge in response to a preceding liberalism and so is just as much part of the secularisation process as the liberalism it opposes. It represents an attempt to reassert the total authority which has been thus challenged and to turn back the process of modernisation (at whatever period).[1]

Most texts which are held to be infallible do have a definite historical situation, as is recognised by liberal theologians and believers, who view the scriptures in the context of the conditions prevailing when they originated or to which they refer and are prepared to reinterpret them in the light of changed circumstances. Fundamentalism, however, tends to view these texts as timelessly valid, thus implying a non-historical or even anti-historical worldview. The most that can be done is to discover truths already revealed in the texts but hidden by our own inability to grasp them. Within Christianity, one of the effects of fundamentalism is that appeal to the authority of the scriptures, or more exactly to a particular, rather narrow interpretation of them has led its adherents to substitute the medium for the message, to take a few texts and make shibboleths of them rather than to be open to the living Word of God. In its most extreme form fundamentalism can lead to bibliolatry. It is often based not merely on selective interpretation of scripture (commonly by taking a brief statement uncritically out of its context and so failing to take into account the underlying sense of the whole passage) but sometimes on incorrect understanding through refusal to accept the validity of textual scholarship. This is shown in partiality for a particular translation, usually the longest established (for example, among English speakers, the Authorised Version of 1611), and in a failure to realise that the favoured version may present an incorrect rendering of the original, or, more often, that the meaning of words has altered, so that statements which once were clear or accurate are now misunderstood. This position can come very close to the use of incantations, where it is the form of words alone which is important, not the meaning; this is then a little like the degeneration of the use of *mantras* within Hinduism, where at first the Vedic hymns used in the ritual were those that were most apposite but later, as the meaning was no longer understood by most, the emphasis shifted to the exactness of the repetition of ever shorter forms of words.

It is interesting to observe that there was indeed a somewhat similar development in the conservative Mīmāṃsā system, of which we have already seen something above. In the interests of the correct interpretation of the Vedas, it sought to prove that the Vedas were eternal (and thus inerrant, but also lacking a divine author). The basic standpoint of the Mīmāṃsā system is that the Vedas, being eternal and uncreated, possess absolute authority and that the Vedic commands constitute man's entire duty (*dharma*). In concentrating on the actual mechanics of the Vedic sacrificial ritual, it further reached the position where its earliest author, Jaimini, regards deity as a redundant category irrelevant to his central concern, the discussion of *dharma*. Thus, effectively Mīmāṃsā becomes atheistic through a fundamentalist concentration on the scriptures themselves, or rather on one part of them.

The Mīmāṃsā method of exegesis is designed to demonstrate the consistency and non-ambiguity of the Vedic revelation. The textual material is arranged in such a way that conflicts and ambiguities can as far as possible be eliminated: an explanatory passage cannot contradict a command and the testimony of *śruti* is by definition stronger than that of *smṛti*.[2] Even where certain sentences in the Vedas appear incoherent or meaningless, this is not really so, for it is invalid to take any Vedic utterance out of context and treat it in isolation; in this respect, then, there is less analogy to the fundamentalist use of scripture within Christianity. The Mīmāṃsā system thus carries forward the exegesis and the defence of the Vedic sacrificial *dharma* into the period of the classical philosophical systems, which operate under quite a different framework of methods and presuppositions.

As the example of the Mīmāṃsā shows, the phenomenon of reaction is by no means limited to the modern West, as some writers have assumed. There have also been similar figures or movements within more modern Hinduism, such as Dayānanda Sarasvatī, who points to the Vedas as 'the supreme authority in the ascertainment of true religion' and asserts that all men should believe in them as the only true revelation, since they are absolutely free from error and self-authenticating. What is commanded by them is right and what is condemned by them is wrong. Through his Ārya Samāj he sought to promote the authority of the Vedas as the Word of God and the source of true revelation.

There is another type of attitude, not uncommonly found within the commentary tradition of the Hindu philosophical systems, which may be compared with fundamentalism in its approach, although in some respects its effects were the reverse. To the extent that such philosophical commentators, mainly in the period between the fourth and tenth centuries, cultivated the myth that their founder's thought could be endlessly extended, since universally valid, their outlook resembled a fundamentalist one. But, whereas the fundamentalism associated with Christianity tries on the whole to reverse the historical process, the philosophical commentators' outlook did not attempt to reject change but only to deny its operation. They did not in reality attempt in their commentaries to return to the insights of the original writer and expound those, as was their declared intention, but rather they sought to present their own philosophical ideas as being already logically implicit in the *sūtra,* the basic text which forms the foundation of the system. Too exact a definition of what precisely the original writer meant would have limited its scope and risked easy rebuttal by rival schools.[3] There had to be room for change and development if these schools were to retain philosophical credibility but equally the original insight had to be represented as being a timeless truth, the more so as these philosophical systems developed ever closer ties with the religious orthodoxy. A prime example of this is the very divergent interpretation of the *Brahmasūtra* or *Vedāntasūtra* offered within the Vedānta system by its various commentators, of whom the two best known are Śaṅkara (traditionally 788–820) and Rāmānuja (traditionally 1017–1137), the founders respectively of the Advaita and Viśiṣṭādvaita subschools; even more, perhaps, can it be seen in the numerous commentaries on the *Bhagavadgītā* which joined the *Brahmasūtra* and the Upaniṣads as the three authoritative texts for the Vedānta system.

The role of brāhmans as the major religious specialists within Hinduism can be traced back at least as far as the Brāhmaṇas (and it is no accident that the name of the group and of the texts is in fact the same, meaning in both cases 'related to Brahman'). One of the features of the Brāhmaṇas is the extent of the emphasis placed on the sacrificial ritual and its efficacy in maintaining the world in its proper order. One result was that the gods, to whom the sacrifice was once directed for their gratification, became less and less relevant as the act itself assumed greater significance, while the importance of the priestly officiants correspondingly increased, to the point where one of the Brāhmaṇas asserts that there are two sorts of gods – deities in heaven and brāhmans as human gods – and two sorts of sacrifice – oblations to the deities and fees to the brāhmans – with the implicit suggestion that the nearer ones are the more effective or relevant (*Śatapatha Brāhmaṇa* 2.2.2.6). Despite the challenge to their supremacy which can perhaps be glimpsed in the linking of some of the teaching of the Upaniṣads with the second class, the kṣatriyas, in general the hold of the brāhman class on the religious life of India has tended only to increase. The two great Sanskrit epics, which in their origins clearly belong to the secular culture of the kṣatriya aristocracy, in due course acquired religious significance when Rāma and Kṛṣṇa were identified with Viṣṇu as transmission of the texts passed into the hands of the brāhmans, who by this time were well established as the guardians and teachers of tradition.

Such authority has always been exercised by the brāhmans as a class and hence, in the absence of a single authority figure, it has tended to be a leadership by consent rather than a dictatorial control. Hinduism as a whole lacks a clear hierarchy of control (although this may well be found within specific sects and is indeed something of a characteristic of such groups); but in this it is not actually so different from Christianity as a whole, which has no unified structure, even though the hierarchical principal is very apparent in two major components, the Roman Catholic and Orthodox Churches, and present in slightly less marked degree in others, such as the Church of England. What is different is the way in which the brāhmans carry out their activities. For example, the group called the Smārta ('traditional', from *smṛti*) brāhmans tend to advocate rituals directed to the group of five deities (Viṣṇu, Śiva, Devī, Sūrya and Gaṇeśa) who are largely acceptable to most Hindus, but they also regard themselves as followers of Śaṇkara's Advaita Vedānta, as a sign of intellectual orthodoxy; in the absence of Śrīvaiṣṇava priests, it is they who are called upon by members of that sect to perform the various day-to-day rituals, and they play a similar role in relation to several other groups.

The extent to which the brāhmans as a group had continually to make accommodations with the civil power in order to maintain (and where possible enhance) their position as religious leaders is well illustrated in provisions recorded in perhaps the earliest of the Dharmaśāstras (textbooks of legal theory, composed by brāhmans from a brāhman perspective), the one ascribed to Manu and assignable to around the second century; as we shall see in chapter six, some of the foreign groups who invaded India around the beginning of the Christian era are there described as lapsed kṣatriyas, a legal fiction which opens the way to their (re)admittance into the orthodox community after performance of the appropriate rituals. This means that their *de facto* status as rulers can be given religious sanction (in effect *de jure* status), provided that they acknowledge the brāhmans as religious leaders. This kind of symbiotic relationship between religious and civil leadership can then be traced throughout much of Indian history.

The schism between the Eastern and the Western branches of

Christendom, conventionally dated at 1054 (the excommunication of Patriarch Michael Cerularius by Cardinal Humbert) but in fact occurring more gradually over a longer period, involved a number of factors; one of the more significant was their different understanding of the structure of the Christian community. The Western church saw the church on the model of a monarchy and regarded the Pope as the source of all authority in teaching and administration, whereas the Eastern church rejected a papacy of that kind, regarding the Patriarchs as leaders rather than sovereigns (perhaps partly because the Byzantine emperors exercised close control over the church). The various churches of the Byzantine Orthodox communion still exhibit this feature; they comprise some twenty churches, all theoretically enjoying equality of status and self-government, so that no decision is made in the name of the Orthodox Church unless it is approved by all. The Ecumenical Patriarch of Constantinople occupies the most senior position among the ancient Patriarchates (the others being of Alexandria, Antioch, Jerusalem and Cyprus). However, in many ways the most important organisation nowadays is into the five major national churches of Russia, Rumania, Greece, Yugoslavia and Bulgaria (most of them headed by Patriarchs; the heads of other churches may be called Catholicos, Metropolitan or Archbishop).

By contrast, the Roman Catholic Church, following the collapse of the Western Roman Empire, came in its dealings with the barbarian tribes converting to Christianity to function almost as another state. In addition, in such mass conversions we see the kings bringing their people into Christianity with them, the king and the state being seen as basically the same; this was to lead to the concept of the establishment of religion, of the union of church and state, which has dominated most Roman Catholic thought until this century. It was indeed a principle which many of the Protestant Reformers were content to take over from the Roman Catholic Church. As the head of a quasi-state, however, the Pope came to exercise autocratic powers over the rest of the clergy and the Roman Catholic Church is marked by a strongly authoritarian structure.

One factor in facilitating the development of such a rigidly hierarchical structure may well have been the institution of celibacy (in which the Roman Catholic Church is unique among Christian churches), since a celibate priest is perhaps more easily subject to such control, having fewer counter-claims on his allegiance. Even its rule of celibacy was not universal before the First Lateran Council in 1123, which established as generally obligatory what was by then prevalent in most dioceses and was quite possibly due to monastic influence. Priestly celibacy also served to reinforce the pattern common in the Renaissance and early modern Europe of a close association between spiritual and temporal power, with cardinals often being younger brothers of important rulers, for with celibacy hereditary succession is in theory impossible and so inheritance of high ecclesiastical office returned at each generation to the seat of temporal power. Thus, whereas in Hinduism the *varṇa* system separates brāhmans as religious specialists from kṣatriyas as wielders of temporal power, the organisation of the Christian clergy tended in the past to encourage links between religious and secular authority.

The Protestant churches after the Reformation asserted the principle of the priesthood of all believers and in some cases did initially do away with a separate clergy; this is a position that the Society of Friends have maintained to this day in many countries, although in others pastoral leadership is accepted. In practice, however, the great majority of Protestant denominations do nowadays have an ordained clergy but their status is inevitably not the same as that of the Roman Catholic or Orthodox priests, since ultimately the minister or pastor (the difference in terminology serving to underline the difference in function) is just another believer along with the other members of the church. Martin Luther (1483–1546) envisaged the church largely in terms of pastors who, though sharing in the common priesthood of believers, had as their function the conduct of public worship. Calvin in his *Institutes* set out a fourfold order of pastors, teachers, elders and deacons, claiming scriptural authority for this scheme, and laid down that only a duly ordained man might preach or administer the sacraments; for Calvin, ministers were elected by the consent and approval of the people (and he cites St Cyprian in his support).

The ordination of women is accepted by virtually all Protestant denominations that have a permanent ministry (the main exception at present being parts of the Anglican communion), reinforcing the break with the Roman Catholic doctrine of the priesthood. His or her function is not one of mediation between the laity and God but ideally one of leadership in encouraging the whole church to exercise its ministry both in the worship of God and in witness and service to others. Typically, the minister will have had an extensive theological training which serves to set him or her apart from the rest of the local church, and ordination, though to the local church, will have involved other clergy (and indeed in the Anglican and some other denominations will be performed by a bishop in a pattern close to the Roman Catholic one). Also, in practice most denominations have evolved forms of association which, however great the emphasis in theory on the independence of the local church (or more exactly its responsibility directly to God), have introduced a measure of centralisation, which nonetheless falls far short of the hierarchical structure of the Roman Catholic Church. In this more diffuse pattern of leadership rather than authority the Protestant clergy are, indeed, perhaps more similar to the brāhmans within Hinduism than to the Roman Catholic clergy, though sharing with the latter a vocation to the task as against the brāhmans' hereditary entitlement.

Both Hinduism and Christianity at the popular level show a blending of monotheistic and polytheistic elements. The individual worships one deity but also venerates other figures. The figures of the Christian saints, though in principle real historical individuals, do include the mythical (such as St George, the slayer of the dragon) and fairly transparent adoptions of pagan deities (such as St Joasaph, who is a version of the Buddha, or St Bridget, who is related to the Celtic goddess Brigantia, patroness of arts and crafts and fertility, and in Irish Christianity became the midwife of the Virgin Mary). Though originally applied to all Christians and so used in the New Testament, the term saint came to be restricted from around 200 to a few outstanding individuals. The cult of the saints was originally intended to honour those martyred in the church's persecution by the Roman state, who had thus made the supreme witness to their faith (martyr is the Greek word for a witness), but it then continued as a means to edify the faithful with Christian ideals.

Orthodox Christians, in both public and private prayers, ask the saints to pray for them and they also pray for the saints, in a vivid affirmation of the concept of 'the communion of saints'. They do not regard them so much as mediators but rather as teachers and friends who by their Christlike character can bring others nearer to God. Canonisation in the Orthodox Churches begins locally with popular feeling for an outstanding individual, followed by examination by the local church of the record left by that individual and is concluded by pronouncement of canonisation by the hierarchy of that church and announcement of the fact to the other Orthodox Churches.

Devotion to the saints and in particular to Mary is a characteristic feature of the Roman Catholic Church. The saints are thought to represent examples of successful leading of the Christian life, respect for and imitation of which is only natural. They are also regarded as intercessors, being as it were more intimate with God; they are held to have pre-eminently the power of intercessory prayer which all Christians have. Mary as mother of Jesus is held to be closer to him than any other human being, while her position has been enhanced over the centuries by the doctrines of her immaculate conception (long vigorously debated and denied, for instance, by Aquinas but declared as dogma by Pope Pius IX in 1854) and bodily assumption into heaven. It is clear that Mary forms the main channel for the feminine element within Roman Catholicism, uniting at all periods the two ideals of womanhood as virgin and as mother. Significantly there is a story that when Vasco da Gama first arrived in India in 1498, he worshipped in the temple of a local goddess, taking it to be a shrine to Mary, while it is by no means unknown in modern South India for Mary to be conflated with Māriyamman, one of the major goddesses there, or even to be regarded as the sister of such a goddess. The cult of Mary reached its peak in the Middle Ages, when it came to influence western European secular literature; the devotion of the faithful to the virgin Queen of Heaven was reflected and even parodied in the courtly romances as the devotion of the lover to his unattainable mistress. The multiple Madonnas (strictly not multiple Marys but appearances of her to individuals or groups) show a pattern of localisation of religion which may well owe something to preceding pagan worship. In more modern times, in the nineteenth and twentieth centuries, new centres of pilgrimage in the Roman Catholic Church have mainly been established as a result of visions of the Virgin Mary; examples range from Lourdes (where Bernadette Soubirous had visions of the Virgin in 1858), through Fátima (in 1917), to Međugorje (in 1981).

Practically from the beginning, however, elements of supplication were mixed with the veneration and before long the spiritual power of the saints was popularly located in their material remains. Indeed, it is clear that to many ordinary people in mediæval Europe the relics of the saints were sought after because they were identical with the saints themselves. Thus, paradoxically, whereas many saints had seen their bodies as enemies of their spirit and sources of sin, their remains were regarded as vehicles of supernatural power. In addition to this reversal of values, the cult of the saints also tended to foster among those who prayed to them for intercession a religious viewpoint which saw God as remote or inaccessible to ordinary people, the opposite of that direct vision and communion with God which characterised the saints themselves. The life of a saint was a lesson in attaining holiness through self-denial for the love of God or in service of God's creatures, and was thus both a model for others and also a temptation towards vicarious piety; while some were inspired to imitate the saints, many asked only for their help. Although orthodox teaching insisted that the saints merely interceded with God for the suppliant, practice by clerics as well as the laity in the Middle Ages often turned the saint into a worker of miracles and generally a provider of material benefits, again particularly through the relics which were regarded as being the actual saint.

With the Reformation such views were fiercely challenged. In the late Middle Ages, the cult of the saints had so degenerated into crude materialism, with the trafficking in relics, worship of images and votive gifts to saints, that the Protestants rejected it outright, invoking the First and Second Commandments: 'You must have no other god besides me. You must not make a carved image for yourself, nor the likeness of anything in the heavens above, or on the earth below, or in the waters under the earth' (Exodus 20.3–4). In fact, somewhat less effectual criticisms had already been raised by John Wycliffe (c.1330–84) in Britain and Jan Huss (c.1372–1415) in Bohemia, while the Lollards objected strongly to indulgences and to the veneration of images and relics, which they regarded as synonymous with idolatry. Martin Luther's doctrine of justification by faith alone ruled out the saints' efforts to earn divine grace by acts of charity and personal asceticism. He noted that Christ had come to be represented as an awesome judge rather than a loving saviour and suggested that this was the origin of the growth in the cult of the saints. He was convinced that Christ was the sole mediator, exercising an eternal highpriesthood, and attacked the saints as rivals to his position. His attack on indulgences in the 95 Theses of 1517, fixed to the door of the Schloßkirche at Wittenberg, raised the whole issue of individual responsibility for salvation. Rejecting the traditional

Catholic distinction between veneration and worship, Protestants argued that prayers to the saints violated the first commandment. They declared that saints were those who lived by God's grace, which was a free gift, and so the saints were the whole community of the faithful.

The Counter Reformation, while continuing to affirm the value of the cult of saints, was also concerned to curb its excesses, all the more so as it could be seen as a manifestation of lay piety and out of tune with the centralising hierarchical aspect of the Roman Catholic Church, now re-emphasised. The saints themselves by their outstanding virtues were a challenge to the frailties of the clergy, while their supernatural powers detracted from the centrality of the priestly celebration of the Eucharist. Also, saints' cults were often localised and so could become the focus of local, civic or national pride and even of nationalism. Increasingly, therefore, the veneration of saints was brought under strict papal control.

The attitude of the Church of England has been ambiguous, as might be expected where the break with the Roman Catholic Church was inspired by political at least as much as by theological considerations. In the long run, Mary and the apostles lost their roles as intercessors but were not excluded from reverence, while saints' cults were abolished; unofficially though, at least, they retain a certain hold.

In Hinduism, the figures who correspond most closely to the Christian saints, the Vedic seers and the great religious achievers, especially the yogins, of later periods have not on the whole attracted the same veneration as mediating figures. Some have done so and for example, several of the Āḻvārs, the Vaiṣṇava *bhakti* poets in Tamil, were considered to be incarnations of Viṣṇu or his consort or of his attributes, such as his conch and mace, and as such attracted some worship. However, for the most significant mediatory figures, one must look elsewhere. The figure of Hanumān is one that is very popular with the masses of the Hindu population, especially in Maharashtra, where he is commonly known as Māruti, 'the son of the wind'. In literature he occurs primarily in the *Rāmāyaṇa* and its derivatives, where he is the monkey leader who is the great helper and loyal servant of Rāma. At the popular level, though, Hanumān is worshipped both as a great devotee of Rāma and as a powerful magician. The great Hindi poet, Tulsīdās, whose own attitude to Rāma is mainly the devotion of a servant for his loving master, wrote a version of the Rāma story, the *Rāmcaritmānas*, in which he quite naturally finds a special place for Hanumān, who by his time had become the pattern of whole-hearted service to the deity, despite his all too human failings of lack of application and forgetfulness. In another of his works, Tulsīdās appeals to Hanumān to act as intermediary between himself and Rāma; this mediatory role has subsequently been a frequent one in popular devotion.

The role of the consort as a mediator between the devotee and his deity in Hinduism has already been treated in Chapter 2 as one model of divine interaction with the world, but it is also relevant here. Invocation of Pārvatī or Lakṣmī by worshippers of Śiva or Viṣṇu respectively would be more nearly analogous to Christian intercession with, for example, St Michael the Archangel, since there is no suggestion that they have ever been part of the human condition (except in so far as Śrī or Lakṣmī becomes incarnate to accompany Viṣṇu in his descents to earth). The position of Nandin in relation to Śiva is also in some ways similar to that of Hanumān in relation to Rāma but he has not normally been the focus of any significant cult of his own, his worship simply forming part of the worship addressed to Śiva.

Channels of mediation between the human and divine levels need not be only personal, however, and forms of mediation based on the authority of the community as a whole and thus more institutional – Christian sacraments and Hindu *saṃskāras* – are just as significant. The Roman Catholic Church clearly affirms that there are seven sacraments – baptism, confirmation, Eucharist (Mass), penance (confession), extreme unction, orders and marriage – and that they were instituted by Jesus Christ; up to the twelfth century the number was not in fact fixed but since Peter Lombard (c.1100–60) the number has been settled at seven. The Orthodox Churches, which prefer to call them 'mysteries', for a long time not only accepted these seven but also regarded as sacraments various other rituals (for example, the Blessing of the Waters at Epiphany, a monk's or nun's vows and the consecration of a church); more recently there has been a tendency to accept just the seven but sacramental practice has remained less formalised than in the Roman Catholic Church and, indeed, Orthodox prayer books generally include, beside these major sacraments, over forty other rites and sacramental blessings. From the

Reformation onwards, the various Protestant churches have argued that not all the seven are found in the New Testament, tending generally to recognise just baptism and communion as central, although some – in particular the Society of Friends and the Salvation Army – have rejected the use of sacraments altogether.

Roman Catholic belief is that the sacraments are effective symbols but that the manner of their operation belongs in the area of mystery. St Thomas Aquinas cast his explanation of the sacraments in terms of the Aristotelian concept of matter and form as the two components of material reality. According to this, the matter, such as the water in baptism and the bread and wine in the Eucharist, in itself has no sacramental significance but receives that from the accompanying words, which constitute the form; both must be ritually correct and concurrent for the sign to be valid. Baptism is administered by the pouring of water over the head and the utterance of the Trinitarian formula (deriving from Matthew 28:19) 'I baptise you in the name of the Father and of the Son and of the Holy Spirit'. Since baptism is the sign of entry into the church, the baptistery is separated from the rest of the church by a screen or grill or, in some older churches, is actually a separate building. Confirmation is intended to be administered at the start of adolescence but has been preceded during most of this century by the first communion, since the age for that was lowered to seven;[4] it is administered by a bishop (though not necessarily the diocesan bishop) and the biblical basis for it is claimed in the laying on of hands in Acts (8:17 and 19:1–7). The Eucharist (often called the Mass or Holy Communion) is held to be a sacrifice, a symbolic re-enactment of the atoning death of Jesus Christ as prefigured in the Last Supper; the Council of Trent (1545–63) declared that the offering in the Mass is not merely an offering of praise or thanksgiving, nor just a remembrance of Christ's offering of himself on the cross, but a reconciling offering. The bread and the wine are changed into the body of Christ, the doctrine of transsubstantiation endorsed by the Fourth Lateran Council of 1215, interpreted in the Aristotelian categories of St Thomas Aquinas. Communicants receive only the bread, in practice a wafer, while the celebrant alone drinks the wine, and this has been the practice since at least the fifteenth century. Penance, more commonly called confession, is justified on the basis of the risen Christ's words to his disciples: 'If you forgive anyone's sins, they are forgiven; if you pronounce them unforgiven, unforgiven they remain' (John 20:23). It is obligatory before receiving the Eucharist if one has committed a mortal sin but frequency of confession varies greatly; the priest hears the confession of the penitent and declares absolution. Extreme unction was formerly the last anointing with consecrated oil administered to those near to death, accompanied by confession and communion (and given the specific name of *viaticum*), and its sacramental effect was held to be the removal of 'the remains of sin' as a key part of the preparation for death; since the liturgical reforms inaugurated by the Second Vatican Council, it has become a rite to strengthen the sick.

These five sacraments form a complete life-cycle of rituals in religious terms and would do so in sociological terms were it not for the absence of marriage from among them. Thomas Aquinas was indeed aware of this when he noted a similarity between spiritual and natural life and applied it to the sacraments (*Summa Theologiae* 3.65.1). The two remaining sacraments of the Roman Catholic Church can be seen as in a sense optional, in that no one has to become a priest or to marry. The sacrament of holy orders is strictly a series of seven orders, of which only the last few are truly sacramental. The four minor orders (janitor, lector, exorcist and acolyte) had tended to become obsolete but there have been moves to revive them since the Second Vatican Council. Of the three major orders of subdeacon, deacon and priest (the bishop not strictly being a separate order), the first two are seen mainly as preliminaries to the third. The priest is empowered to administer all the sacraments except orders and usually confirmation, and ordination (of males only) is conferred on the candidate by the bishop delivering to him the Eucharistic vessels and laying his hands on him, signifying the claim to an unbroken succession from Apostolic times. In the sacrament of marriage, the consent of the partners to the union is seen as the sacrament, with the priest there essentially as a witness, but the contract is sacramental only if it is between two baptised individuals; a consummated marriage is also regarded as indissoluble.

In the Orthodox Churches, the life-cycle pattern is very evident at birth, when the standard practice is for the priest to visit the home on the day of the birth to bless the child and on the eighth day to name the child, even before the ceremony of baptism. These churches have on the whole been much less concerned to create precise definitions of the nature and efficacy of the sacraments, being content to term them 'mysteries' and to interpret them as symbols of the divine interaction with mankind. The general Orthodox practice in baptism is a three-fold immersion, accompanied by a Trinitarian formula. Baptism is combined with Chrismation, which corresponds to confirmation,[5] being seen as the receiving of the gift of the Holy Spirit and being performed with holy oil (which must have been previously consecrated by a gathering of bishops, although the ceremony is performed by the priest); as a result children are accepted as communicants from infancy. In the sacrament of confession the priest commonly stands alongside the penitent and at the end asks Christ's forgiveness for the penitent in a way that distances them less from each other; among Russian Orthodox in particular it is regarded as a necessary part of preparation for communion.

The Orthodox Churches centre their liturgy very much on the Eucharist, in which they ask God to change the bread and wine into the body and blood of Christ without on the whole attempting to define matters further. There are a number of different forms of the liturgy among the various churches but several features are general. The Eucharist is usually celebrated at an altar concealed by a screen, with a deacon linking the congregation and the priests celebrating the liturgy at the altar; the laity normally receive both elements. Unction, anointing with holy oil, is a regular practice in cases of illness (not confined to those expected to die) and even, in the Russian Orthodox Church, often offered during Lent to all members of the congregation who wish to receive it; it is regarded as a vehicle of the healing power of the church. The ritual of ordination involves the whole community: the ordinand is presented for approval to the laity and then to the assembled clergy before kneeling in front of the bishop to receive the laying on of hands. There is thus a combination of the claim to Apostolic succession through the bishop with choice by the local congregation. Marriage is commonly called 'crowning' and in its form the sacrament combines some features of ordination and the Eucharist, invoking the symbolism of the Church as the Bride of Christ the King in the crowning which forms a part of the ritual and expressing the couple's new unity by their drinking the wine from the same cup. The priest then takes them by the hand and leads them thrice round the lectern.

The views of the Protestant churches on the sacraments have

varied. Martin Luther, for example, in his catechism includes just the two sacraments and refers to them as instituted by Christ, the Heidelberg Catechism of 1562 states that the Reformed Church recognises only the sacraments of Baptism and the Lord's Supper, but Philip Melanchthon (1497–1560), defining the sacraments as rites which have the command of God, accepts three: Baptism, the Lord's Supper and Absolution. Luther, nevertheless, includes penance in his Small Catechism between Baptism and the Lord's Supper, though not giving it sacramental status. In due course both Lutheran and Reformed churches have come to accept just the two sacraments of Baptism and the Lord's Supper as alone having a biblical basis. It was recognised that baptism in the New Testament was a mark of conversion and connected with the confession of sins, with the one to be baptised asking for baptism (e.g. Acts 8:36–8, 22:16), but most Protestant churches have continued the practice of infant baptism, basing this on the accounts of the baptism of whole households or families (e.g. Acts 10:48 and 16:33) and on analogies with the Jewish rite of circumcision. Some, however, have emphasised the aspects of conversion and confession and affirmed that baptism should be of believers only; the main groups to take this stance in the wake of the Reformation were those generically labelled Anabaptist, among whom the present-day Mennonites are probably the best known, and at later dates the Baptists, Disciples of Christ, most Plymouth Brethren, and Seventh-day Adventists, while in the last half century the issue has received renewed attention in the wake of Karl Barth's criticism of infant baptism. The Lord's Supper is often seen as a commemoration rather than a sacrament, with the real presence of Christ coming through the renewal by the individual participants of their faith in and fellowship with him rather than through anything that is done in the celebration. The Reformers as a whole rejected the idea that Christ was offered in the celebration, which was rather the eating of the bread and drinking of the wine in grateful remembrance of Christ's death, and most Protestant churches, apart from Lutherans and some Anglicans, also reject the idea that any transformation takes place in the bread and the wine.

Hinduism has a considerably more elaborate system of *saṃskāras*, literally 'perfectings', rites which prepare an individual or object for a function, but applied more specifically in the texts on domestic ritual (Gṛhyasūtras) and the law books (Dharmaśāstras) to the series of personal life-cycle rituals or sacraments which begin even before birth. These texts do not agree on the number of *saṃskāras* and the total varies between forty and twelve, although the most usual figure is sixteen. The descriptions of the rites also diverge considerably, with explicit recognition in the texts of local and caste differences, and the importance of the different ceremonies varies. Here too, at any rate in the Gṛhyasūtras, marriage is taken outside its natural place in the sequence but precedes the rest. This reflects its centrality to Hinduism, in which only a married man accompanied by his wife is regarded as entitled to perform the major ritual acts; already Vedic texts declare that a man becomes complete only after gaining wife and producing a son.

After detailed instructions about the selection of suitable partners, about the proper age of marriage for boys and girls, about the auspicious time for the marriage and so forth, the texts list the various rites, which are more subject to local variation than for any other *saṃskāra* (a situation that seems always to have existed since the Gṛhyasūtras acknowledge the variety of customs existing), although there are four core components which usually are present. The bride is given away by her father; the bridegroom takes the bride's hand and says 'I take your hand for happiness'; he leads her three times round the sacred fire and after each circumambulation makes her step on a stone with appropriate words; and he makes her take seven steps towards the northeast, again uttering a standard formula. The circumambulation of the sacred fire in the Hindu ritual and the circumambulation of the lectern in the Orthodox ritual are presumably both calling on divine witness of the ceremony. The seven steps are often regarded as the essential act of the marriage, which comes into being at that point; in India the Hindu Marriage Act of 1955 provides both that Hindu marriages may be solemnised in accordance with the customs of either party and also that, where the seven steps are included, 'the marriage becomes complete and binding when the seventh step is taken.'

The list of *saṃskāras* continues with three performed during pregnancy (one to promote conception, one to secure a male child and one to ensure the safety of the child in the womb), then come the birth ceremony, the naming ceremony on the tenth or twelfth day after the birth, coming out of the birth chamber between the twelfth day and the fourth month from birth, the first feeding of solid food in the sixth month, ear-piercing performed between the twelfth day and the fifth year and tonsure in the fifth year; the main aim of these childhood *saṃskāras* is the protection and well-being of the child. The subsequent *saṃskāras* have a clearly social significance; these are investiture with the sacred thread, return from studentship accompanied by a ritual bath, and the funeral rituals (both after death and subsequent memorial rituals). There could in addition, according to the traditional texts, be various further rituals but most of these are now rarely if ever practised; even of the major rituals, some are applicable only to males and in particular to male brāhmans.

The ceremony of investiture with the sacred thread (*upanayana*) was originally open to all males of the three upper *varṇas* (brāhmans standardly receiving it at eight, kṣatriyas at eleven and vaiśyas at twelve) and marked their admission by a 'second birth' into the life of the full adult community, but later it came to be almost entirely restricted to brāhmans, with the result that the term 'twice-born', denoting those who had undergone the ceremony, became synonymous with brāhman. In the earliest texts prescribing the ritual, the boy becomes the pupil of a teacher (*guru*) who places the sacred thread (a cord of three threads, each made of nine strands) over his left shoulder to hang across his chest and under his right arm and imparts to him the *Gāyatrī* (the *mantra* drawn from *Ṛgveda* 3.62.10 which is still to be muttered each morning and in all rituals). Traditionally, this was followed by a period of studentship and celibacy under the teacher, during which the student (*brahmacārin*) learnt the Vedas and related material, but this has long been reduced to a mere token for most. Originally this period of studentship could last for up to twelve years, although this figure may have been symbolic of completeness, and only after the student had ceremonially completed the period and taken a ritual bath could he assume the duties and privileges of full adult status, in particular by marrying and setting up as a householder. This ritual in particular has suffered most from the trend among educated Hindus to drop some rites and abbreviate others. Although habit and a sense of obligation encourage educated Hindus to maintain traditional worship in this sense more strongly than would be the case in the West, there is a marked tendency towards simplification. Usually, this is a matter of individual initiative but there are some instances of formal attempts to remodel the rituals; for example, the Dharma Nirnaya

Mandal in Maharashtra, as part of its aim to re-establish *dharma* in the modern world, has produced a new investiture ceremony in which the now irrelevant taking leave of her son by the mother is omitted and the child promises to study truth as a school pupil and student rather than under a *guru*.

Although there are signs that investiture was possible in the Vedic period for girls also (as well as for males of the first three classes, but not of the fourth class, the śūdras), since they too could receive a full education, before long they lost that privilege and the only ceremony to mark their admission into adulthood was that of marriage. The age of marriage in India has long been low and indeed the proper time for a girl is before puberty according to many texts, as well as popular practice. The general view is that failure to marry a daughter before her first menstruation causes the father to incur the same guilt as if he had procured an abortion (itself considered more heinous than many kinds of murder, but sharply distinguished in its terminology from accidental miscarriage) and there is regularly an extreme emphasis on the procreative function of marriage; there are also some similarities to the official Roman Catholic condemnation of contraception and abortion.

The last *saṃskāra* is the funeral, standardly in Hinduism by cremation and regarded from the late Vedic period onwards as the last sacrifice, in which one's own body is offered in the sacrificial fire to be born again into a new existence. There are in fact a series of events comprising this *saṃskāra* and so the term 'funeral' is really too narrow. The first stage should be preparation for death: purification by bathing, laying on the earth (usually with the head to the north and in some cases out of doors), Gaṅgā-water and *tulasī* leaves being placed in the mouth. Immediately after death come the washing and dressing of the corpse and it is then placed on a kind of stretcher for the journey to the cremation ground, during which balls of rice (*piṇḍa*) are placed at specific points along the way. Traditionally the cremation itself takes place within a day of death. The cremation ritual does not complete the funeral, for the spirit of the dead person in a ghost-like form (*preta*) lingers in a liminal state for twelve days or a year, during which special offerings of food and water are made; on the twelfth day (as is current practice) or after a year, the dead person is united with his or her ancestors in a rite involving the amalgamation of rice balls, signifying the generations. The best known exception to the practice of cremation is that renouncers (*saṃnyāsins*) are buried, often in a seated position as though continuing their meditation, since their act of renunciation marks their death to society and indeed incorporates significant elements of the funeral ritual.[6]

4

Devotionalism and Personal Piety

It has commonly been said that by contrast with Christianity there is no true prayer in Hinduism and, if by prayer is meant intercessory prayer (with which in any case some liberal Christians have certain problems with regard to its meaningfulness or efficacy), then there is a measure of truth in the statement. However, if the more contemplative and meditative aspects (which will mainly be examined in Chapter 5) are intended, the statement is rather misleading, since both the *bhakti* movement and popular Hinduism in general show ample evidence for the loving devotion to the deity which underlies prayer. It will be helpful to outline the history of the *bhakti* movement before proceeding further with an examination of devotionalism and personal piety.

The earliest significant use of the term *bhakti* is in the *Bhagavadgītā* but in a somewhat different sense from that which it later acquires. Typical of the *Bhagavadgītā*'s use of the term is the way that Kṛṣṇa's self-revelation produces in Arjuna a spirit of humble adoration, although a hint of the future development of the term can also be seen in Kṛṣṇa's declaration at the end of the whole poem of his attachment (*bhakti*) to Arjuna and his promise that he can be attained and entered into through his grace. The nature of this devotion (which is probably the best translation for *bhakti* in its various nuances) is, however, rather more formal than later, for its hallmarks are sacrifice and discipline and there is little room for spontaneity, but rather a stress on one's duty (*dharma*), by which is meant one's caste-specific duties. Nor is there much suggestion of intimacy, except as part of the goal, and the attitude of the devotee should be that of Arjuna, subservience and awe. Nevertheless, this way of devotion, which is available to all, is placed above the ways of knowledge (*jñāna*) and action (*karma*).

A new and more intense meaning was given to the term *bhakti* by the emergence around the seventh century of a movement in the south of India, in the Tamil-speaking area, usually known simply as the *bhakti* movement. This was characterised by an intense personal relationship between the deity and the devotee such that worship became an ardent response of total commitment through experience of divine grace. The intensity of the emotion so engendered was such that the movement can only be described as monotheistic, although it had two parallel branches, each centred on one of the two major deities, Viṣṇu or Śiva, or rather on one or another of the local deities identified or related to these two. There is, indeed, what seems at first sight a paradoxical blending of the localisation of the deity with his universality, for between about the seventh and ninth centuries the Tamil poets of this movement delighted in praising the deity of a particular locality, as enshrined in a specific temple and as represented there, while being at the same time fully aware of his transcendence. What underlies this apparent paradox is precisely the intensity of the poets' experience of the deity here and now in their own particular situation, which included the shrines at which they worshipped. It is also worth noting that within the Vaiṣṇava branch of the *bhakti* movement the focus shifts from the theme of Viṣṇu's occasional intervention in the world's affairs by direct incarnation to that of his abiding presence through grace in the heart of every devotee, which has the result that the mythology of the *avatāras* did not develop significantly thereafter, except to the extent that either Rāma or Kṛṣṇa were themselves the focus of this devotion.

Whether they belong to the Vaiṣṇava or the Śaiva branch of this movement, these mystical poets emphasise the same recurrent themes. Religion is no longer a question of contemplating a transcendent and impersonal absolute but consists rather of rapturous response to a very personal deity in all his immanence. This results in a deep sense of the worshipper's own inadequacy and so to an appeal to the deity's forgiveness and grace, accompanied by a total surrender to him. This divine love should find expression in one's concern for one's fellows and cannot be limited by the bounds of caste and sex. Indeed, one of the frequent metaphors used in the *bhakti* poetry is that of conjugal love. Parallels to this can be found within the Christian tradition: the church as a whole can be seen as the Bride of Christ, individual nuns are regarded as being wedded to Christ, and in the *Odes of Solomon* (a series of early Christian poems dating to around 100) the believer's rapturous response to Christ is expressed in sexual and conjugal terms.

The collecting together of these *bhakti* poets' works in the tenth century began the process of systematising these fundamentally individual perceptions and thus producing theological schools. In South India these were first and foremost the Śrīvaiṣṇava and the Śaiva Siddhānta movements, the first of these centred in particular round the figure of Rāmānuja (traditionally 1017–1137) and the other formulated by a series of teachers between the twelfth and fourteenth centuries in the fourteen Śaiva Siddhānta Śāstras. As the movement spread beyond the Tamil-speaking area, first into other parts of South India and then into North India, a series of other movements emerged, usually centred around a particularly charismatic figure or an especially able teacher. Thus, there developed in Karnataka the Liṅgāyat or Vīraśaiva movement headed by Basava (c.1105–67) – a highly idiosyncratic development – and the Vaiṣṇava movement founded by Madhva, in Maharashtra the cult of Viṭṭhala (a local deity regarded as a form of Kṛṣṇa and thus of Viṣṇu) usually called the Vārkarī Panth, 'the pilgrims' path', and in North India a mass of often only half distinct groups, among which two of the most important have been those centred on Caitanya (1486–1533) and Vallabha (1479–1531), while the blending of Vaiṣṇava *bhakti* with certain other strands of Hinduism led to the wide-spread but rather ill-defined movement called the *sant* tradition.

Naturally, each of these have their distinctive emphases but it is also possible to identify certain common themes. The deity's loving involvement with his worshipper is clearly the most basic but this leads to a cluster of others: a higher valuation on life in the world than in much of Hinduism, a social concern based on the fact that the grace of the deity is open to all, a stress on the right religious response as being surrender to the deity and correspondingly a trusting expectation of his grace (*prasāda*), a tendency to see the goal not so much as *mokṣa* (simply, that is, as liberation from *saṃsāra*) but more as union with the deity both now and hereafter, and in some groups (though emphatically not in others) a trend towards rejecting the externals of religion in favour of the inner experience of the deity's presence. Most of these will be examined in later chapters but the theme of the deity's love for the devotee and the devotee's response to that love deserves further exploration here.

Meykaṇṭar (who wrote his main work around 1221) and other writers of the Śaiva Siddhānta school emphasise that *bhakti* produces in the individual the necessary attitude for receiving Śiva's grace in order to love him properly. They utilise four types or stages of *bhakti*. The first stage, which finds expression in tending the shrine and in service to other devotees, is regarded as the attitude of a servant towards his master; the second stage, expressed in offerings to the deity and the like, resembles the affection of a child for its parents; the third stage, which consists of loving meditation on Śiva as intelligence, is compared with the relationship of friends; and the fourth stage, comprising knowledge or direct intuition of Śiva, brings union with Śiva comparable to that of lovers. The *Bhāgavata Purāṇa*, a South Indian work of the ninth or tenth century devoted to Vaiṣṇava *bhakti*, recognises a ninefold classification of *bhakti* (7.5.23): these are *śravaṇa* (listening to the name of the deity or to narrative about him), *kīrtana* (chanting his name), *smaraṇa* (remembering or meditating on him), *pādasevana*, *arcana* and *vandana* (serving, worshipping and bowing to him), *dāsya* (servitude), *sakhya* (friendship) and *ātmanivedana* (self-offering). This comprehensive classification has been adopted by many later authors and schools.

For Rāmānuja, the most important figure in the corresponding Śrīvaiṣṇava movement, *bhakti* is the best means of salvation and consists of intense devotion and submission to Nārāyaṇa, the name by which Rāmānuja usually designates Viṣṇu, in which the worshipper realises his utter dependence on him. The essence of the *ātman* is to stand in a serving and subservient relationship to the deity and Rāmānuja declares that the universal desire for independence is an illusion, based on the mistaken identification of body and soul. Surrender (*prapatti*) to him as one's sole refuge is both the commencement and the continuance of devotion to the deity; it demands accepting one's dependence and so submitting entirely to the deity, trusting in his will and awaiting his grace. Though inaccessible to men in the fullness of his majesty, Viṣṇu is full of grace and love for his creation. The concept of *prapatti* is found earlier in some Pāñcarātra texts, where the term is used interchangeably with *bhakti* and it is stressed that such surrender works for everyone, no matter what his situation, for there are no prior conditions of fitness.

Rāmānuja's understanding of *prapatti* is most clearly revealed in his three devotional works, the *Gadyatraya*, the most revered of his writings and the most frequently recited by modern Śrīvaiṣṇavas. The first takes the form of an appeal by Rāmānuja to Nārāyaṇa and Śrī, his consort, at the festival which celebrates their marriage, and so is seen as the record of Rāmānuja's own act of taking refuge at the feet of the deity in surrender to his mercy. The second, shorter one consists of a prayer of surrender addressed to Raṅganātha (the form of Viṣṇu worshipped at Śrīraṅgam) and asking to be accepted as an eternal servant of the Lord. The third consists mainly of a detailed description of Viṣṇu's heaven, Vaikuṇṭha, to be meditated on regularly after performing the act of surrender. Together they reveal how Rāmānuja thought of the practice of *bhakti* as repeated, disciplined meditation on the deity's perfections. In a further work, a ritual handbook, Rāmānuja lays down the daily routine for an orthodox Śrīvaiṣṇava on the basis of the five daily acts of the Pāñcarātra and details the five sacraments specific to the community, which begin with the branding of Viṣṇu's symbols on the initiate's body.

Since, in the philosophical presentation of his ideas, Rāmānuja also defines the body-soul relationship between individual souls and Īśvara as the relationship between part and whole (more exactly, possessor of the part), which implies complete determination of souls by the deity, Rāmānuja directly addresses the question of whether the *ātman* acts by its own will or is dependent on the Supreme Self (*Śrībhāṣya* 2.3.40). His answer is in terms of the concept of 'permission' (*anumati*), whereby the deity as the 'inner controller' (*antaryāmin*) stands within the individual soul as the permitter and, while in respect of any action the volitional effort must come from the individual, the deity allows it to take effect. The individual has to realise that in all his actions he is dependent on the control, support and permission of the Supreme Self but this should lead, not to a passive resignation, but to an active desire to co-operate with his will. In this way Rāmānuja endeavours to preserve the agent's moral freedom to act, while affirming that Īśvara oversees it as a function of his universal causality. There are obvious analogies in this aspect of Rāmānuja's thought with process theology, with its idea of God undergoing real change and development in interaction with individuals. It also seeks to resolve the problems raised in Western philosophy over omniscience and freewill, in particular whether God knows now what the individual will freely do tomorrow, since if he does then freewill cannot really exist, while if he does not there must be additions to his knowledge and hence change in him – both of which are repugnant to the classical theist. The sophistication of Rāmānuja's thought is here clearly apparent.

Within two centuries of Rāmānuja's death the Śrīvaiṣṇava community had split in two. The schism centred on the question of *prapatti* in relation to divine grace, with both schools appealing to Rāmānuja's writings in support of their understanding of the issue. The Northern school (the Vaṭakalai) held that the worshipper had to make some effort to win the grace of the deity and so stressed the performance of *karma*, a position regularly summed up as being 'on the analogy of the monkey and its baby', since just as the monkey mother carries her young while they cling to her, so Viṣṇu saves the devotee if he himself make some effort. Vedāntadeśika, a leading exponent of this Northern school, affirms the need for an 'occasion' provided by human devotional effort, especially an initial ritual act of surrender, through which divine sovereign grace can function effectively. The Southern school (the Teṅkalai) held that the Lord's grace alone conferred salvation, a position 'on the analogy of the cat and its kittens', since just as the cat picks up her kittens in her mouth and carries them off willy-nilly, so Viṣṇu saves those whom he wills without effort on their part.

This controversy has often and with some reason been compared to the differences between the Arminian and Calvinist positions within Protestantism (it could also be said to be roughly analogous to a Pelagian as against an Augustinian stance, to take an earlier phase in Christian theological history). Equally, some of the Southern school adopt the rather dubious doctrine that God enjoys sin, since it gives a larger scope for the display of his grace – a view which again has analogies with the antinomian views of, for example, some early Anabaptists, while its rebuttal by other Śrīvaiṣṇavas has parallels with the emphatic rejection of antinomian ideas by other early Protestants, as well as with Paul's condemnation of them (Romans 6). In the Protestant churches, of course, the issue of election could divide denominations (and the rift subsequently be bridged); for example, the majority of English Methodists followed the Arminian views of John Wesley (1703–91) but the largest group among the Welsh were the Calvinistic Methodists, while in the Separatist tradition the generally moderate Calvinism of the Particular Baptists and the Congregationalists was flanked on one sideby the ultra-Calvinist Strict and Particular Baptists and on the other by the Arminian General Baptists.

There were in fact various other issues besides this doctrinal one which divided the two Śrīvaiṣṇava schools. In general the Southern school reveals a more liberal attitude, shown in its definite preference for the use of the local language, Tamil, and in teaching the same *mantra* to initiates of all castes, whereas the Northern school abbreviated the *mantra* given to brāhmans when teaching it to other castes, and reverted to the use of Sanskrit with its more conservative overtones; Rāmānuja himself had used Sanskrit in the interests of reaching as wide an audience as possible among the educated in other parts of India.

In the thought too of the later Vaiṣṇava Madhva (probably 1198–1278), as in Rāmānuja's, there is a subtle interplay between the grace of the deity and the worshipper's seeking. The Vedas, according to Madhva, teach that we can enter into relation with the transcendent deity; he also cites the *Bhagavadgītā* to demonstrate that this deity manifests himself to us. His grace (*prasāda*) can liberate us from the cycle of rebirth (*saṃsāra*) when we understand his nature and our total dependence on him through *bhakti*. We can know only as much about the deity as he chooses to reveal and so the growth of *bhakti* both is dependent on Viṣṇu's grace and in turn calls it forth.

In contrast to the trends visible in much of the *bhakti* movement to stress the equal worth of all worshippers, since all are of concern to the deity, Madhva develops a strongly hierarchical principle in his concept of the capability of each soul (*yogyatā*), a kind of inherent capacity which will be fully realised only in liberation, for even there distinctions remain and so released souls will gain a spiritual body corresponding to their capability, through which they can know Viṣṇu in his entirely spiritual form and attain one of the four types of association with him. What makes the working out of this concept so distinctive is Madhva's view that mankind is divided into three kinds: those chosen for eventual liberation, those doomed to eternal damnation and those destined to perpetual rebirth. This feature and one or two others have incidentally been seized on by some to suggest that Madhva was influenced by Christian ideas, perhaps through the Syrian Christians of Malabar,[1] but the parallels in ideas are not really very close (although some details of the hagiography around Madhva may more plausibly be owed to this source) and such convergence as there is should probably be attributed to the similarity of starting point.

A characteristic feature of the *bhakti* movement as it manifested itself in Maharashtra is the emphasis on devotion to the deity even by the lowest castes and concomitantly on the direct relationship between deity and devotee. One of the earliest figures in this area, Nāmdev (c.1270–1350) presents in his poetry the theme that the deity (who for these *bhakti* poets is Viṭṭhala, a local form of Kṛṣṇa and thus of Viṣṇu) is present everywhere and accessible to everyone, so that religious practices open only to the higher castes and even renunciation are unnecessary, since the one necessity is to love the deity and sing his name. Nāmdev emphasises the transcendence of his deity whom he identifies with Brahman (rather in the fashion of *nirguṇa bhakti*) and sees images simply as a token of his presence rather than as being imbued with any divine essence. Somewhat later Tukārām (d. 1650), coming from a poor and low caste family, declares that it is devotion to Viṭṭhala alone that produces holiness, and not one's caste status or even the experience of *mokṣa*. He thus puts the love of god first in the religious life and claims that without love (which necessarily implies duality) there cannot be real spiritual growth; his impassioned devotional hymns have remained highly popular in Maharashtra.

In the spread of the *bhakti* movement to the heart of North India a key role was played by Rāmānanda, a rather shadowy figure who probably belonged to the fourteenth century. The sect that he founded, the Rāmānandins or Rāmāvats, is the first clear manifestation of the cult of Rāma and Sītā, here regarded as the supreme deity and his consort rather than as *avatāras* of Viṣṇu. However, Rāmānanda's main significance is in terms of other individuals whom he apparently inspired, such as Kabīr and Tulsīdās.

Kabīr (probably early fifteenth century) was a highly complex figure with a tangled background and by tradition was a disciple of Rāmānanda. Born into a Muslim weaver community, he nevertheless shows in his religious language far greater acquaintance with the Hindu traditions of the Nāths (a Śaiva tantric group active in North India between the twelfth and fifteenth centuries) and the Vaiṣṇava *bhaktas*. Kabīr's approach to god was through *jñāna* as much as *bhakti*, since his deity is an absolute being without either an earthly incarnation or a personal form; he thus belongs to what has been termed the *sant* tradition. Nevertheless, his approach to this unqualified Brahman is suffused with a very real sense of love in the *bhakti* tradition, despite being linked with views of such love as a way of suffering which may reveal some indebtedness to the Sūfī mystics. He expresses very movingly in his poetry the seeking of the soul for the hidden deity who is yet deep within one's own heart, the hardships of the search and the sense of separation from the deity, while also affirming that the deity's grace is available to the devotee who loves him and presenting the goal of the mystical quest through the symbolism of the union of the soul with the deity as his bride, as well as describing it as a merging with the One in which all duality is abolished.

If Kabīr represents a monistic tendency emerging against a *bhakti* background, Caitanya (1486–1533) and Vallabha (1479–1531) are prime examples of the highly emotional aspect most characteristic of it. There had already been quite a tradition of Vaiṣṇava devotional songs in Bengali before the time of Caitanya but he is the first to institute a distinct sectarian community in Bengal. He underwent a relatively sudden conversion experience as a young man, when in 1508 he travelled to Gayā to perform memorial rites for his father; at this critical point he met again an ascetic whom previously he had rebuffed and was initiated by him into the worship of Kṛṣṇa. On his return to his home town, he became the centre of a group which met to sing devotional songs to Kṛṣṇa every night and soon began to have the periods of ecstasy and possession by Kṛṣṇa which became such a feature of his life and were to attract many others to this charismatic figure. Before long he had become a *saṃnyāsin*, a renouncer or ascetic,[2] as a sign of his complete commitment to the worship of the deity and had moved from Bengal to the great pilgrimage centre of Puri, the seat of the Jagannāth temple (to Kṛṣṇa, in his form as lord of the world). Here he stood out as a leader of the singers and dancers who performed in the processions round the deities' cars in the annual festival. He was not himself in any sense a teacher but was sufficiently aware of the needs of the large numbers drawn to him to commission others to give the incipient movement some theological shape (these were the six Gosvāmins). Among the mass of his followers the view undoubtedly emerged, even while he was alive, that Caitanya was an *avatāra* of Kṛṣṇa and for some this took the form that he was in fact the dual incarnation of Kṛṣṇa and Rādhā in one body. Though not given recognition in the formal theology of the Gosvāmins, such views were widespread in Bengal and in their most elaborate form held that Kṛṣṇa became incarnate in the form of Caitanya, assuming the fair complexion and the emotions of Rādhā, in order to experience within one body the bliss of union with his *śakti*. The erotic aspect obvious here is visible also in the worship of the devotee, who becomes a *gopī* in relation to Kṛṣṇa, feminising himself and regarding himself as the beloved of Kṛṣṇa. Rādhā's status as a married woman is even used to develop an elaborate analogy, suggesting that the worshipper should similarly overcome all such mundane obstacles to achieve union with the deity.

Vallabha definitely set out to establish a new community, called in its religious or cultic form the Puṣṭimārga, centred on worship of Kṛṣṇa, which is discussed further below. According to his ideas, devotion to Kṛṣṇa should find expression in elaborate ritual worship of the deity in the form of the images which are thought to be actual embodiments of him. Despite this strong ritual orientation, the Vallabha movement did have a significant place for devotional poetry within its worship and tries to claim for its own the most outstanding poet of Kṛṣṇa *bhakti* in the Hindi language, Sūrdās (c.1478–1564). Sūrdās traditionally composed an enormous work based on the tenth book of the *Bhāgavata Purāṇa*, of which much is certainly later than his time; within that work there nonetheless seems to be discernible a devotee of Kṛṣṇa who was very conscious of his own failings and moved by feelings both of remorse and of trust, who sometimes even gives expression to his feeling in a challenge to Kṛṣṇa to save even him, the chief of sinners. Other topics visible in the core of the work include Kṛṣṇa's birth and infancy, as well as some of the feats of his youth, such as the lifting of Mt Govardhana, but the theme most emphasised is that of the separation of the *gopīs* of Vraj from Kṛṣṇa when he leaves the region permanently (a symbol of the separation of the soul from the deity closer to Kabīr's thought than to Vallabha's).

The most famous *bhakti* poet in Hindi, however, is undoubtedly Tulsīdās, author of the best known adaptation of the *Rāmāyaṇa* into any of the modern languages of India, the *Rāmcaritmānas* ('lake of the deeds of Rāma'), which eclipsed even the highly popular Tamil version by Kampaṉ (ninth or tenth century). There are indications in the poem that Tulsīdās was a follower of Rāmānanda but he draws from several sources and the breadth of treatment of the subject has made it one of the most popular of all texts throughout the Hindi-speaking area of North India. Tulsīdās tends to distinguish Rāma from Viṣṇu, elevating him directly to the status of Īśvara or even of the unqualified, formless Brahman. Despite this tendency towards monism, Tulsīdās is mainly concerned to express loving devotion to his deity. Taking his cue from the *Rāmāyaṇa* story itself, he identifies very much with the figure of Hanumān, the pattern of loyal if sometimes limited service. In general Tulsīdās shows a relatively open attitude to other deities, provided that the supremacy of Rāma is not compromised in any way. His concern to give his message as wide an appeal as possible may underlie his emphasis on the name of Rāma, which had become in some ways a generic name for Īśvara at this period; for him the name is the essence of the supreme deity and its saving power is infinite. Tulsīdās states, indeed, that the name surpasses Rāma himself, since Rāma as an *avatāra* saved only a few individuals, whereas his name continues to bring salvation. In this Tulsīdās is developing ideas about the worship of Rāma seen in an earlier text of the Rāma cult, the *Agastyasaṃhitā* (twelfth century), which lays great stress on the name; it declares that the ancient sages secured Rāma's incarnation by chanting his name, and that uttering his name – whether by singing his praise, remembrance of him or listening to the story of his deeds – is central to his worship.

Jesus himself in the account given of him in the New Testament places most emphasis on the inner component of worship and indicates that true service is adoring and obedient love of God, coupled with loving concern for one's fellows; this does not mean that ritual forms of worship are valueless but that they are simply one part of the believer's total attitude to God. Worship in the early church included both a formal ritual element in the celebration of the Communion and a freer element in which inspiration of the individual was more apparent (cf. for example, Paul's recommendation: 'when you meet for worship, each of you contributing a hymn, some instruction, a revelation, an ecstatic utterance, or its interpretation, see that all of these aim to build up the church', 1 Cor. 14:26). These two types present in the earliest worship, broadly the sacramental and the prophetic, have continued thereafter, with the tendency towards greater formality every so often reversed by a move towards a more direct and prophetic form of worship. Apart from the celebration of the Communion, there seems to have been little uniformity in the earliest worship, which was evolving rapidly from the synagogue style of worship to more distinctively Christian forms, and certainly there were no special places of worship. Instead, the weekly meetings for the common meal which formed the focus of activity took place in the houses of those able to accommodate them. The Epistles indicate a concern for an orderly conduct of worship and suggest that it was gradually becoming more formally organised, although the element of teaching and proclamation seems still to be the dominant one after the celebration of the Eucharist.

The celebration of the Eucharist has remained central to the liturgical life of the Orthodox Churches, as we have already seen,[3] and was gradually elaborated up to about the fifteenth century, although its basis is recognisably Byzantine. Christians in the Orthodox traditions are also taught to pray every morning and evening at home, using selections of prayers contained in special manuals, which also contain the office of preparation for Holy Communion and the thanksgiving following it.

The liturgy of the Roman Catholic Church was similarly centred on the celebration of the Mass, which came increasingly to be a ritual enactment by the clergy witnessed by a laity who, as time passed, had less and less understanding of the Latin wording; in these circumstances, elaboration and a proliferation of usages and observances ensued in the later Middle Ages. In reaction both to this and to the Reformation, the Council of Trent (1545–63) laid down a corpus of rubrics to control every detail of the liturgy and bring uniformity of practice. The Second Vatican Council (1962–65) initiated major reforms which reaffirmed communal celebration of the Eucharist and the proclamation of God's word as the foundations of the theology of the liturgy and therefore decreed that the language of the liturgy would be changed from Latin to the modern vernacular languages; it also gave official recognition to the much freer form of service, generically called Bible Services and containing both the reading of the Bible together with homilies on it and response to it by the congregation, which had arisen out of the Liturgical Movement, originating in the nineteenth century. The Constitution on the Sacred Liturgy, in which the programme of liturgical reform was delineated, stresses the active participation of the laity, seeing the purpose of the reform as being to restore to the faithful the full and active part in liturgical celebrations which is their right and duty. It thus emphasises that the liturgy is not a clerical preserve but the worship of the whole people of

God and the congregation is said to offer Mass not merely through the priest but along with him, while the traditional view of the Mass as a sacrifice is complemented by the understanding of it as a meal. In contrast to the previous four hundred years of liturgical rigidity, there is now an acceptance of liturgical adaptation and experiment, along with an emphasis on conscious participation that is enhanced by the use of the vernacular.

Martin Luther in his own writings was relatively conservative about the ceremonial aspect of the liturgy, though radical in pruning the rites of anything that he regarded as anti-biblical theology, but gave a much greater emphasis to preaching of the word and introduced the use of the vernacular to increase the involvement of the people and teach them the basis of their faith. Similarly, the beginnings of worship in the Calvinist tradition of the Reformed Churches started with a translation of the Latin Eucharist into German, but this was rapidly followed by a string of changes which aimed to restore the weekly celebration of communion but also elevated the sermon to a central position. The worship of the Presbyterian Churches derives from the Reformed tradition (John Knox's *Book of Common Order* of 1564 was based on Calvin's *La Forme de Prières*) but places even greater emphasis on the sermon, as God's word to man, while until recently the celebration of communion was an infrequent event (quite commonly quarterly). Although the Anglican liturgy is distinct from those of the Lutheran and Reformed Churches, it rests on much the same historical and theological foundations; one unique Anglican feature is a daily office of morning and evening prayer. An initial emphasis on uniformity has over time given rise to a greater acceptance of variety, especially with the growth of the Anglican communion overseas.

Perhaps the most distinctive emphasis of the other Protestant churches, those called in Britain the Nonconformist denominations, has been that public prayer should not be in any prescribed form but entirely guided by the Holy Spirit, although they have regularly also stressed the biblical basis of their worship, given expression in the importance of the reading of the scriptures and preaching; the typical pattern of worship in these churches consists of reading and proclamation of the word, prayer and hymns. This emphasis on free prayer was supported by various arguments denouncing the limitations of set forms of prayer and emphasising the directness of the worshippers' relationship with their heavenly Father, but it has commonly given way nowadays to a blending of spontaneous and prepared prayer in the conduct of public worship, while the introduction of denominational service books for optional use by congregations represents a shift to a more liturgically oriented form of worship, although the extent of its acceptance is very uneven.

Prayer in any tradition is most often thought of in terms of a worshipper addressing a deity in some kind of speech act and this underlies the frequent division of prayer into different types, such as petition or intercession. Yet, alongside this understanding which lays stress on words and often texts (in, for example, the use of prayer books), there is also quite often the feeling that prayer is a free and spontaneous response of the worshipper to the deity, as Mahatma Gandhi (1869–1948) suggested when he wrote about prayer: 'It seems to me that it is a yearning of the heart to be one with the Maker, an invocation for his blessing.'[4] The first of these aspects is by its nature relatively easy to document, whereas the second is much less accessible to investigation, while the formulaic character of ritual prayer does not rule out its expressing heartfelt emotions any more than it requires it. Most generally prayer is an act of communication: as act it has its effects on the participants and as communication it concerns the transmission of thoughts or ideas from one party to the other. It should not therefore be separated too sharply from other acts of worship, as has been done by those who regard prayer as a feature of Christianity but not of Hinduism. Within Christianity a ritual prayer of invocation, both in form and content, serves to bring the participants into a suitably worshipping mood; it thus has functional analogies with the Hindu ritual of *nyāsa*, even though that is not usually termed prayer. There are a number of Christian hymns which were originally written as prayers and should still be regarded as such, even when sung, while the general theme of praise characteristic of many hymns is not really distinct from prayers of praise to God. Categories and forms of worship should be considered as complementary components of the whole. Nevertheless, there probably is a significant point underlying the suggestion that prayer is typical of Christianity and not of Hinduism but, if so, it is that, at the popular level of religious behaviour to which such judgements have been applied Christianity is oriented more towards linguistic expression and Hinduism more towards ritual and similar activities; even this is a matter of relative emphasis and not of absolute differentiation. Much of Christian religious expression is predominantly verbal, in line with its cultural context, and ordinary Christian worship is a matter of words in various forms as much as it is a liturgy, whereas the value of silence and openness to truth through intuition is an important strand within Hinduism, which has perhaps a wider acceptance – if not always practice – than the recognition of the power of silence by Christian mystics. However, one definition of Christian prayer that has had some currency – the practice of the presence of God – is broad enough to cover both aspects.

The Pāñcarātra system within Vaiṣṇavism shows a marked concern for ritual. This is justified by its doctrine of the five modes of Viṣṇu's self-revelation, of which the last is the *arcā avatāra* (the descent as the image for worship). The Pāñcarātra texts devote much attention to the construction of the image, its installation and consecration, and the liturgies offered to it. This expresses their understanding of Viṣṇu's gracious descent (*avatāra*) to be present thus within the world as the focus of image worship. Those who turn to him are saved by worshipping him in the simple ritual of offering (*pūjā*) but those who neglect this chance to receive his grace or are inattentive to the details of worship affront his dignity and must make expiation. A worthy response to divine grace consists of building a suitable residence for the image, installing it and ensuring that worship is performed suitably.

Another early Vaiṣṇava school, that of the Vaikhānasas, provides a relatively detailed account not just of the external acts of worship but also of the logic underlying them. The worshipper begins by deliberately imagining the abandonment of his worldly body and his sins and then identifies his self with the deity, mentally fashioning a new and ritually pure body, inviting the various forms of the deity into each part, until it is completely filled with the deity. When his body has been prepared in this way as the deity's abode, the worshipper meditates on the aspect that he wishes to worship. He considers his body as a temple and his heart as the inner sanctum, within which he prepares a lotus throne as the deity's seat. When the worshipper has thus been completely filled with Viṣṇu, he applies the same process to the image, until the deity residing in his heart can also reside in and animate it. Only now does the worshipper begin the series of ritual offerings to the image which are all that an external observer would see.

The liturgy performed in most Hindu temples basically treats the deity in the same way as a great temporal ruler. The daily routine thus begins with the deity as represented by his image being woken with music, bathed and dressed; thereafter follow meals, audiences and periods of entertainment in royal style. The deity is honoured with flowers and garlands and surrounded by incense and lamps, as his worshippers come to do him homage; in the past such entertainment of the deity included performances by the dancing girls who were maintained as part of the temple staff. These regular acts of worship carried out by the officiants, the temple priests (*arcakas, pūjāris*), may well be observed by a considerable number of lay people, particularly in the larger temples on special occasions, but as an audience rather than as direct participants. There is no real element of congregational worship, in marked contrast to Christian worship, and an individual would go to the temple alone or with his family to perform his own particular act of worship or to pay a temple priest to perform a ritual on his behalf; the fact that large numbers gather on special occasions does not basically affect this point.

The major exception to this generalisation is constituted by the devotional movement established by Vallabha (1479–1531), known as the 'way of well-being' (Puṣṭimārga). In this movement the path of devotion to Kṛṣṇa is seen to consist essentially in Kṛṣṇa's service (*sevā* – a term which, like the English 'service', can mean both being a servant and an act of worship), which is held to consist of the congregational worship of Kṛṣṇa in the movement's own temples. The image is regarded as Kṛṣṇa himself, as the term used for it within the sect indicates (*svarūpa*, literally 'own form'); it is worshipped in a pattern based on the earthly life of Kṛṣṇa in eight stages from first waking to going to bed. The elaboration of the ritual, with expensive costumes and ornaments, flowers, music and singing and on special occasions dancing, makes of this worship a definite aesthetic experience. The grand and luxurious fashion in which the images are worshipped is in keeping with the movement's rejection of asceticism and celibacy and its providing for householders a religion in which they can enjoy their wealth and the good things of life, provided that they first make a token dedication of them to Kṛṣṇa. There are thus several senses in which the movement can be said to be relatively materialistic.

Worship (*pūjā*) is, along with Yoga, one of the two basic components of tantric religious practice. Ritualised worship is obligatory for every tantric, even those who have reached higher levels. Tantric ritual involves constituents taken from many sources and typically is performed in addition to the ordinary rituals belonging to the tantric's caste or sectarian background. There is a daily ritual of worship of the goddess, as well as more elaborate occasional rituals. Underlying all of them is the realisation of the identity of the deity with the worshipper through the *guru*, who is the deity herself manifest on earth, and through the *mantra* imparted by him. After meticulous purification of everything connected with the rite, there follow the main components of the ritual, central to which is the consecration of the worshipper's own self by divesting himself of his own body and investing himself with a pure body into which the goddess descends limb by limb by the process of *nyāsa*.

The religious life of the ordinary Hindu is expressed through participation in worship and festivals, without regard for the elaborate doctrinal systems typical of more intellectual Hinduism. It has rightly been said that to a large extent Hinduism is a matter of orthopraxy rather than orthodoxy, that is of performing the prescribed acts rather than subscribing to the correct beliefs. Indeed, some features of belief implicit in such ritual action may actually be at odds with orthodoxy, representing on occasion extremely archaic as well as popular attitudes.[5] The rite of *pūjā* is just as much characteristic of worship in the home as of worship at temples or shrines. Most Hindus have a household shrine for the family deity, either in a separate room or in a shrine-cabinet contained within another room, which may house pictures or images of the deity. Many pictures of the gods are mass produced by photolithography and are widely on sale in the form of calendars and the like; their artistic quality is often execrable, like so much popular religious art in all cultures. A particularly elaborate household *pūjā* may contain all sixteen of the traditional components which also constitute the core of temple *pūjā* but more commonly only a selection is included. This series of actions includes – literally or symbolically – invocation of the deity, offering of a seat and various other gestures of greeting, bathing the image, clothing it, offering perfumes, flowers and incense, waving a lighted lamp in front of it (*āratī*), offering various sorts of food, bowing or prostration before the image, and leave-taking; it can readily be seen how far it coincides with the standard pattern of temple worship indicated above. The officiant in household *pūjā* will of course be one of the family, with the other family members essentially as spectators, although in Vaiṣṇava households they may eat the food that the deity has sanctified by tasting it. Temple officiants are usually brāhmans, although such temple priests have a lower status than other brāhmans; here too normally one officiant acts for the benefit of others and may perform optional *pūjās* for worshippers on payment of the requisite fees, more commonly at one of the many subsidiary shrines that are included within major temples' precincts. At local village shrines the officiant is more likely to be drawn from one of the lower castes (though still on the hereditary principle) and the ritual will be somewhat different, principally in the offering of blood sacrifices to the goddess, for most village deities are goddesses of a relatively fierce nature. Occasionally such cults have attained a more than local status; the best known example is that of the goddess Kālī, who regularly receives sacrifices of goats in the course of her daily worship, especially at her most famous temple in Calcutta (the anglicised form of Kālīghāṭa, 'the bathing place of Kālī').

Festivals are very much part of the annual pattern of worship at all major temples. Commonly these take the form of the 'car festivals' (*rathayātrā*) in which a movable image of the deity – not the immovable main image – is mounted on a large wooden wagon or car with an elaborate superstructure and hauled through the streets of the town near the temple on a set processional path; the influence of this custom can be seen in the actual layout of major temple towns, most notably at Madurai and Puri. Devotees thus have a chance to obtain a closer sight of the deity, throw flowers or break coconuts over the car, and sprinkle the image with water as the car proceeds on its cumbersome way, normally dragged by willing bands of devotees.[6] These car festivals are especially, though not solely, characteristic of South India. Another frequent occasion for a festival is the annual celebration of the marriage of the deity and his consort, which in some of the South Indian temples is sufficiently elaborate for a separate building to be dedicated to it, termed the marriage pavilion.

Other festivals may not be so much temple as community events. In North India, and especially in Bengal, it is common for community associations or families to sponsor festivals at which elaborate and expensive clay images of the deities are placed on public display, are feted with music and other entertainment, carried in procession through the streets and finally immersed in the local river or reservoir, there to dissolve. Another such popular religious institution organised by many local communities in North India is the Rāmlīlā, literally 'Rāma's sport or play', which is enacted in dramatic form over several days during the annual Daśahrā festival. In Hindi-speaking areas the text on which the performance is based is the *Rāmcaritmānas* of Tulsīdās, mentioned above. The actors are drawn from the local community, which organises and finances the performance; those portraying the main characters, who as their embodiments are offered worship by the audience, must be young brāhmans under the age of puberty (that is, both ritually pure and sexually innocent). Successive days' performances are often staged at different locations, normally outdoors, around the village or town in a way that suggests the setting of the story in the community concerned (such locations sometimes bearing their mythic names throughout the rest of the year). The whole event is as much a religious ceremony as a dramatic performance, while also serving as a significant vehicle for the transmission of the mythology to an illiterate audience. In both these respects the Rāmlīlā has a function in the Hindu context similar to that of the mystery plays in mediæval Europe; the mystery plays, usually performed out of doors, probably developed from the dramatic parts of the liturgy and the most important were the passion plays, although Corpus Christi processions provided opportunities for elaborate representation of Gospel stories. Similar, but much more localised, is the performance of the Rāslīlā, a re-enactment of Kṛṣṇa's life and especially his dance with the *gopīs* in the Vraj region near Mathura (in which each one thinks that Kṛṣṇa is dancing exclusively with her), where alone it is now performed by professional troupes of actors (unlike the Rāmlīlā).

At the individual rather than the corporate level of worship, a feature common to both religions is the practice of vows. Officially within the Christian church there has been on the one hand an emphasis on the three vows of poverty, chastity and obedience undertaken by those entering the monastic life or on the vows associated with entering the priesthood and on the other a disparagement of other types of vow on the basis of various biblical texts about the taking of oaths (e.g. Matt. 5:34–7). In fact, there are indications within the New Testament of the performance of the more popular type of vow when, for example Paul 'had his hair cut off at Chenchreae in fulfilment of a vow' (Acts 18:18; cf. also Acts 21:23–4). Augustine records that it was his mother's custom to make votive offerings to the shrines of saints on their memorial days but that she was forbidden to do so because they were too similar to pagan offerings to the dead (*Confessiones* 6.2). In the Middle Ages private vows – to make a pilgrimage, to build a church or to make some votive offering – were certainly quite common and were quite frequently reinforced by an oath; indeed, they became so common that by the eleventh and twelfth centuries attempts were made to regulate them by limiting their dispensation to bishops or the Pope. The shrines of the saints received large numbers of votive offerings, whether items of value or symbols of the purpose of the vow (models of limbs afflicted with disease, crutches that were no longer needed or the like); these offerings could be made in anticipation or more often in thanksgiving after the benefit was received. Such practices indicate a transactional approach to religion and still exist at the popular level in both the Roman Catholic and the Orthodox Churches.

Sometimes associated with the observance of festivals but more commonly undertaken at other times are the numerous *vratas* (roughly, 'vows') that have long been a feature of day-to-day Hindu life; there are nowadays weekly, monthly and annual *vratas*, as well as some without a fixed time. These commonly involve abstention from certain foods for a fixed period, reading or hearing of the appropriate story about the *vrata* (of which there are enormous numbers in the Purāṇic literature) and performing the appropriate acts of worship. The Purāṇas and related texts extol the benefits of *vratas* in extravagent terms, suggesting that their performance is equivalent to many Vedic sacrifices (the standard currency in effect for rating all religious activities, despite their obsolescence by now). Individuals of all castes, including śūdras and women, are entitled to perform *vratas*; indeed, many texts prescribe several such vows for women alone, though usually also requiring that a wife seek her husband's consent first. The majority of the *vratas* undertaken in mediæval and modern times are regarded as being optional, since they are performed in order to secure some benefit in this life or the next; most are in fact primarily secular in intent and have as their purpose the gaining of success in business or in studies, health or recovery from disease, and various similar material benefits. Most are undertaken by women with the purpose of ensuring family welfare but some, such as the Saturday *vrata* for Hanumān, are observed by men. For Vaiṣṇavas the fast on the eleventh day of each half of the month (*ekādaśī*)[7] is a particularly important one and there are a number of texts specifically devoted to it, with each of the twenty-four occasions during the year being given different names; the two occurring at either end of the monsoon season, during which according to the mythology Viṣṇu goes to sleep, are particularly important. Incidentally, Vaiṣṇavas are so commonly vegetarians that in everyday speech the name is used to mean 'vegetarian' and many stricter Vaiṣṇavas avoid not only meat, fish and eggs but also any red-coloured foods, because of the association with blood, as well as onions and garlic, because they are thought to inflame the passions.

Corresponding to the importance of *ekādaśī* for Vaiṣṇavas is that of *Śivarātri* (on the fourteenth day of the dark half of each month) for Śaivas; one in particular during the year is important and so designated as *Mahāśivarātri*. The main feature of its celebration and the accompanying *vrata* is the all-night vigil undertaken the night before, punctuated at intervals by offerings to Śiva, continuing with a fast on the day itself and concluding with feeding and making gifts to brāhmans. This use of a vigil as part of the preparation for *Mahāśivarātri* is closely analogous to the Christian practice of holding a service on the eve of a festival. In the early centuries vigils often preceded Sundays as well as major festivals such as Easter and Pentecost; by about the ninth century vigil services as a form of preparation for a festival had become linked with fasting. Watch-night services which began spontaneously in early Methodism in the middle of the eighteenth century soon became regularised and linked especially with New Year's Eve, spreading subsequently to many other denominations.

Pilgrimage is a feature which marks the more popular aspects of both Hinduism and Christianity. Within Hinduism it therefore features naturally in the Purāṇas, although its first attestation is as early as the *Mahābhārata*, where one of the passages inserted into the epic as it grew consists of a tour of the sacred sites (*Mbh.* 3.80–8).[8] The cult of pilgrimage to sacred places or *tīrthas*, literally 'crossing-places' or 'fords', became quite widespread by the mediæval period and is still a popular way for the ordinary man or woman to remove sins and accumulate merit. The merit acquired by visiting them is commonly reckoned in terms of the performance of so many Vedic sacrifices; however, unlike the sacrifices that were thus replaced, the sacred places are available to all. As their name *tīrtha* indicates, such pilgrimage centres are normally, but not invariably, associated with rivers. In Hindu thought all rivers are to some extent sacred and purifying, although the Gaṅgā is much the most sacred and especially sacred at Prayāga, the modern Allahabad, at its confluence with the Yamunā and, according to the legend, with the Sarasvatī (a river of great importance in Vedic times but later lost, perhaps as the result of geological changes). Other sites along the Gaṅgā are also very significant, most notably the ancient city of Kāśī or Varanasi, which is regarded as the seat of Śiva and is the premier cremation site in north India, partly because of the belief that those who die in Varanasi gain heaven thereby (a belief which is consistent with the basic meaning of *tīrtha* as a place to cross over, here from one life to the next or more exactly from *saṃsāra* to *mokṣa*). By stages other rivers and other sites came to be recognised as centres of pilgrimage, in several cases no doubt as older traditions associated with local, tribal cults gained orthodox recognition. As part of this process, passages eulogising these *tīrthas* were incorporated into one or another of the Purāṇas or retained a separate existence as Māhātmyas.

Pilgrimage is basically an individual affair, with the pilgrim sometimes undertaking all kinds of austerities in his solitary travel. Sometimes pilgrimages were undertaken in order to perform the memorial ritual for a dead relative (especially at Gayā) or to consign their ashes to a river, especially the Gaṅgā, or as a way of seeking the recovery of a sick person; here again the meaning of *tīrthas* as places to cross over is manifest in this link with the rites of passage. At some places, however, particular occasions are favoured and, for instance, at Hardwar and Prayāga (both on the Gaṅgā), where the most favoured occasion occurs only at intervals of twelve years, there are enormous gatherings of pilgrims, among whom wandering ascetics are particularly prominent. Although some *tīrthas* are more popular with worshippers of one particular deity, the major ones are revered by all Hindus.

One exception to the generally individual nature of Hindu pilgrimage is the Vārkarī Panth or 'pilgrims' path' in Maharashtra, which brings together the worshippers of Viṭṭhala, the Marathi form of Kṛṣṇa or Viṣṇu popularised by the *bhakti* poets such as Nāmdev and Tukārām. The main feature of this regional movement, and the one which gives it its cohesion, is the annual pilgrimage to the main shrine of the deity in the south of Maharashtra at Pandharpur, in which groups from all over the state converge on the town, starting nowadays from the places associated with the great poet devotees of the past, although the custom already existed in their day. Tukārām, for example, asks the pilgrims on their way to intercede for him with the deity. As the group associated with each such figure makes its way towards the destination, bearing a palanquin containing some relic of the poet saint, they sing his hymns and those of the movement's other poets; they thus keep the hymns alive in a largely oral tradition and through their use heighten their mood of expectant devotion. The strong group feeling thus engendered (and shown in a considerable sharing in the common life of the group, which stops short however of complete obliteration of caste distinctions) constitutes a unique combination of the otherwise more traditionalist feature of pilgrimage with sectarian devotionalism.

In Christianity the tradition of pilgrimage was certainly well under way in the fourth century and received a considerable boost from the visit of the empress Helena in 326 to Jerusalem, as well as from her son the emperor Constantine's erection of imposing buildings there and at Bethlehem. Cyril of Jerusalem (c.315–86) devised a series of liturgies, especially for Holy Week, linked to the various sites in the city, a central feature of which was the reading of the relevant passage from the Bible. The Holy Land, as it is most often termed in this context, has remained a favourite area of Christian pilgrimage over the centuries but pilgrimages to Rome to visit the tombs of the Apostles Peter and Paul, as well as many other sites in the city, were hardly less popular in the Western Church. There were also thousands of small churches visited mainly by local pilgrims, in particular on the feast day of the patron saint. From the twelfth century the worship of Mary flourished and gave rise to a number of pilgrimage centres, as has already been noted in Chapter 3. The period between the eleventh and fourteenth centuries saw a rise both in the number of centres of pilgrimage and in the totals of pilgrims going to them, before the Reformation caused a rapid decline in the popularity of pilgrimage, only partially reversed since.

Because of the considerable hardships involved in such travel, every pilgrimage was to a certain extent an exercise in penance and asceticism. From the eighth century, however, there developed the practice of imposing a pilgrimage as a form of penance and by the thirteenth century this had become fully institutionalised. Penitential pilgrimage, incidentally, contributed to the importance of Rome as a destination for Western pilgrims, since sometimes a bishop referred a person to the Pope for an appropriate penance. It also led to the system of granting indulgences which became common from the twelfth century; this involved the remission by the church of the temporal penalty through the merits of Christ and the saints, which constituted an inexhaustible treasury on which the Pope as the holder of the keys may draw.[9] Eventually they were no longer linked to specific sins committed and became a general remission of the penalties to which all human beings are liable as part of their fallen state, but they still continued to be reckoned in days, weeks or years just as they were when they were the equivalent of precise penalties. Increasingly the attractions of different pilgrimage centres were calculated according to the scale of the indulgences associated with them, in a way that has close analogies to the calculation of the merit of Hindu *tīrthas* according to the scale of equivalences in terms of sacrifices (even to the tendency over time to the inflation of the figures involved). Books of indulgences began to be produced which listed holy places and the corresponding benefits to be gained by a visit to them (again closely analogous to the Māhātmya literature of Purāṇic Hinduism).

The pilgrims were frequently distinguished by their special attire, in the Middle Ages often including a grey gown with a red cross and a monk's cowl. The two most general signs of the pilgrim, though, were the scrip and the staff with their biblical resonances and not infrequently they were buried with the returned pilgrim; these suggest the itinerant and ascetic side of pilgrimage (and may be compared with the Hindu ascetic's use of a staff – of different types according to the group – and a begging bowl). In the Sarum Missal the ceremony of presenting a gown with a cross to a pilgrim bound for Jerusalem is followed by a rubric which points out that branding a cross on the pilgrim's body is forbidden by canon law, while in the seventeenth century various travellers (such as Thomas Coryate who was in Jerusalem in 1614 on a journey to India, of which he has left an account) record, and often underwent, the tattooing of a cross on their arms in Jerusalem as a mark of a completed pilgrimage. Just as this external feature of practice can be paralleled by the use of branding in Śrīvaiṣṇava initiation noted earlier in this chapter, so too the use of shells as badges by Christian pilgrims who had been to Santiago de Compostela and by Hindus visiting Rāmeśvaram is an example of common but trivial features.

The Eastern Church shared with the Western Church the same interest in the Holy Land, especially Jerusalem, as a pilgrimage destination but also had others of its own, not always in its own areas; an interesting instance of this is Orthodox pilgrims going to Cologne to venerate the sepulchre of the three Magi. Many Orthodox pilgrims to Jerusalem, who tend to be going late in life, take with them a white shroud to have it consecrated on the site of Christ's resurrection and some then seek to remain in Jerusalem to die, seeing death in that place as especially sanctified, just as some Hindus go to Varanasi to die. Mt Athos, of course, has long been a major focus for all the Orthodox churches, while many pilgrims still go to various monasteries in Egypt, Syria and elsewhere. In Egypt the best known is the monastery of Dair al-Muḥarraq, where the holy family is held to have rested and taken refuge in their flight from Herod.

Martin Luther, who had himself gone to Rome in 1510 and visited the seven great basilicas as well as the *scala santa*, asserted as part of his attack on indulgences that all pilgrimages should be stopped and that the churches which were their focus should be levelled; he argued that pilgrimages were a means of seeking merit and so were in conflict with the doctrine of justification by faith alone. Jean Calvin was in agreement with Luther in condemning pilgrimages and in general this has been the Protestant attitude ever since, although not uniformly so. On the one hand, there has been the allegorical trend of viewing the whole of life as a pilgrimage (seen most notably in English in John Bunyan's *Pilgrim's Progress*, first published in 1678) and, on the other hand, the attitude of the Church of England in particular has tended to change over time, reverting from a more Protestant to a more Catholic position, as shown for example in the resumption of pilgrimage to Walsingham. An entirely modern development has been the founding by Lord MacLeod in 1938 of the Iona Community, with the subsequent growth of what can really only be called pilgrimage to the island where St Columba brought Christianity to Scotland in 563 and indeed with the establishment of a local pilgrimage circuit round the island.

5

Meditation and Asceticism

In the area of the contemplative life, of meditation, mysticism and asceticism, the problem of terminology is particularly acute: apparently different terms may well be pointing to the same phenomena in the two religions, while in other instances there may be a substantial overlap but not identity of meaning. Thus, the contemplative life and monastic discipline are terms commonly applied to aspects of the Christian tradition, Yoga and asceticism to aspects of the Hindu tradition. Other terms are apparently more neutral but in fact conceal differences of approach. Mysticism, for example, is a term for which the Indian languages have no generally employed equivalent (although some specialised terms do exist) and the nearest single term would in fact be Yoga, which is however a whole system of thought. Part at least of the answer in this instance is that, whereas in the West mysticism is often distinguished rather sharply from other aspects of religion, it could be argued that all of the more intellectual side of Hinduism is mystical to the extent that it deals with what cannot be communicated directly to others but must be discovered by turning inwards, by discovering eternity within oneself.

In many forms of mysticism the emphasis is on union rather than communion, on the abolition of separation and on identity. In Hinduism this is the realisation that the self is nothing else than the ultimate reality, that *ātman* is Brahman. Within Christianity the same kind of insight has been expressed, for example, by Meister Eckhart (1260–1328?), who talks of God and the soul becoming completely one and even of the soul being most perfect when it enters the desert of the Godhead and its identity is destroyed, and by St Catherine of Genoa (1447–1510), who claims: 'My "I" is God and I know no other "I" but this is my God.' More recently there have been those, such as Fr Jules Monchanin (1895–1957), Swami Abhishiktananda (Dom Henri le Saux, 1910–73) and Dom Bede Griffiths (b. 1906), who have found the language of Advaita useful in expressing their understanding of union with God.

Before dealing with the different types of Hindu mysticism, it would be as well to define what we understand by mysticism in general. It is most simply described as a direct perception of an eternal being or state, whether conceived of in personal or impersonal terms or as a state of consciousness. It is a transcendental experience, in that it is above the categories of time and space, and an intuitive experience of a timeless and spaceless, and thus eternal and unchanging entity. It is the realisation of oneness with or in something that transcends the empirical self, whether this oneness is experienced as complete identity or as intimate union with this transcendent being. These features are common to virtually all types of mysticism, although there are problems even with these definitions in regard to *dhyāna* in Theravāda Buddhism, but that is outside our present concerns; each type is also, however, distinguished by certain specific features. These more distinctive features concern the theological or metaphysical doctrine which is based on that experience and the techniques used to lead to its realisation. The experience of unity with nature that is found, for example, in Wordsworth's poetry cannot really be included within the ambit of mysticism proper, which consists not of turning outward, but rather of turning inward in interior contemplation; indeed, within the Roman Catholic tradition the term 'contemplative' is often preferred for mystics, who in their meditative discipline might be said to be practising a Christian Yoga.

The origins of Yoga are rather obscure. Efforts have been made to see precursors of the later yogins in the Vrātyas who figure so prominently in the *Atharvaveda* or in the long-haired sage who is described in one late hymn of the *Ṛgveda* (10.136). These hymns' emphasis on inner meditation and various kinds of asceticism leading to experiences of ecstasy may point in that direction but there is no real evidence of continuity. Elements of Yoga must, however, have been present quite early in the Indian tradition, since they are found not only in the Upaniṣads but also in Buddhism and Jainism, which became distinct in the sixth to fifth centuries B.C. One of the first clear references to yogic concepts of self-discipline is to be found in the *Kaṭha Upaniṣad* (3.3–6), where Yoga is compared to a chariot in which the *ātman* sits (as the passenger) with reason as the driver and the body itself as the chariot. There is further material on Yoga in the didactic parts of the *Mahābhārata*, which in addition begins to link it with the Sāṅkhya system which later provides it with its theoretical superstructure.

The first separate exposition of the Yoga system is in the *Yogasūtra* of Patañjali, a composite text put together between the second century B.C. and the fourth century A.D. It contains four chapters, the first on the nature and aim of meditation, the second on the means of attaining the aim, the third on the goal together with the achievements along the way, and the fourth on the nature of the state of detachment from matter reached through Yoga. The main body of the text distinguishes eight stages or 'limbs' of Yoga, of which the first five relate to the training of the body and the last three deal with the perfecting of the self. Some of the early stages are quite well known in the West, where the use of them as a method of physical relaxation has had something of a vogue, but it should be emphasised that for the Yoga system itself they are merely the necessary preliminaries in a disciplined path of ascent to release. The basic aim of the classical Yoga system is the pursuit of interiorisation and the reduction of the apparent multiplicity of the world back to an original unity. The first stage, restraint (*yama*), consists of the more or less universal moral principles of non-injury (*ahiṃsā*), honesty, not stealing, chastity, and freedom from greed, while the second stage, observances (*niyama*) adds five positive components of personal behaviour: purity, contentment, austerity, study of the scriptures and devotion to the Lord. Superficially, the last of these (on which the *Yogasūtra* has more to say at 1.23–51) gives the system a theistic flavour, but in reality this Īśvara is neither active nor creative (and indeed has never become involved in any way in this world) and so cannot be an object of true devotion but is simply an aid to meditation as supplying an example of the state aimed at. The third stage, posture (*āsana*), though the first of the typically Yoga techniques, is little emphasised in the *Yogasūtra*, where it is basically a case of taking up a suitable position, but some later forms of Yoga elaborate it greatly. The fourth stage, breath-control (*prāṇāyāma*), consists of bringing the involuntary process of breathing under the conscious control and regulation of the will. The last of the five stages of training the body is then the withdrawal (*pratyāhāra*) of the senses from their interaction with the external world, which is held to be what binds the self to *saṃsāra*. One method is to concentrate on a single point until all else disappears from consciousness and then transfer the attention from an object to a mental image. The three remaining stages of perfecting the self form a closer progression, from fixing the thoughts (*dhāraṇā*) without the aid of the senses through meditation (*dhyāna*), when the self remains thus without distraction, to the final stage of ecstasy or trance (*samādhi*), when the individual is no longer conscious of meditating and reaches identification of subject and object, thus achieving the goal of 'isolation' (*kaivalya*), though not necessarily immediately (since some traces of this existence may have to be eliminated first).

Yoga practice, however, is by no means limited to the Yoga school and has been used in one way or another by many different traditions within Hinduism; consequently, the distinct and divergent aims with which it is practised need to be recognised. In the classical school of Yoga, as outlined above from Patañjali's *Yogasūtra*, the objective is to 'yoke' the mind (the root *yuj*, from which Yoga comes, meaning basically 'to join', is cognate with the English word) so that the self (*puruṣa*) can rid itself of attachment to sense-objects, by stilling the senses and controlling the mind until the self is set free to experience the pure 'isolation' of its true nature. If Īśvara, as the most perfect and liberated self (which is all that Yoga makes of him, denying him any active role), can be made to serve as an aid to concentration, then so much the better, but it is the 'isolation' of the self that is the final goal of classical Yoga; it is not Īśvara, or meditation on Īśvara, or union with Īśvara as such.

However, when yogic practice is utilised within the framework of a theistic system, as in the various sects of Vaiṣṇavism and Śaivism, its role in relation to the ultimate goal is radically altered. In this context union with the deity is what is aimed at and so yogic techniques are inevitably subordinated to this different goal, which is indeed radically different because the sense of dependence on the soul's supreme Lord, and the experience of such a dependent relationship with him, is essential to this kind of theistic perspective. However, to the extent that attachment to the Supreme Self can best be achieved by detachment from everything else, yogic discipline is valid at this level. It can also be an aid to meditation on the supreme deity, helping the worshipper to concentrate on his many perfections – as part of the later stages of the discipline, whereas in classical Yoga this theistic dimension has only a lower-level significance. For example, the Pāñcarātra texts include Yoga (interpreted very much as in the *Bhagavadgītā* as a means of delivering the soul entirely to the deity) as one of their four main subjects. Again, in Rāmānuja's Yoga, the object to be concentrated on in *dhāraṇā* is the Supreme Person alone and this is intended to generate devotion and a closer personal relationship with the deity (in this emphasis on contemplative meditation Rāmānuja is closer to the Roman Catholic or Orthodox traditions than to the Protestant tradition, with which his emphasis on *bhakti* otherwise aligns him). The goal being aimed at must always be taken into account if a proper evaluation is to be made.[1]

Perhaps the prime example of this is Tantrism, where the two parts of its religious practice are ritual worship (*pūjā*) and meditation or Yoga. Although Tantrism has developed the meditative techniques of Yoga in distinctive ways (*mantrayoga* consisting of meditation on mystical syllables and *layayoga* based on an elaborate mystical physiology), the goal they lead to is merging with the deity. Yet another example of a reformulation of Yoga is the Integral Yoga of Aurobindo Ghose (1872–1950), which he claims to be a blending of the different Yoga systems each with its own approach through body, mind and so on; here the goal is union with the Divine principle, a union that, according to Aurobindo, is at once transcendental, cosmic and individual. The main originality in Aurobindo's synthesis is the attempt to incorporate modern evolutionary ideas; he sees the goal of evolution as the divinisation of man – an extension to the whole of humanity of tantric ideas about perfecting the body of the individual – and the ultimate transformation thereby of the material world through the upward pull of the Spirit. In this regard there are distinct similarities between the ideas expressed by Aurobindo and those of Pierre Teilhard de Chardin (1881–1955), for both posit an evolutionary universe in which there is progressive spiritualisation through a movement towards higher levels of consciousness and both reinterpret their respective theologies in the light of new biological understandings.

Aurobindo's thought is also quite strongly influenced by Advaita Vedānta, which adopts an approach to reality often labelled as mystical, in that it regards the goal of religion as being the existential realisation of the identity of one's *ātman* with Brahman. Many followers of neo-Vedānta have then attempted, on the basis that all mystical experience is essentially the same and that it consists in realising the Self which is Ultimate Reality, to suggest that this unity of mystical experience favours the view of religious unity that they embrace, that all religions point to the same truth (but that neo-Vedānta does so more clearly than others). Even if mystical experience is essentially the same and the differences are solely in the explanatory systems used to interpret it (a proposition that many would contest in any case), this does not establish that the Vedāntin interpretation is the correct one.

After all, within Hinduism many would see elements of the approach of the *bhakti* poets as being basically mystical in the way that they rejected outward forms and emphasised direct personal experience of the deity, but they also emphasise separation between the devotee and the deity in contrast to the Advaitin model. The image of love in separation, developed in romantic and sexual metaphors, is a favourite one of many of the *bhakti* poets, none more so than the Rājasthāni princess, Mīrābāī (1403–70 or a century later), who rejected the values of the society in which she was reared to become a wandering ascetic, totally committed to her devotion to Kṛṣṇa. She expresses this in the sensual imagery of the 'mystical marriage' but also speaks of the lovesickness and even madness produced by Kṛṣṇa's absence, talking of the inner fire brought about by the pain of separation from the deity or of the arrow of love which pierces the heart. The same images or symbols are used by many other *bhakti* poets, prominently including another woman, the Liṅgāyat poet Mahādevīyakka, in the twelfth century, who is said similarly to have rejected society in order to give her whole self to the deity, in her case a form of Śiva; she speaks in concrete terms of marrying and making love to Śiva in a spiritual union, yet she also alludes to the flameless fire and the bloodless wound of the love-sickness produced by her acute sense of separation at times from her deity. The fifteenth-century *sant* poet, Kabīr, can still more clearly be seen as a mystic, since the main emphasis in all his poetry is on the realisation of the deity in the inner self, and he often refers to the absorption of the self in the deity, blending together the personal and impersonal strands in his experience of such union and speaking of the brightness of mystical illumination.

Despite the example of the *bhakti* and *sant* poets, with their emphasis on realisation of the deity in day-to-day life, there is a strong tendency in Hinduism to see meditation and asceticism as going together and as being the preserve of the religious specialist, whether yogin or renouncer. Asceticism is seen as the choice of discipline (*yoga*) over desire (*kāma*) and, for the Hindu ascetic, women often came to symbolise desire and to represent sexuality, reproduction and all the other ties that acted as obstacles to his release. This was frequently depicted mythologically in stories of *apsarases*, a kind of celestial nymph (or nymphomaniac), who seduce ascetics at the behest of the gods who fear for their own position, and was expressed also in the concern in Tantric Yoga for the retention of the semen. This resulted quite often in a distinctly misogynist outlook, which is by no means foreign to Christian monasticism either.

The earlier texts on social conduct recognise the possibility of several alternative lifestyles, among which is included that of the renouncer (*saṃnyāsin*), but from about the beginning of the Christian era these alternatives were remodelled into a sequence, with reunuciation as the last.[2] Thus one could only properly reach the state of the renouncer after passing through the preceding three stages (student, householder, forest-dweller), which considerably limited its availability; this was no doubt part of the rationale behind the development, since there are signs that opting out of society was more popular at the period than was acceptable to the orthodox authorities. Initiation (*dīkṣā*) into *saṃnyāsa* parallels both the funeral rituals and the initiation into studentship, for it symbolically enacts the death of the novice and his rebirth into the ascetic way of life. As a preliminary the intending renouncer had to perform a sacrifice in which he distributed all his possessions to priests and the poor; at this point he lost all rights of property and inheritance in his family. At the end of the ritual the novice was given a new name by the *guru* to symbolise his new life (along with a *mantra* and the accoutrements of his new status – the robe of rags, tonsure, staff and begging bowl) and quite often a period of instruction, as with the student, then followed. The renouncer had to leave his wife and thereafter remain celibate; he was forbidden to kindle fires (whether for cooking or for ritual purposes) and instead had to beg all his food, eating only enough to keep him alive; he no longer performed the sacrificial ritual and abandoned his sacred thread as the outward sign of his death to society; he was to cultivate detachment by meditation on the loathsomeness of the body and to purify his mind by the practice of Yoga; and, according to most of the older texts, he was to observe silence except when reciting the Vedas. Some of these ascetics lived in the depths of forests in order to carry out self-mortification through hunger, thirst, heat or cold, while others frequented deserted areas on the edges of towns or villages and engaged in more exhibitionist asceticism, such as sitting between the 'five fires' (four fires surrounding him towards the points of the compass and the sun above) or standing in fixed positions so long that they eventually could not abandon them; they were homeless and ideally wanderers, never staying long in one place. As the ascetic progressed in his self-discipline he was thought to acquire various powers, *siddhis* (that is, '<signs of> success'), just as the yogin did in his practice of Yoga, and equally could be deflected by them into achievements of a magical character (levitation, clairvoyance and the like) but ideally pressed forward to his goal of direct insight into reality. Passing 'from darkness to darkness deeper still', he finally grasped the truth about himself and the universe and so found release (*mokṣa*).

This model was directed at the individual and for many centuries there was no kind of organisation of those who had reached the fourth stage of *saṃnyāsa* or renunciation, although the forest-dwellers in earlier periods (before this stage was rendered obsolete by the growth of renunciation), as well as maintaining some basic ritual practices, did on occasion at least live in groups. Nevertheless, there have always been individuals who have become *saṃnyāsins* at an earlier age than this model would allow, most notably Śaṅkara (traditionally 788–820), who is said to have gone directly from student to renouncer. Although Śaṅkara is best known as a philosopher, his concerns were basically religious. This is clearly illustrated by the tradition that he organised the first order of *saṃnyāsins* and founded teaching organisations or seminaries (*maṭhas*) at the four corners of India to propagate his doctrine. The order is now represented by ten groups, hence its usual name of Daśnāmī; three are restricted to brāhmans (nowadays often termed *daṇḍins* from the staff that they carry) and the rest are open to the four *varṇas*, despite the fact that Śaṅkara himself, following older precedent, declared that only brāhmans could become *saṃnyāsins*. These orders are Śaiva in affiliation and there are a number of other Śaiva ascetic groups, such as the Aghoris, Kānphaṭa Yogins and Nāths. There are also Vaiṣṇava ascetic orders in the traditions of Rāmānuja (commonly called the *tridaṇḍins* from their triple staff) and Madhva, as well as some smaller ones.

Although in theory the members of these orders follow the rules enjoining lack of property for all *saṃnyāsins*, the *maṭhas* or other institutions received large donations from pious lay people and so large properties came to be controlled by their heads, who were often therefore influential figures for material as well as spiritual reasons. In contemporary India, the Śaṅkarācāryas (as the heads of the four *maṭhas* established by Śaṅkara are called) are a major conservative influence politically, while the Śaṅkarācārya of Śṛṅgeri is also the head of the orthodox Aiyār brāhman community. There were also at some periods instances of the abuse of succession to the headship of such *maṭhas* when nepotism was as rife as at certain times within the mediæval Christian church in the West. Another perversion of the earlier aims of *saṃnyāsa* is seen in the emergence during the period of Muslim rule, in response to attacks on Hindu ascetics by Muslims, of armed ascetics, the *nāgās* (so called from their going naked – now largely confined to ceremonial occasions such as the Kumbha Mela festivals), organised into orders to which even śūdras were then admitted.

The repeated exhortations to self-denial in the New Testament are one starting point for the development of asceticism within Christianity, while the writings of Clement of Alexandria (c.150–215) and Origen (c.185–254) developed its theoretical foundations, for they saw ascetic practice as a purification of the soul from its passions and thus as a necessary means of loving God more perfectly. Asceticism also came to be regarded as a means of expiation of one's sins. By the third century the ascetic ideal as a way of life was widespread and the idea of withdrawal became attractive, as the Desert Fathers began to direct their isolated lives to prayer, fasting, mortification, humility and meditation. The terms used to designate them, monk ('solitary') and anchorite ('withdrawer'), illustrate very clearly the aspect of isolation from the temptations of the world. Such separation from the world regularly involved the separation of recruits to the monastic life from their families to join a 'new family', justified by the words of Jesus about abandoning family to follow him (Matt. 10:35–9, cf. Luke 12:52–3).

The origins of Christian monasticism are usually linked with St Antony (traditionally 251–356), who withdrew into the desert of Nitria in Egypt around 270.[3] His struggle against spiritual and material temptation attracted many admirers to his cell and some began to imitate his austerities; before long the movement acquired mass dimensions and popular enthusiasm even began to consider that monks alone were truly following Christ by obeying his commandments without compromise. Pachomius (c.290–346) made the first moves to organise these ascetics into a communal life – his organisation was developed in Cappadocia by St Basil the Great (c.330–79) – and his sister Mary founded the first community for women nearby. Monasticism soon spread from Egypt into other areas of the Eastern church. In Palestine, an early centre directly influenced by Egypt, a characteristic feature was the *laura* system of hermits sharing certain activities under the direction of an *abba* (abbot). In Syria monasticism reached the heights of St Simeon Stylites (c.390–459) spending thirty years on top of his pillar and becoming the focus of popular adulation by both Christians and pagans. From the tenth century Mount Athos in northern Greece became a great monastic centre with many monasteries and hermit cells; to this day no women are allowed to set foot anywhere on the peninsula. Monasticism was basically a corporate movement directed at achieving within the community the fullness of the Christian life; all the varied activities of hospitality to the poor, tending the sick, giving advice to seekers and the like were seen as aspects of the worship and adoration of God. The monks and nuns also enriched the worship of the church and the services of the Orthodox Church evolved to a great extent within the monastic setting. The emphasis on defeating sexual temptation and also a fear of heresy were factors in encouraging an intolerant attitude which at some periods marred their otherwise notable contribution to the life of the church.[4]

Monasticism spread into Western Christianity in the second half of the fourth century and by the end of it monastic communities existed in Italy, Gaul, Spain and North Africa. The monasteries attracted a number of the wealthy and aristocratic, as well as having strong connections with the ecclesiastical hierarchy from the start. The early monasteries in the West were often small compared with those in the East with less need initially, therefore, to develop elaborate formal organisations. St Augustine of Hippo (354–430) followed the model already set by Ambrose of Milan (c.339–97) and others in laying down for his clergy a monastic form of life, out of which arose the *Rule of St Augustine*, probably drawn up by one of his followers, though perhaps in his lifetime, and adopted by the later Augustinian Canons and the Dominicans among others. In the fifth and sixth centuries monasticism proliferated in the West, spreading to Ireland, where it became the main form of ecclesiastical organisation (often borrowing in its organisation from the secular forms of government) and developed the distinctively Irish feature of exile as an ideal; wandering monks, such as most famously St Columba (c.521–97), did much to spread Christianity in barbarian kingdoms. The founding of monasteries and the subsequent migration of their members to new areas became a key pattern in the spread of Christianity in Western Europe.

The tonsure which became the normal hair style of monks until modern times was adopted from the hairstyle required of Roman slaves, as a sign that monks were the slaves of Christ, while female religious had their hair cut fairly short and covered; both practices also, of course, reduced the individuality which distinctive hair styles express. Similarly, the habits adopted by the different monastic orders seem originally to have been closely patterned on the ordinary lower-class, peasant dress of the period of their foundation, but usually then became fixed and so in due course marked their members out as separate rather than identifying them with the poor and needy. Again, though, the precise and uniform dress requirements helped to emphasise the shared community of its members.

Communal monastic life regularised the ascetic activities of the solitary anchorites but it still embraced a range of activities: fasting, chastity, self-mortification (for example, by flagellation), the adopting of uncomfortable postures, meagre clothing and acceptance of humility and even humiliation. These activities, in being regularised, came under collective control and so some of the wilder excesses were no doubt curbed but the discipline generally remained severe. The aim of monastic life was seen as being both the development of the monks' spiritual welfare and, at least as the orders developed, service to the community, and the methods by which these were to be achieved were primarily withdrawal from the world, austerities and contemplation. Whereas these methods were entirely appropriate to an anchorite seeking only the first aim of spiritual advance, there is a certain tension between the aim of service to the community and the means of withdrawal from the community. In modern times the aim of service to others has been favoured more but, interestingly, one of the forms of this service has been the provision for the laity of facilities for temporary withdrawal from the world in retreats. The aspect of service in performing religious worship on behalf of the laity at large is perhaps less stressed but remains significant, while social work and education in their broadest sense have long been important. However, the contemplative life continues to be of paramount importance for certain orders, involving a very austere regime with much time devoted to prayer, both vocal and mental. Enclosed monastic orders have regularly seen their justification in the declaration that 'Man's chief end is to glorify God'. It is also worth noting that the rules governing the various orders are regularly designated by the name of the founder and, while it is recognised that he rarely acted entirely on his own, it is routinely stressed that the creation of the order is due to the founder. This sense of the role of the founder can lead almost to a personality cult, which contrasts with the training in self-abnegation imposed on ordinary members, while the identification of the order with the characteristics of its founder provides a strong role model at the expense of flexibility in changed situations. Some of these themes will be illustrated as we look briefly at the development of monasticism in the West.

St Benedict of Nursia (c.480–547) is well known for composing his rule for religious life, which eventually became the main, indeed almost the only, rule followed by Roman Catholic monastic orders; it was originally drafted for the ordering of the group of small monasteries that he established for monks around that at Monte Cassino, of which he was abbot, but was adapted at an early stage for the use of orders for women. His sister, St Scholastica, is held to have founded a women's monastery nearby (the earliest communities for women were also termed monasteries and only later were separate terms used, such as nunnery). Even when other Rules were composed, the *Rule of St Benedict* continued in use and in any case often influenced them; its stress on humility and obedience, on a well-planned novitiate, on stability (staying in one house) and on the Christ-like authority of the abbot were major factors in its success. Its prime purpose was to enable the monks living in community to lead lives that would lead to salvation and accordingly it required monks to spend much time in the oratory, chanting or reading the Divine Office. A substantial part of the day would also be devoted to the manual pursuits necessary to keep the monastery going, although over time there developed a tendency for those monks who were ordained priests to concentrate their energies on performing Divine Office, while the secular work was done by lay brothers or monastic servants. Female religious communities were not expected to be economically self-sufficient in the same way but regularly received support from outside, although their members still engaged in productive labour in such tasks as sewing and embroidering ecclesiastical vestments. Sometimes, in earlier periods, male and female monasteries were established close together and the monks were expected to help the nuns with their contacts with the outside world, as well as performing Divine Office for them; later this custom was gradually abandoned because of the potential scandal and temptations inherent in it.

A whole chapter of St Benedict's *Rule* relates to the hospitality which the monastery should provide to travellers, who were to be welcomed warmly and seated at the abbot's table. This provision was of considerable significance in the Middle Ages, when travellers had few other facilities available to them and when in any case many were on pilgrimage. It has been general in both Eastern and Western Christianity that monasteries and convents kept their doors open to anyone in need of spiritual or material assistance; commonly they offered free hospitality for three nights to all visitors. Among Orthodox churches, even now it is not uncommon that a lay Christian who wants to make a more careful preparation for his communion, or to spend a time in retreat, will go to a monastery, where he will usually find an experienced confessor; such a period of spiritual concentration, fasting and prayer is most popular among the Russians (who call it *govenie*). Another activity that was important at an early period was the reading and copying of the literature of the church, with the formation of monastic libraries. Gradually copying became a significant part of monks' work, especially as such clerical activity was regarded as a more acceptable alternative to manual labour for those monks who were priests.

Periodically throughout the history of Western monasticism there have been movements to return to the strictness of the original discipline which was felt to have been compromised by later developments. The monastery of Cluny (founded in 909) was the focus of one such development, when the high standard of monastic observance there led to other monasteries coming under its control, until by the end of the eleventh century a large system of monasteries was controlled by the abbot of Cluny (who was exceptionally under the sole authority of the Pope). The wealth and influence so acquired led in turn to activities that were seen as incompatible with Benedictine ideals and the emergence of a new reforming movement, resulting in the establishment of the monastery of Cîteaux in 1098; the most notable figure in this new Cistercian order was St Bernard (1090–1153), abbot of Clairvaux. The Cistercian reforms spread rapidly in the twelfth century and proved very popular, with their emphasis on a community of *caritas*, Christian love. The Cistercians reacted strongly to the elaboration of Cluniac monasteries by adopting an austere and dignified building style; however, their emphasis on agricultural activity in accordance with St Benedict's ideas, led to increased distinction in function and also in status between priests and lay brothers within the community. Somewhat later, St Bridget of Sweden (1303–73), impressed by the virtues of Cistercian life, established the Order of Brigittines (Ordo Sanctissimi Salvatoris), which was originally organised as double communities: separate communities of male and female religious living in separate parts of one monastery and sharing one chapel, in which the monks were responsible for the liturgy. This arrangement was abandoned in the sixteenth century. By the seventeenth century some felt that the Cistercians were becoming decadent and broke away to form the Trappists (the Order of Cistercians of the Strict Observance), best known for their strict rules of silence; the reform was introduced at the monastery of La Trappe in 1662 by Abbot Jean de Rance (1626–1700), who sought a return to St Benedict's strict requirements (including abstinence from meat), as well as adding austerities of his own.

A different early monastic order, that of the Carmelites (founded in Palestine around 1154), was committed to extreme asceticism by its *Primitive Rule* laid down in 1209 but, after the decline of the Crusades and the order's retreat to Europe, its rigour declined. Again, a movement of reform emerged, centred on St Teresa of Avila (1515–82) and St John of the Cross (1542–91), both Spanish Carmelites, who restored the *Primitive Rule* in many monasteries and convents, with some additions to encourage the contemplative life, which formed the mainstay of their personal mystical devotion. The number of great mystics produced by the order is noteworthy. Mental prayer, comprising the various forms of internal communication with God and developing into mysticism, is in general a characteristic of monastic discipline but nowhere is it more evident than among the Carmelites. Distinctions gradually evolved between different types of mental prayer: meditation (which was the discursive form consisting of devout meditation on a chosen, usually Biblical, theme in order to deepen spiritual insight), contemplation (its non-discursive form) and affective prayer (in which intellect and imagination are subordinated to acts of will to unite the soul with God). While monastic orders have encouraged their members to practise mental prayer, the complexity of the process has been recognised and provision made for even advanced practitioners to have spiritual advisers, as is clear, for example, from the life of St Teresa. The progression within mental prayer and the need for an adviser have obvious analogies with the higher stages of Yoga (while some of the lower ones can be paralleled in monastic austerities more generally) and with the role of the *guru* in so much of Hinduism, not only the Yoga schools.

Another motive is evident in the establishment of the Dominican Order (formally the Ordo Praedicatorum, 'Order of Preachers', and commonly known as Black Friars). St Dominic (1170–1221) was impelled to found the order as a result of a preaching tour undertaken with his bishop against the Albigensians in Languedoc (southern France); he became part of a group of clerics seeking to win them back to orthodoxy, which stressed the combined importance of good preaching and exemplary lives, for the local clergy by their poor standards were part of the cause for this dissent. Because of a ban on the proliferation of religious orders and rules by the Fourth Lateran Council (1215), when St Dominic received permission from Pope Honorius III (1216–27) to found his order, it adopted a version of the Augustinian *Rule*. The Dominicans placed great emphasis both on preaching and on study, including the adaptation of Aristotelian thought to Christian theology which is particularly associated with St Thomas Aquinas, while at a later date they gained notoriety through the Inquisition. This was established by Pope Gregory IX around 1233 as a means of suppressing heresy (whereas St Dominic had sought to convert the Albigensians by preaching) and he assigned to the Dominican Order the main responsibility for operating it; the degree of its effectiveness depended very much on the amount of support it received from the secular government, being limited in Britain and elsewhere in Northern Europe and most vigorous in Spain, where it became practically an arm of the state and lasted longer than elsewhere (between about 1480 and 1800).

St Dominic's contemporary, St Francis of Assisi (1182–1226), in the founding of his order was most concerned with the practice of poverty in the monastic discipline. The son of a well-to-do merchant family, he reacted against a worldly youth and parental materialism by abandoning everything and soon gathered other young men around him who were equally committed to the practice of poverty. The Franciscan Order was a mendicant order, living solely by begging, with the concomitant need to move from one area to another in search of alms. Saint Francis placed great stress on the order's obedience to the church authorities, while emphasising egalitarian relationships among members; he never became a priest himself and laid down that lay brothers should have the same voice in the policies of the order as ordained members (although this was soon modified). The order's continuing success is closely linked with the spontaneity and devotion shown in St Francis's own life, although repeated controversies over the principle of poverty have seen the order split into a number of distinct groups. St Francis's ideals inspired St Clare of Assisi (1194–1253) to found a parallel female religious community, ultimately known as the Poor Clares, which was equally vowed to strict poverty but followed a contemplative life.

The two main aims of the Society of Jesus, founded by St Ignatius Loyola (1491–1556), were to encourage reform within the Roman Catholic Church (especially in the light of the Reformation) and to undertake missionary work and higher-level education, while one of its unique features was that its constitution laid down that its services should be at the disposal of the Pope. Consequently, Jesuit rules do not require the group life typical of monastic orders, the wearing of distinctive clothing, or the performance of the Divine Office, none of which were entirely conducive to these aims; however, there was still an obligation to engage in daily meditational prayer along the lines established by St Ignatius in his *Spiritual Exercises*. The Jesuits' role in education was often to give them an outstanding position on the mission field but the order's international outlook also aroused resentment within nationally-oriented hierarchies in Europe. The order was expelled from Portugal in 1759, from France in 1764 and from Spain in 1767, and it was suppressed by Pope Clement XVI in 1773, leading to the collapse of several missionary activities, but restored by Pius VII in 1814 to spearhead a renewed militancy in the Roman Catholic Church.

There was a significant revival and spread of Roman Catholic monasticism in the nineteenth century which has continued in the present century, although there has been a continuing debate on the forms and purposes of monasticism since the Second Vatican Council (1962–5). Orders continue to be founded in the Roman Catholic Church up to the present. For example, following an appeal from the Archbishop of Calcutta, the Sisters of the Immaculate Blessed Virgin Mary (Loreto) embarked on the creation of schools for the children of European Catholics in India and one of its members was Mother Teresa (b. 1910), who in 1960 instituted the Congregation of the Missionaries of Charity to carry out the mission to the destitute and dying in Calcutta which had by then become her life's work.[5]

At the Reformation the Reformed Churches vigorously repudiated the monastic life. The suppression of monasteries and confiscation of their wealth by secular rulers followed in its wake. However, we may note the subsequent emergence of orders within the Church of England, such as the establishment of a Franciscan-inspired group at Cerne Abbas in 1921, and, more particularly, the establishment of the Reformed brotherhood of Taizé in France half a century ago (founded in 1940); the oldest religious community for men in the Church of England is in fact the Society of St John the Evangelist, the 'Cowley Fathers', started in 1866 by R. M. Benson, the vicar of Cowley. It is also important to recognise that the emphasis on the contemplative life can flourish outside the confines of monastic orders – a notable example of this is the Society of Friends, whose whole way of life manifests a disciplined openness to the presence of Christ.

From its beginnings, Christian monasticism was an effort to achieve a close communion with God by withdrawing from ordinary society and its pleasures, while the introduction of community life added the further aspect of the discipline of communal living as a training in self-abnegation. Ideally, however, the motive of all Christian monasticism was the individual's growth in the spiritual life, becoming like Christ and, as the monastic theologians would put it, the restoration of the image of God in humanity. St Symeon the New Theologian (949–1022), who is linked with a return to strict monasticism in Constantinople, is one of the greatest mystical writers of the Byzantine church, noted for his emphasis on the vision of the Divine Light. The fourteenth-century mystical movement called Hesychasm, 'quietism', originated in Mount Athos (as well as looking back to St Symeon). Its most outstanding figure, Gregory Palamas (1296–1359), taught that, although God is inaccessible in his inner self, his divine light or energy pervades the whole of creation and forms the closest personal relations between man and God; he defends the discipline of the 'prayer of quiet, or of the heart', by which is meant the rhythmic repetition of the name of Jesus in order to gain the vision of this divine light by purifying the heart and mind. The Hesychasts recommended a specific bodily posture and the use of breath control to keep time with the recitation of the Jesus prayer ('Lord Jesus Christ, Son of God, have mercy upon me'); their aim was to achieve what they call 'the union of the mind with the heart', so that their prayer became 'prayer of the heart' and to gain the vision of the Divine Light, which they believed could be seen with the material eyes of the body. The similarity of their basic techniques to Yoga are obvious. For the continuing significance attached to meditative prayer in the Christian tradition, we have only to look at the popularity of the form of prayer recommended by St Sulpicius (d. 647) with its devout concentration on 'Jesus before the eyes, Jesus in the hands, Jesus in the heart' or the *Spiritual Exercises* of St Ignatius. Within our own time, in the Roman Catholic tradition, one can point to figures such as Thomas Merton (1915–68), the Trappist monk who wrote extensively on the Christian meditative tradition and also in the later years of his life became interested in Hindu and Buddhist spirituality, especially Zen Buddhism.

St John of the Cross in the sixteenth century presents the mystical path in his writings as being composed of successive stages of attainment of ever higher levels of religious consciousness and understanding, while accepting that the stages merge into each other. He makes use of the three stages typical of Roman Catholic mysticism (*via purgativa, via illuminativa, via unitiva*), which go back through Dionysius the pseudo-Areopagite to the neo-Platonist Plotinus, but he places between them what he terms the Night of Sense and the Night of Spirit, both characterised by feelings of inner emptiness and separation from God. In his poem, 'The Spiritual Canticle', he uses the imagery of the Songs of Songs in narrating the seeking of the soul as the bride for her divine bridegroom. His contemporary, St Teresa of Avila (1515–82), recognises four stages or degrees of prayer, in which the degree of effort decreases as God takes over; she provides an elaborate scheme of spiritual progress in her *Interior Castle* and develops the symbolism of the spiritual betrothal and marriage, which cannot however 'be consummated in perfection while we live here below'. Despite her very different personality, she thus makes use of the same imagery as St John of the Cross and also speaks of the pain of separation from God in terms of a burning inner fire or of the heart being pierced by a fiery arrow or spear. There are a number of close parallels here with the *bhakti* poets of the Hindu tradition, even to the way that St Teresa in introducing her reforms sought to minimise hierarchy within the order, just as the *bhakti* poets tended to oppose the implications of the caste system.[6]

The more specific content of the imagery used by these saints to describe the mystical state has an obvious relation to the visions that are recorded by various mystics, for both in contemplation and in visions they are entirely taken up with spiritual realities. Visions have, however, a specific visual and aural content which distinguishes them from the ineffability of the mystic experience in itself (before the use of imagery to interpret it). Nonetheless, many of those noted in the Christian tradition as contemplative also had visions. Thus, for example, Julian of Norwich (c.1342–1413) had vivid visions of the crucifixion which she described in her book, *The Sixteen Revelations of Divine Love*, St Catherine of Siena (1347–80) had a number of visions, including her 'mystical marriage' to Christ, and St Catherine of Genoa (1447–1510) also experienced visions as well as expressing her experience of God in unitive terms, as we note at the beginning of this chapter.

Fasting as a religious discipline is nearly universal and certainly it plays a considerable role in both Christianity and Hinduism. In both it tends to be linked with the ascetic tradition, though not exclusively so, and one can see a natural connection between fasting and the withdrawal from the world found in asceticism or monasticism. The practice is designed to strengthen the religious life by lessening the attachment to the pleasures of the senses. In Hinduism fasting is often a major aspect of the observance of *vratas*, as we saw in the last chapter, and is also a form of penance laid down for various minor sins in the lawbooks (e.g. *Manu*

11.167–9), where the term is extended to cover various restrictions on one's intake of food short of complete abstinence. For the *saṃnyāsin* it was a necessary part of his whole way of life, since he was enjoined never to eat his fill but only to eat as much as was needed to survive, often being limited to eight mouthfuls, and not to feel either elation or dejection whether he got much or little from his begging, for which elaborate rules were laid down to restrict his choice (e.g. *Manu* 6.27–8, and 55–9); it is not too much to say that he was engaged in a continuous fast.

Fasting seems to have been accepted as a natural enough discipline by Jesus but given little significance, at least during the period of his presence with his disciples (Matthew 6:16–18 and 9:14–16, cf. Mark 2:18–20), although he himself fasted during the temptation in the wilderness (Matthew 4:2, Luke 4:1–2). It seems to have been one of the most favoured ascetic practices of the desert dwellers and monks of the early period, who regarded it as necessary to free the soul from worldly attachments. No doubt its popularity is the reason why at a later stage most monastic manuals or rules warn monks against excessive fasting, which could harm both body and soul. However, it has also had a place in lay life. Already in the *Didache*, the Church's earliest manual on morals and practice, the custom of fasting on Wednesdays and Fridays is found (8.1; contrasted with Jewish fasting on Mondays and Thursdays). The fast of Lent came to extend to forty days before Easter, although in the early centuries the period was of different length in different churches. In the early church fasting meant complete abstention from food during the whole or part of the fast day but over the centuries came to be reinterpreted in terms of various dietary restrictions; elaborate definitions had to be made and widespread subterfuges were adopted to get round the letter of the law, just as in the comparable situations in Hinduism. In the Orthodox Churches fasting is usually one of the acts of purification preparatory to participation in the liturgical mysteries, especially the Eucharist. In the Roman Catholic Church the severity of fasting has been much reduced in recent times but partial fasting and abstinence from meat on Ash Wednesday and Good Friday is still generally observed, while the penitential character of Lent is reflected in certain features of the liturgy. There also gradually developed certain seasonal fasts, most obviously and importantly of course the period of Lent but also the Rogation Days (in spring, associated in particular with praying for good crops), Ember Days (four groups of three days distributed through the year, regarded as times of spiritual renewal, though perhaps originating from ceremonies associated with the crops) and the eve of major feasts. In 1969 the Roman Catholic Church replaced the Rogation and Ember days by periods of prayer for the needs of mankind, the fruits of the earth and the work of men's hands, which could be observed by local arrangement.

Fasting is not the only form of abstinence common to both Hinduism and Christianity. Sexual abstinence, not only in the form of permanent chastity but also in the form of abstention for a specific period, has played a definite role in both. Sexual intercourse was banned on many days in the Christian church and in connection with many Hindu rituals, including marriage. The motivation for this temporary abstinence is, however, often rather different, since the purpose of such abstention in many early societies was in fact to build up the sexual energies in order to produce better offspring or to redirect those energies elsewhere (the rationale of abstaining from intercourse by participants before battle in earlier periods and, presumably, nowadays before sporting events such as football matches). When the practice was taken into the Christian church, these aims were no longer so appropriate and were reformulated in terms of a more general spiritual benefit. Thus, chastity came to be seen as something desirable in itself to such an extent that eventually the practice had to be discouraged for those outside monastic orders (and the priesthood in Roman Catholicism). Within Hinduism, celibacy was considered appropriate for the student phase of life and again after the householder phase, after social obligations have been fulfilled. Continence for three nights after the marriage ceremony is also prescribed in many of the Gṛhyasūtras and other Hindu texts as a defence against the demons who might otherwise kill or harm the new husband and to ensure the birth of a son. When a similar practice entered Christianity from paganism it was called the Tobias Nights (following a Vulgate interpolation into Tobit, 6:18–22, cf. 8:4). The original purpose was lost but the custom remained in vogue in parts of Europe till quite recently; the nights of chastity, often consigned successively to God, the Virgin and a saint, were assumed to confer some more or less vague spiritual benefit on the couple.[7] Pagan superstition was thus rationalised into a positive virtue but one that lacked any particular social merit, unlike conjugal fidelity, virginity before marriage and avoidance of promiscuity, all of which are social virtues with positive benefits to society, endorsed by Christianity, Hinduism and indeed most religions.

6

Social Values and Morality

Within Hinduism the principle of *karma* (the belief that one's present state is determined by the sum total of one's actions in previous lives) tends to emphasise the autonomous character of the sphere of morality, since *karma* is inbuilt into the nature of the universe. The concept has at times had a similar function in Hinduism to the idea of history in Western thought, though with the important qualification that it operates at the individual rather than the societal level. For *karma* relates to this world, of which it supplies the causal structure and as such is distinct from the Absolute (but not necessarily from the deity, especially in *bhakti* Hinduism); it is, therefore linear in operation, since it necessarily proceeds from cause to effect. Incidentally, the common notion that belief in *karma* amounts to fatalism is based on a misconception, through failing to take into account the timescale involved; one's present condition is determined by one's own past actions and one's future condition is being determined in the present by one's actions, and thus a man is essentially what he has made himself and can make himself what he chooses. This is not, of course, to deny that there may be greater obstacles for some than for others (but then those obstacles will have been of the individual's own making).

The understanding of the operation of *karma* will naturally be dependent on the way in which the world itself is seen. In the monistic viewpoint, which in some sense goes back to the Upaniṣads and is fully developed in the Advaita Vedānta, the world, made up of pairs of opposites, such as pleasure and pain, good and evil, is an appearance only, and release is achieved by recognising Brahman as the sole reality. Thus, *karma* is operative only so long as one is bound to *saṃsāra* and equally suffering is a problem only so long as it is thought to be something real and inescapable. Criticisms have sometimes been raised that this view leads to indifference to the problems of the world as it is and that Hindus are therefore indifferent to the sufferings of their fellows. The attitude of detachment, found not only in Advaita but also for example in the *Bhagavadgītā*, can shade off into indifference, since the *karma* doctrine, that an individual's present position and suffering are a consequence of his own actions, can lead to a passive acceptance of the *status quo*; however, while this certainly does happen, it is clearly recognised by Hindus themselves as a perversion of the real meaning of *karma*. Indeed, we can see this awareness already in the *Bhagavadgītā* – one of the most important texts in Hinduism for its treatment of questions of morality – where Kṛṣṇa puts forward two lines of argument to encourage Arjuna to fight, despite the suffering this will cause (2.11–38). The first is that he should recognise the identity of the *ātman* with Brahman and the second is that it is Arjuna's caste duty as a warrior to fight. To overcome the apparent contradiction between the call to detachment implicit in the first and the call to commitment of the second Kṛṣṇa starts to propound the main theme of the *Bhagavadgītā,* that of action without attachment and the cultivation of equanimity in the midst of all the ups and downs of life, when *karma* will no longer have its binding force. Much later, Rāmānuja regards human action as an appropriate form of response to the knowledge of the deity and suggests that fulfilling one's *dharma* and offering one's virtuous actions to the Lord is pleasing to him; the devotee will, therefore, naturally perform such actions without any personal desire for the benefits which may accrue.

The doctrine of *karma* raises a major problem when it is linked with the concept of an omnipotent deity, as in many theistic forms of Hinduism. Either the deity grants his grace (*prasāda*) and his liberation because of the law of *karma,* in which case they are in fact superfluous and he is not omnipotent, since liberation would come anyway through the operation of *karma* and without the deity's intervention. Or else the deity acts despite the law of *karma* and so overrides it, in which case he is omnipotent but is responsible for the operation of *karma* and hence also responsible for suffering. Rāmānuja, for example, asserts that Nārāyaṇa has the power to override the workings of *karma* to which he is not in any way subject, while vigorously denying that he has any connection with evil or suffering, which affect only the divine body not the highest self. This is, one might say, the specifically Hindu version of the problem of theodicy. The *karma* doctrine also implies that all suffering is the result of action by moral agents (whether at the divine, human or subhuman level) and it could be argued that it does not take account of natural disasters or of sheer chance. The defence, which has been implicitly recognised ever since the *Bhagavadgītā,* would be that natural disasters, such as floods or earthquakes, or accidents, such as a falling tile, cause suffering only when there is someone affected by them and that an individual's presence would be the result of past *karma* having brought the individual there at that particular time. Thus, it is the individual's own actions that brought the suffering about and nothing else is responsible.

This is the strict theory but, as so often, it is not always adhered to in actual circumstances. A notable case in point is Mahatma Gandhi's violent assassination in 1948, which ought to be seen as evidence of some past misdeed according to the *karma* doctrine but which in the popular imagination has been seen rather as further evidence of his saintliness, almost it seems along Christian lines of his martyrdom; there is, indeed, a broad parallel to the mediæval Christian view that Christian warriors who died in conflict with the heathen would go straight to Heaven without passing through Purgatory and that this applied all the more to martyrs for the faith.

The caste system, which is the most obvious and distinctive feature of Indian society, is intimately linked with Hinduism and, indeed, it is given a religious basis in the doctrine of *karma.* Whether it is in fact a necessary component of Hinduism is another matter, and there is evidence both in the way that many Hindus outside India are radically simplifying the system and in the protests raised against it by some movements within Hinduism that it is by no means indispensable. It is also true to say that historically the caste system has been nowhere near as monolithic and rigid as has often been implied. In addition, a distinction must be made between the older, and nowadays largely theoretical, division into four broad classes or *varṇas* (a classification which is attested as early as the Vedic period) and the later multiplicity of closed castes and subcastes, the *jātis,* which form the actual social framework at the present day.

Whether intrinsically necessary or not, caste has traditionally been viewed as the basis of society in Hinduism, and Hindu legal texts have regularly laid down that it is the duty of the ruler to see to its proper ordering and maintenance. There is thus no equivalent of the distinction between church and state which has so exercised Christian writers in defining their relationship; the caste system is both a social and a religious concept and thus the roper concern both of the ruler and of the brāhman, although it hould be stressed that matters of caste discipline are normally andled within the caste grouping with appeal to an outside uthority only as a last resort. Whereas for many Christians in ecent times there is a gulf between religion and ordinary life, in Iinduism they have regularly been coterminous in the mechansms of caste and caste-*dharma*. It should also be remembered hat Hinduism as a whole lacks the ecclesiastical hierarchy or rganisational structure which within Christianity has tended to ive the church-state issue a sharper focus. There is, therefore, o single individual or institution to give voice to authoritative ronouncements on behalf of the religion as a whole. By contrast, eaders of particular sects may well adopt a much more dogmatic tance. For example, the various Śaṅkarācāryas have become in nodern times definite authority figures in the Hindu tradition and re often called on, or take it upon themselves, to rally the masses n social and political issues with a religious dimension, such as ommunal harmony or the slaughter of cows. There were some igns during the independencemovement of political allegiances long religious lines but the events leading up to partition and Gandhi's assassination in 1948 ensured a decisive turning away rom that pattern for many years. Nevertheless, there was always n undercurrent of Hindu chauvinism and the last few years have een the rise of the Bharatiya Janata Party as an explicitly rightving Hindu party challenging what it sees as the socialist and ecularising tendencies of Congress. However, in an important ense the precise nature of the government is irrelevant for Hindusm, since what matters is simply that the government should nsure the proper functioning of Hindu society, in particular the aste system.

Particularly influential in recent years have been Louis Dumont's fforts to interpret the caste system in terms of a ritual hierarchy ased on an opposition between purity and pollution. The whole oncept of hierarchy is somewhat alien to Western modes of hought, which in modern times at least have put a high value on quality, and it has therefore not been sufficiently understood n the West. Dumont suggests that in Hindu society status is etermined not by political or economic superiority (broadly by ower) but by religious purity. Purity is meaningful only in terms f its opposite, pollution, which is regarded as being contagious nd thus has to be avoided by elaborate rules of behaviour.

The issue of purity and pollution is, indeed, closely tied in with the caste system. The origin of castes is a complex matter, involving the development of guilds or occupational groups into self-contained communities and the assimilation of tribal groups as distinct units into traditional society. Nevertheless, the basic elements which affect their ranking are almost entirely connected with their orthodoxy or otherwise in matters of ritual purity. Indeed, castes as a whole can over a period of time alter their ranking by moving closer to the customs of the brāhmans. Brāhmans, as the group from which alone priests and ritual specialists for the major cults can be drawn, have to guard themselves strictly against pollution and observe caste restrictions as a matter of religious and moral duty. Such rules have become increasingly rigid over the centuries. For example, there are nowadays many detailed restrictions about the types of food that one caste may accept from another, although the general rule is that one may accept cooked food only from someone of equal or higher status. One slightly incongruous result of this is that some brāhmans have become cooks, since anyone can receive food from them; this deviation from their proper duties is justified by appeal to notions of permitted occupations in time of distress, which are wider than the recommended or proper occupations. More generally, there is virtually no trace within Hinduism of the fellowship at a common meal found in many other religions (and in Christianity primarily in the Eucharist or communion, originally part of a complete meal even if now symbolic); there is a limited exception to this in the distribution to worshippers of *prasāda* (normally denoting the deity's grace, here the consecrated food offered first to the deity), which occurs as part of the ritual at some temples.[1]

At the opposite end of the hierarchy are those groups which are permanently polluted by their occupations: the untouchables or outcastes, as they used to be called, or the Harijans, as they are termed now. These groups were involved in contact with dead animals, as scavengers and leather-workers, or with the waste products of other humans as 'sweepers', that is those who cleaned out the latrines for other households, or with similarly defiling substances. They are regarded as being outside the system of the four *varṇas*, hence the term outcastes (although they are divided into *jātis* in the same manner as other Hindus), and as being so polluting that caste Hindus should not come into contact with them; there were indeed, especially in South India, elaborate rules about the distances to be maintained between caste Hindus and such untouchables (a few groups of whom were too polluting even to be seen by brāhmans). The social stigma attaching to them within Hinduism has encouraged different groups at various times to seek relief in mass conversion to other religions (whether Islam, Sikhism or Christianity) but this has not really alleviated the situation, since it has not removed the root causes in their occupation and general lifestyle. The efforts by Mahatma Gandhi (1869–1948) on their behalf had only a limited impact and the official abolition of untouchability by the constitution of independent India has been largely ignored in practice. Recently there has emerged a trend to assertion of their own worth, often focused on the celebrated fifteenth-century *sant* poet Ravidās, who was a leather-worker, with many from that caste forming themselves, as Ravidāsīs, into a distinct sect.[2]

Historically, the arrival of successive foreign groups to dominate the Northwest of India around the beginning of the Christian era posed a serious challenge to the existing *varṇa* system, for their rulers clearly had the *de facto* status of aristocrats but not the hereditary qualifications. It is interesting to see how the great legal theoretician, Manu, deals with this situation, writing as he most probably was in the second century A.D. in the immediate aftermath of this series of invasions. In the part of his textbook dealing with the four *varṇas* he recognises not only the emergence of the numerous occupational groups, erstwhile tribal groups and other small social units which are evidently the forerunners of the modern *jātis* but also assigns these rulers of foreign origin a place in the scheme of things, in both cases making use of what one can only call a legal fiction. He explains the many 'mixed castes' as he terms them as originating from a miscegenation between the basic four *varṇas* that produced a large number of separate groups, with their relative ranking being dependent on the parents' status and in particular those of lowest rank coming from a union of a woman of higher status with a man of lower status. The device he uses to account for the discrepancy between the actual and the notional status of the Yavana, Śaka and Pahlava rulers is to assert that they had in fact once been resident within India, when they had the status of kṣatriyas, but became 'degraded' as a result of their wandering away; thus, their status is open to change since, if they are purified of their 'degradation' – by suitably lavish ceremonies with their attendant gifts to the brāhmans and recognition of their supremacy in religious matters – and thus recover their former position in the hierarchy, everything will be as it should. We see here an excellent example of accommodation of theory to reality under the guise of affirming the *status quo*, something that the legal theorists were to practise extensively later.

Another social change which is already apparent in this textbook of Manu is the decline in the status of women resulting, it seems, from the lowering of the age of marriage. Boys of the first three *varṇas* undertook a period of celibate studentship in their teens (the precise age varied from one class to another) as a necessary preliminary to membership of adult society; at the beginning of this period they received the sacred thread, a symbol of rebirth which marked their admission into adulthood. This pattern was no longer followed by girls, who were standardly married at or before the onset of puberty. The result was two-fold: on the one hand, girls no longer took part in the higher levels of education associated with study under a *guru*, and on the other they no longer received the sacred thread and so technically were not full members of their *varṇa*. Thus, women joined śūdras, the fourth *varṇa*, and outcastes, who were outside the system altogether, as groups ineligible to hear the recitation of the Vedas. This decline in the status of women continues steadily in the theoretical literature and, so far as our rather sporadic evidence goes, equally in reality, although there is not really any evidence for the seclusion of women (except perhaps among the rulers and the very wealthy) until considerably later. Paradoxically, this decline in the status of women to one in many respects on a par with that of śūdras goes side by side with an extreme emphasis on maintaining caste identity through marriage only within one's own caste (or in a few instances a closely related caste grouping) which makes the woman's caste a matter of paramount importance when finding a bride. Indeed, the emphasis on endogamy is even stronger than the restrictions on commensality as an index of caste identity.

The youthfulness of the couple at marriage (for, while the girl is regularly younger than the boy, both are often below puberty) may well also be connected with the fact that marriages are arranged; this is a practice which is still nearly universal, even among Hindus living outside India in cultures where it can lead to severe social problems. A similar system of arranged marriages existed among the nobility in mediæval Europe, and a binding betrothal often took place while the couple were still children. In both situations the underlying factor is social rather than religious: the concern to secure the family's position through marital alliances. Equally, the actual consummation of the marriage was normally delayed until the girl reached puberty in both cultures. The European parallel to Hindu practice also helps to make the point that for the past our textual evidence relates to the upper levels of society and practice among lower levels may be different; pre-puberty marriage seems to be virtually universal among caste Hindus but there is evidence that among marginal groups, particularly tribals, this is far from true.

Another reason for the inferior position of women in Hindu society may well lie in the notion of purity. Whereas some substances are not only pure in themselves but can also purify other things (for example, water from the Gaṅgā, cow's urine and the sacred thread), other substances are impure and defiling, among which the discharges of one's own body are particularly defiling. Since women have the particularly obvious discharge of menstruation, they are seen as being necessarily more impure;[3] there are elaborate rules for the segregation of menstruating women and in particular they should not prepare the family food, a prohibition which could readily enough be observed in the traditional extended family, where there were other women around to take on the task, but which poses problems for many contemporary urban Hindus living in nuclear families. Other types of impurity may be mitigated by another important concept of Hinduism, that of auspiciousness. Thus, childbirth is impure, involving as it does the discharge of bodily fluids, but this impurity, though requiring segregation and purification of the mother, is more than balanced by the auspiciousness of the birth of a child, especially a son. Marriage is an event characterised by both purity and auspiciousness. Death, however, involves both inauspiciousness and impurity, and it is particularly inauspicious for a wife if her husband dies before her.

Traditionally women are seen entirely in terms of their husbands and children, of which a simple illustration is that a woman will normally be referred to and even addressed as the wife of so-and-so or the mother of her eldest son. As a result of their exclusion from education as early as the period of the Brāhmaṇas, women were restricted to pursuing the spiritual through their husbands, who would have the necessary education to know the rituals; indeed, they were recommended in the legal textbooks to see their husbands as their gods. A woman's devotion to her husband in feeding him and caring for all his wants and desires was understood as a religious offering comparable to that given to the deity. Most strikingly, even when women did undertake the vows (*vratas*) addressed to the gods which were typical of their religious practice, the purpose was commonly to secure from the deity some benefit for the husband, while the method was also frequently that of self-denial in a fast or the like. For the man self-denial in whatever form would typically form part of a Yoga discipline aimed at direct union with the ultimate, but for the woman such ascetic ideals are domesticated and directed towards her husband.

The supreme evidence of a woman's devotion to her husband, her ultimate self-sacrifice, was to accompany him in death through the act of becoming a *satī* (literally 'a good woman') by burning herself on his funeral pyre. In this sacrificial act involving the purifying fire, she burnt away not only her own bad *karma* but also the pollution resulting from her husband's death,[4] and thus she purified the family and, according to many texts, ensured that she would be reunited with her husband in heaven. By contrast, the plight of the widow was bleak, for she was felt to be guilty of failing to secure her husband's longevity through her vows and her caring and regarded as extremely inauspicious; the rest of her life had therefore to be an expiation for this bad *karma* by becoming a female ascetic practising chastity, rejection (or denial) of possessions and endurance. There is evidence that the practice of *satī* was originally a kṣatriya custom but it gradually extended more widely and certainly by about the fourteenth century is being put forward as the ideal for all women, even though some objections continued to be raised, such as that it was not applicable to brāhman widows or that it was not conducive to *mokṣa*. The latter objection exploits the shift in the goals of Hinduism from heaven (*svarga*), promised to the widow and her husband if she became a *satī*, to total liberation from *saṃsāra*, not achievable by one who dies before the end of the natural life span. In practice, no doubt, there were also social pressures for a widow to become a *satī* operating alongside the religious reasons. The woman herself may well have preferred what she had been encouraged to see as a glorious death to the severe restrictions and misery of life as a widow, while relatives might have seen it as a convenient way to eliminate a dependent female and claim her resources (limited as these would be).

Despite its banning in 1829 during British rule (and sporadic earlier attempts to eliminate it, for example by the Mughal emperor, Akbar), instances of women becoming a *satī* still occur. For example, on 4 September 1987 a widow of eighteen, Roop Kanwar, was burnt to death on her husband's pyre in the Rajasthan village of Deorala and within weeks the site had become a centre of pilgrimage; the central government took various ineffectual steps to quell the upsurge of popular feeling, including the gesture in December 1987 of passing a law imposing the death penalty on anyone abetting the act of *satī*.

Although this view of women as subordinate dominates Hindu thought, there are other facets. Even for the average Hindu, women are also seen more positively as a necessary link in the goal of *artha*, the second in the series of four goals (to be discussed below) which together constitute the proper aims of life, comprising wealth and other material benefits. The concept of motherhood is related to that of *śakti*, the divine creative power, and in the various forms of Hinduism influenced by tantric ideas this female power or energy is regarded as a means both to material wealth and to *mokṣa*, the fourth of the series of goals. Worship of the goddess is above all connected with Tantrism, which gave women an important place in their cult and instituted orders of female ascetics; some tantric texts also condemn the custom of a widow becoming a *satī* (they even declare that the woman burning herself on her husband's pyre goes straight to hell), denounce prostitution and advocate remarriage of widows. On the other hand, in the more popular tantric literature, such as that of the celibate Nāths, women are depicted as evil beings from whom man must save himself, as enchantresses by day but tigresses by night. By contrast, the Sahajiyā Yogins followed the tantric technique of having intercourse with a woman after mastering the temptation that she offered; often the woman was only present mentally as part of the meditative exercise in the form of *śakti* but in some cases actual intercourse was used to induce the experience of being taken out of oneself, regarded as divine bliss (the woman in these cases sometimes participating in the spiritual discipline but often being regarded simply as a means).

One of the Pāñcarātra texts, the *Lakṣmī Tantra*, is notable for its treatment of Lakṣmī as the power or *śakti* of Viṣṇu and for its glorification of women in general as created in her form. Lakṣmī, as Viṣṇu's *śakti*, is creatively active and the world is thus a part not directly of Viṣṇu but of his consort Lakṣmī, who is in reality identical with him and yet distinct as an attribute; this paradox is used to explain the coexistence of an infinite and perfect deity with a limited and transient creation. Later, the northern school of the Śrīvaiṣṇava movement believes that Lakṣmī, as well as Viṣṇu, is capable of granting liberation. Such exaltation of the goddess did have some impact on the view of women, though limited, in a similar fashion to the mediæval Christian veneration of Mary.

The element of social protest which is apparent from time to time in the *bhakti* movement flows essentially from its understanding that all devotees are of equal value in the sight of the deity; this appreciation may well of course be confined to the religious sphere but it has not infrequently been broadened to a more general concern for social justice. Something of this can already be seen in the accounts – largely hagiographical – of the lives of the Tamil *bhakti* poets. For example, the Vaiṣṇava Tiruppāṇ (probably ninth century), attached to the great Śrīraṅgam temple in the lowly position of a lute-player (regarded, later at least, as a śūdra occupation), is supposed one day to have been so lost in his contemplation of Viṣṇu on the bank of the nearby river that he failed to heed the warning shouts of a temple priest to get out of his way. Stoned by the brāhman, Tiruppāṇ fled but the brāhman found on his return to the temple that its gates were closed against him. In due course Viṣṇu revealed that this was his doing, for the stone thrown at the lute-player had in effect been thrown at him, since Tiruppāṇ was an *avatāra* of the deity (there is a striking similarity here to Jesus's words about feeding the hungry, clothing the naked and so on, in Matthew 25:31–46). To make amends the brāhman had to circumambulate the temple carrying Tiruppāṇ on his shoulders, thus dramatically purging the original offence by undergoing what orthodox opinion would see as a humiliation.

At a slightly later date, Rāmānuja in the twelfth century apparently devised for the untouchables the term *Tirukulattar*, 'those of the holy family', which is probably the origin, through the later *bhakti* poet in Gujarat, Narasiṃha Mehtā (traditionally 1415–81), of the term *Harijan*, 'people of Hari (= Viṣṇu)' popularised by Mahatma Gandhi. Rāmānuja also introduced changes into the conduct of worship at Śrīraṅgam which led to more complete participation of worshippers of all social levels and assigned definite ritual roles to certain śudras.[5] It has sometimes been argued that, however slow the process or however long the delay, it was the spread of Christianity with its attendant high valuation of all men as having a God-given soul that led to the recognition that slavery was unacceptable. If this argument has any validity, it may equally be argued in the Hindu context that the rise of the *bhakti* movement, for the same kind of reasons, has begun to mitigate the worst features of the caste system. It is perhaps significant that Gandhi's name for the untouchables derives ultimately from Rāmānuja.

The tensions and problems that continued to exist in this context are movingly illustrated in the life of one of the noted *bhakti* poets of Maharashtra, called Cokhāmeḷa (d. 1338), who was a member of the Mahars, an untouchable group. Despite manifestations of the deity Viṭṭhala's favour to him, the inhabitants of his village continue to harass him as an untouchable and even his death is related to his status, since the Mahars were liable for forced labour on behalf of the village and Cokhāmeḷa is killed by a collapsing village wall that they have been required to repair. The deity's final favour is to get his fellow *bhakta* Nāmdev (c.1270–1350) to seek out his body and bury it near Viṭṭhala's temple at Pandharpur; his *samādhi*, the memorial erected over the spot, marked both his recognition as one who had reached the final stage of union with the deity and the limit beyond which, before 1947, untouchables might not approach the temple. The majority of Cokhāmeḷa's poems describe his devotion to the deity but several express very poignantly the tension between his love for Viṭṭhala and the difficulties in showing it because of his untouchability, which means a life of constant pollution; Cokhāmeḷa concludes that untouchability is an act of divine providence beyond human understanding but that it is still possible to reach the deity through faith, for in the eyes of the deity there is no inherent impurity in the tasks that an untouchable must do.

This *bhakti* emphasis on the irrelevance of caste, in the religious sphere if not always in the secular, is clearly one contributory element in the violent rejection by Kabīr (probably early fifteenth century) of the whole socio-religious system based on brahmanical dominance, but another stimulant is very probably the presence in North India by then of Islam, with its egalitarian emphasis. However, the Islamic domination of North India produced two opposite reactions within Hinduism: on the one hand, it stimulated some, such as Kabīr, to stress further the trends toward equality already present and, on the other hand, it prompted many to retreat as it were into the protective shell of their traditional ways and values, thus encouraging a stricter application of caste restrictions. A good example of this in an institutional setting is that, at the restoration of temple worship at Śrīraṅgam in 1371 following the Muslim sack of the temple in 1323, the code of Rāmānuja was abandoned in favour of a more traditional form and so the rights and privileges of śūdra functionaries which he had introduced were lost.

The attitudes towards caste by Hindu reformers have tended to be somewhat ambivalent: concern to eliminate the injustices that were undoubtedly part of its actual practice but anxiety for the most part not to reject something seen as central to Hinduism. An interesting example of this is Dayānanda Sarasvatī (1824–83) and his Ārya Samāj, denying that caste was a religious institution but accepting it as a purely social one and advocating a return to the ancient system of the four *varṇas* rather than the multiplicity of *jātis*. In particular, Dayānanda saw the weakness of the contemporary caste system in its treatment of the untouchables and devised a rite of purification first for those among them who had converted to Islam or Christianity and then more generally for all untouchables to make them the equals of caste Hindus, though significantly not abolishing their group identity – one of the key features of the caste system.

Whereas the Syrian Christians had for centuries been integrated into the caste system and were regarded by Hindus as a caste occupying a relatively high position within the hierarchy, the issue of caste became a contentious one among Christians in India right from the start of missionary activity. The vital issue was always whether caste could be regarded as a social order with religious overtones, in which case it could be tolerated (if not exactly approved of), or whether it was an integral part of Hinduism, in which case it must be totally opposed. In general, Roman Catholic and Lutheran missions (especially the Leipzig Missions) took the former line, while British and American missions took the latter. Most Protestants, however, firmly took the line that to become a Christian one must renounce caste, completely and publicly, since they held that caste was a system of legalised inequality sanctioned by Hinduism. As a result, many individual high-caste Hindus might be impressed by the teachings of Jesus but they were reluctant to commit themselves to institutional Christianity because of the consequences involved in social ostracism by out-casting. Sizable numbers did convert to Christianity during the second half of the nineteenth century as a result of 'mass movements' in rural areas, in many cases out of a desire for social betterment. Although the leaders of most Protestant churches continued to be hostile to caste, in the situation of such mass conversions the new Christian communities predictably often came to resemble sub-castes in all but name.

The problems of the Indian Christian community in coming to terms with the issue of caste and the ideas of purity and pollution so fundamental to it have a parallel, of course, in the struggles of the early church to break free from its Judaic background in which ideas of pollution were also important. Jesus himself was opposed to such distinctions, as the story of his meeting with the immoral Samaritan woman (John 4:7–26) clearly shows, while the parable of the Good Samaritan (Luke 10:30–7) points in the same direction. Peter's vision at Joppa, in which he is told to kill and eat animals that for Jews were unclean (Acts 10:9–16, cf. 11.1–18), is directly related to the issue of the admission of Gentiles into the new community, providing as it does the justification for his responding to the Roman centurion, Cornelius, while the whole of Paul's ministry revolves around the issue of Jew and Gentile – 'In Christ there is neither Jew nor Greek' – and this led indeed to his arrest and eventual execution because he was accused (falsely) of taking a Gentile into the Temple (Acts 21:27–9).

Complementing the fourfold division of Hindu society into the *varṇas* is the theoretical division of each individual's life into four stages or *āśramas*; together these form the framework of Hindu social theory in the *varṇāśramadharma*, 'the duties of one's station and stage in life'. The four stages of life are first seen as a succession in the lawbook of Manu (earlier, as we noted in the previous chapter, they had been seen as alternative lifestyles). The four stages in fact ignore childhood and begin with an individual's initiation into the full life of the society at the thread-ceremony (*upanayana*) which inaugurates the first stage as a student (*brahmacārin*), to be followed by those of the householder (*gṛhastha*), of the retired person (*vānaprastha*, literally 'forest-dweller') and renouncer (*saṃnyāsin*). The individual was supposed to pass through each in turn and so only to reach the stage of the renouncer after he had fulfilled all his social obligations, summed up as the three-fold debt, in the stage of the householder (for the stage of the 'forest-dweller', who still maintained some basic ritual practices, was in the long run virtually eliminated). Already in Vedic texts it is said that a man has three debts to pay during his life: to repay his debt to the sages, he should study with a teacher; to repay his debt to the gods, he should sacrifice; and to repay his debt to his ancestors, he should produce sons to continue the pattern of memorial rituals down the generations.[6]

The forming of the *āśramas* into a succession also accords with the brāhman emphasis on living out one's natural life span, already seen in the Vedic idea of the long, good life ideally of a hundred years, whereas the kṣatriya emphasis on warfare encouraged the notion of the heroic death, the death in battle rather than in one's bed. The ideal of a hundred years continues, to be portioned out among the four stages, with the value of longevity upheld by the length of time needed to accomplish all the goals involved and the value of wealth and offspring assigned to the householder stage. The third stage of the 'forest-dweller' may in origin have combined the brāhmanic ideals of ascetic withdrawal with kṣatriya customs of abdication to allow for a peaceful transfer of power to the next generation; certainly, the time for it is marked both by the assurance of a continued line in the birth of grandchildren and by signs of declining powers summed up in the appearance of white hair.

With the transition to the fourth stage of renunciation the individual turns his back on society and therefore also on *dharma* in so far as that comprises morality or the rules for social organisation. For the intending renouncer, however, morality has at least a negative value in that immorality is a sign of imperfection, since immorality is held to be due to ignorance, which leads to desire and thus to action and rebirth. On occasion morality has also a definite, though qualified, merit as a means towards liberation; though not itself the ultimate goal, it is then a necessary, but not sufficient, condition for achieving it. This is commonly seen in the various systems of Yoga both negatively (in for example the ideal of *ahiṃsā*, non-injury) and positively (as in the ideals of friendliness, compassion, and sympathetic joy, e.g. *Yogasūtra* 1.33). More generally, it can be said that 'knowledge', that is spiritual insight, is commonly regarded as standing above moral considerations but equally that morality is a necessary preliminary to such knowledge.

This clear separation between the claims of day-to-day morality in *dharma* and the ultimate goal of intuitive realisation in *mokṣa* is perhaps one reason why modern Indian philosophy has paid relatively little attention to ethical issues. In fact *dharma* as traditionally understood in Hinduism is nearer to morality, in the basic sense of a set of rules and choices, than it is to ethics, in the sense of reasoned reflection on the nature of those rules and choices and our relation to them. On the other hand, *mokṣa* embodies the ultimate value that in Western thought would be associated with ethics but in Hinduism is regarded as lying outside the sphere of *saṃsāra* and thus of *dharma*.

An illustration of this point is that, ever since the appearance of the concept of *mokṣa*, there has been an opposition between it and the other three ends of man or purposes of life, recognised and formalised in Hindu thought; *dharma*, material well-being and satisfaction of desires. The earlier three are intended to sum up human activity in a scale of ascending value, in which, however, each is legitimate and indeed necessary at certain times: it is the duty of the householder to seek prosperity and to raise a family in order to ensure the practice of *dharma*. However, the fourth end, *mokṣa* is added to them in a way which transcends and is opposed to them; indeed, as the value associated with the fourth stage of life, *saṃnyāsa*, it could be said to be anti-social as the purpose for which the renouncer turns his back on society.

Such turning away from the world in the final stages of seeking *mokṣa* is essentially what has given Hinduism the reputation of being world-denying in contrast to Christianity as world-affirming. The picture is in reality more complex. In very broad terms, the basic Christian attitude to the world is not the optimism of modern humanism but a qualified hopefulness that with God's help man can resist evil and suffering enough to be worthwhile, though without complete success in this existence, while the usual Hindu view is that suffering is inevitable in this world and that the only way to deal with it is in fact to reject the world and seek release from it. In the monistic view of the world, this is indeed essentially the attitude adopted. However, the various *bhakti* movements often have rather different attitudes. There is, for example, a much more positive evaluation in the Śrīvaiṣṇava tradition. It is only from the standpoint of human ignorance and sin that the senses and physical existence as a whole are undesirable, whereas from the deity's standpoint the whole world is part of the manifestation of his glory. Thus, embodiment cannot be evil, since Viṣṇu embodies himself in every part of his universe. Although the ordinary person has a material body which is tainted by sinful deeds going back over countless lifetimes, the saint has a body so purified that it can be enjoyed by the deity. The bondage of many souls to beginningless *karma* causes their repeated return, but nonetheless the entire world of material bodies and embodied souls is intended to glorify Viṣṇu, to express his power and goodness in physical terms.

The Christian attitude toward the rest of creation has tended at times to be seen as one of domination over nature, justified by a rather simplistic appeal to Genesis 1.28 ('God blessed them and said to them, "Be fruitful and increase, fill the earth and subdue it, have dominion over the fish in the sea, the birds of the air, and every living thing that moves on the earth"). But this is only one part of the witness of Christianity and at other times the emphasis has rather been on man's stewardship of creation; the Greek Orthodox Church has expressed this well by saying that we are the priests of creation, entrusted therefore with a mediating role between God and the rest of his creation. The Hindu tradition has always seen a much greater continuity between mankind and the rest of creation, all of which takes part in the cycle of *saṃsāra* or rebirth, which means that there is no intrinsic distinction between mankind and other animals. This underlies the emphasis on the concept of *ahiṃsā* with its accompanying preference among brāhmans and various other groups for vegetarianism.

The standard Christian view of society is that both church and state are ordained by God as part of his creative or redemptive purpose. Whether the state is seen along with Augustine as the result of the Fall or whether it is part of the created order, as Aquinas held, it is seen as in some sense divinely ordained. The leaders of the Reformation in the sixteenth century did not essentially challenge this position and it has continued to be the mainstream Christian view ever since. The nature of the relationship envisaged between church and state varies widely, nonetheless. Historically, there have been a number of phases, from the imperial repression of Christianity until the fourth century, through the alliance of church and state, to periods of ecclesiastical domination, as with the Roman Catholic Church under Pope Gregory the Great (c.540–604), or the ecclesiastical state, as with the papal states or Calvin's Geneva.

In the eastern half of the Roman Empire, the period of repression gave way to one of imperial patronage which led to control of the church by the state. The church was established but correspondingly under imperial domination, even in matters of doctrine; so much was this the case that the term Caesaropapism has been used to denote this situation of supreme control by an absolute monarch over the church in his empire. Such an attitude has remained common among the Orthodox Churches; for example, one of the factors in the weakness of the Russian Orthodox Church in the face of Communism was undoubtedly its previous identification with the Czars.

In the West the imperial repression scarcely permitted the growth of any considered views, although it may be noted that the Donatist controversy arose out of Diocletian's persecution of the church at the beginning of the fourth century, when Christians were required to hand over their scriptures and some bishops succumbed to civil threats; the Donatists refused to accept as bishops any who had thus compromised and broke away to form a separate church in North Africa. Augustine (354–430), who grew up in this area, firmly rejects the exclusiveness and puritanical moral stance of the Donatists in favour of a wider understanding of the nature of the church. In his *De Civitate Dei*, he presents his views on social and political theory and argues that, despite the deficiencies of temporal states, social life for man is divinely ordained and natural. Some form of state is needed and this underlies the divine ordination of civil power, the state, although he condemns imperialism and tyranny. Thus the Christian duty of loving one's neighbour in effect teaches civic duty and obedience to the state, within the context of the larger duties to God; this is the essential point of Augustine's distinction between the earthly city, based on self-love, and the heavenly city, based on love of God. Yet, even as he stressed the inherent sinfulness of the secular political order, he accepted that its interest in the preservation of law and order was a kind of recognition of righteousness and suggested that the state ought to place its services at the disposal of the church.

With the collapse of the Western Roman Empire, the popes in an important sense claimed to be the true successors of the Caesars and thus asserted the supremacy of religion over the state. This is starkly seen, for example, in the excommunication by Pope Gregory VII (c.1021–85) of the emperor Henry IV in the controversy over their respective rights in episcopal appointments, which paved the way for the total papal dominance over the Western world seen under Pope Innocent III (1160–1216). Although Thomas Aquinas does not have a great deal to say about the relationship between church and state, he nevertheless recognises that the state has an independent basis in God, the giver of all power, and in the law of nature. Such a view legitimates the autonomy of secular rulers but not to the exclusion of all checks upon them. Although subjects may not depose a ruler, their obligation to obey him in certain circumstances is conditional on the justice of his commands. The emphasis on works in the Roman Catholic Church means that it is still differently related to the societies within which it operates from many Protestant churches with their main emphasis on faith and devotion as the way to salvation, for it becomes directly involved in the total social structure; this has, indeed, at times created problems for the church hierarchy when, for example, worker priests in France turned communist and the experiment had to be abolished, or liberation theology as expressed in South America threatens the church's support from elsewhere.

In Latin America liberation theology emerged in the 1960s as an interpretation of Christian faith out of the experience of the poor, and thus as a critique of the injustices manifest in society, in which the pastoral concerns of church workers seeking to help the poor were given a theological articulation; most of it is specifically Roman Catholic. Liberation is seen as a process of basic change towards a more just and equal society, in which all can share, and the movement focuses on the political and economic causes of social inequality. It first achieved a measure of recognition in the Latin American Bishops' Conference at Medellín in 1968 and gained added relevance from the series of military coups in the region during the 1970s. Considerable stress was laid on the 'base communities' as the basis for pastoral work (arousing at times some suspicion from the ecclesiastical hierarchy) and in this context the question was raised of ordination for married people, including women, by Leonardo Boff. Nevertheless, the central concern remains liberation of the poor, not the generating of ecclesiastical controversies. The concern with social issues and analysis of the actual socio-political situation has naturally led to the use of Marxist terminology by some writers and equally naturally to its denunciation in certain quarters. The term liberation theology has also been extended to other theological movements protesting against oppression and so black theology and feminist theology can be seen as major types of liberation theology. The Roman Catholic Church as a whole has, of course, long claimed the right to comment on the social issues and political structures with which it is faced. Pope Leo XIII's encyclical *Rerum Novarum* of 1891 was the first in a series of papal teachings on human rights in the light of economic development, and its centenary was marked by the Pope John Paul II's issuing of *Centesimus Annus*, in which he criticised the misuse of capitalism at the same time as noting the failure of communism and the explosive situation produced by its injustices.

At the Reformation, Martin Luther sought to establish on a scriptural basis the divine sanction of civil government, free from ecclesiastical control. This government he still saw in terms of the nobility or governing aristocracy and appealed to them to take effective action for the common good of Christendom. He was also distinctly traditional in his attitude to natural law, which for him gave the same duty of obedience to the ruling prince as is given to the parents in the family and indeed legitimated the existing structure of society. The consequence of this has been that to a large extent Lutheranism has accepted the ascendancy of the state over the church denoted by the term erastianism. Luther's emphasis on justification by faith alone thus had major implications for the involvement of the church in the feudal social structure of the period, while it also led to the belief that concern with the world and with good works were not fundamental religious issues. This was not to repudiate the moral aspect of Christianity but to make it firmly subsidiary to faith.

Calvin too insisted that secular government is a divine ordinance, while he remained reluctant to admit any control by the state over man's spiritual life. He affirms the duty of the subject to obey the ruler, since civil law presupposes the divine law on which it should be based. God gives authority separately to both spiritual and temporal government and thus neither is entitled to subordinate the other but must co-operate. However, whereas Luther tried to establish separate areas of jurisdiction and functions for spiritual and temporal government, Calvin assigned to both a common purpose in the maintenance of 'godly discipline', the results of which can be seen in the distinctly theocratic government of Geneva in his time. Subsequently, Calvin's followers in other countries have developed his doctrine of government limited by divine and natural law into a doctrine of constitutional government limited by 'fundamental laws'.

Max Weber (1864–1920) in his discussion of Calvinism and the growth of capitalism put forward the view that, in the context of the Calvinist doctrine of predestination, the effort to prove to one's self and others that one was among the elect encouraged men to greater thrift and industry. In his other writings he attempted to show how the appearance of capitalism was greatly restricted by most religious systems, and in particular that the failure of India to modernise effectively was due to its irrational and ecstatic religion, but in *The Protestant Ethic and the Spirit of Capitalism* (1904–5) he argued specifically that Calvinism provided a suitable seedbed for the growth of capitalism and was thus responsible in a significant degree for its character. He pointed out that in Germany at his time business leaders and owners of capital were overwhelmingly Protestant and posited on this basis a direct causal connection, although accepting that one factor might be that the most developed areas economically had gone over to Protestantism in the sixteenth century. His arguments are undoubtedly somewhat over simplified, especially in concentrating on Calvinism rather than on the whole economic and religious crisis of the sixteenth century and in ignoring the more individualistic aspects of Calvinism which became apparent in the seventeenth century, but his general thesis has been very influential in moulding later ideas on the subject. The linking of certain fields of business with particular religious groups is a well established phenomenon – one has only to think of the extent to which the chocolate industry in Britain owed its beginnings to members of the Society of Friends – but the explanation is at least as likely to lie in the particular social and economic situation of such groups as in their doctrinal formulations. In India, the association between particular communities and capitalist-style exploitation of the economy is well known and indeed a much older phenomenon. Jains have long been known for their success in trade and business (where religious restrictions on the occupations open to them were undoubtedly a significant factor) and the Parsis (as the Zoroastrian community are termed in India) have produced many of contemporary India's leading industrialists; within Hinduism itself, of course, the caste system has historically been decisive in determining individuals' occupations but this does not adequately explain why one trading community, the Marwaris, were the first to move into enterprises which can be called capitalist in anything like the Western sense.

The issue of church and state is also very much bound up with the understanding of the nature of the church itself. In the classic typology of church and sect, the church type of organisation to a large extent accepts the secular order, is integrated into the existing social order and seeks to extend its influence into the whole of life, whereas the sect type characteristically withdraws from society, emphasises the fellowship of the group and regards the state with indifference or even hostility. In both types, of course, there is general acceptance that adherence to the community is an essential part of being a Christian, just as for most Hindus belonging to a specific caste is an integral part of their religious identity. In the modern world, membership of a Christian church is, at least in principle, a matter of individual choice and the church is thus a voluntary community, whereas membership of a caste is preordained by birth. However, for much of the history of the church, its membership has largely comprised individuals born into the religion, as children of Christian parents, brought up in Christian countries or at least Christian groups, so that it was at most a semi-voluntary institution. This contrasts both with the position of the early Christian church in the first and second centuries and with the theology of some Protestant churches, such as the Baptists, who restrict membership to those who actively seek to join through baptism or other personal profession of faith.

There is an obvious contrast between the concept of *karma* and the doctrine of grace which, as we have seen, Hinduism in some of its forms does attempt to address. In the New Testament, the parable of the labourers in the vineyard (Matthew 20:1–16) directly challenges the principle that a man should receive only what he earns, a principle which is contrasted with the free generosity of the owner. While such a passage clearly suggests the paramountcy of divine grace, there are equally passages which indicate the importance of works, at least as evidence of faith (for example, 'Show me this faith you speak of with no actions to prove it, while I by my actions will prove to you my faith', James 2:18).

Within Christianity the ethical demands of belief have commonly been placed alongside worship and, indeed, seen as a form of worship, with love and compassion seen as a practical outworking of one's faith. The parable of the Good Samaritan (Luke 10:30–7) illustrates very clearly that the truly religious man is the one who tended the victim's wounds out of concern for the victim and not the priest or levite who, because they held performance of the temple ritual to be more important than social service, avoided touching what they supposed to be a corpse and so incurring the pollution which would have excluded them from participation in temple service. Such a view of the true meaning of morality makes the welfare of others central and allows importance to rules only in so far as they promote that welfare. But religion is a social phenomenon in a wider sense still, since it expresses itself within communities and its activities have both social causes and social effects.

The Roman Catholic Church rejects the Lutheran dogma of justification by grace through faith alone and insists on justification by faith and works. The Roman Catholic is saved by what he believes and by what he does. The Roman Catholic idea of faith, especially after the Reformation, gives little scope to the emotions, which belong rather to devotions and to mysticism, and theoretically appears to advocate a more intellectual assent; in practice, the situation has been considerably more complex.

The Roman Catholic Church upholds the view that there are certain actions which are inherently wrong and cannot be justified by motives, results or any other circumstances, while also accepting that a large proportion of moral decisions are determined by the situation or circumstances of the particular case. This absolutist tendency (and the problems it causes) are clearly seen, for example, in the way that the doctrine of the sanctity of human life has been given expression in a total ban on artificial methods of contraception and on abortion. There is a trend for Protestant churches, and especially the more liberal elements within them, to move further towards a purely situational ethic, in which the morality of any action is determined entirely by the circumstances surrounding it, within the one overriding principle of love. This has also at times resulted in a greater emphasis on the 'social gospel', on general concern for the well-being of the poor and similar worthy causes, to the neglect of the traditional Christian message. It has also, though, led to some groups developing distinctive attitudes to societal issues, of which perhaps the most notable examples are the involvement of the Free Churches in the temperance movement in the nineteenth century (reacting to the real social evils of alcohol at that period) and of the Society of Friends in both pacifism (given humanitarian expression in their service in the Ambulance Corps during both World Wars) and in international relief.

In reaction against the 'social gospel' trend, the new movement of 'crisis' theology associated with Karl Barth (1886–1968), Emil Brunner (1889–1966) and others, endeavoured to separate the Christian gospel from society (eschewing all connection with the natural sciences, psychology, religious experience and historicism) and to reaffirm the central message of the otherness of God and the unique saving otherness of Christ. Barth's emphasis on the power and sovereignty of God led him to view Christian ethics exclusively in terms of divine commands. The pattern of Christian life is to be found in the obedience of Christ to his heavenly Father and the search for any other or higher criterion is illegitimate; God is the 'transcendent commander' (*überlegener Gebieter*). Man's response, however, is not one of passive acceptance but is active decision. But these human decisions always take place within the context of divine will or command.

Such an emphasis contrasts quite markedly with the kind of attitudes seen in an established church, where the church is seen almost as an arm of the state and conversely the state as the secular expression of the church's values. The difficulties inherent in such a position are clearly seen in the rather uneasy relationship between the British Government and the Church of England, where large sections of the Conservative Party expect the Church of England to share its values and are outraged when it does not. Nevertheless, there have been significant instances of individual courage in rejecting deference to the political arm, for example by Archbishop Davidson in the First World War and Archbishop Runcie after the Falklands War.

7

Teleology: Meaning and Ends

One feature of all religious thought is concern with the purpose of human existence and its ultimate outcome, although the forms that this concern will take are inevitably influenced by views on other fundamental points such as transcendence. The concern for meaning and for salvation is clearly central and equally clearly linked with both the transcendence of the ultimate and the limitations of the human condition, since the failings of mankind, however caused (by sin, evil, desire, lack of insight or whatever else), would seem to call for some state of being not itself subject to those failings in order to remedy them. It is with these two inter-related aspects – included within the term teleology – of the purpose of human existence in the present and of the goal in the future, that is, salvation or liberation, that we shall be concerned in this chapter. Much of the first aspect has already been looked at in Chapter 6 in terms of man's social and moral responsibilities, but there is room for examination of it in relationship to man's ultimate destiny, to eschatology.[1]

The teleological issue of the purpose of human existence may well of course be answered by the denial of a purpose or by the counter-assertion that what is good in itself does not need a further purpose to validate it. Over against the common Christian attitude that the world is here in effect as the place in which individuals are examined for their moral probity, can be set concepts such as that of Śiva as the dancer, who dances the world into being for the sheer joy of it and not for some ulterior motive; it is thus beside the point to ask about the purpose. Yet, even here, there can be a purpose for individuals in conforming to the divine rhythm, and the image of Śiva as the dancer is used just as much to suggest his role in maintaining the universe in existence as to suggest that the cosmos owes its existence to his sport (*līlā*); and of course this particular image does surface in the Christian tradition too, for example in Sidney Carter's modern hymn, 'The

Lord of the Dance', based on the Shaker use of dance in their worship.

Despite the general recognition that developed Hinduism is characterised above all by the concepts of rebirth (*saṃsāra*) and release (*mokṣa*), it must also be remembered that these were absent from the earliest stages of the religion in the Vedic literature. The Vedic hymns are on the whole very little concerned with what happens at death but the predominant picture is that of the passage to an after-life. It is significant that the figure of Yama occurs almost solely in the latest parts of the *Ṛgveda* (books 1 and 10), where he associates with gods and by implication is divine, though only called king of the dead, since he is the first man to die; the realm over which he rules is really rather shadowy but there are hints that his realm is thought of as being subterranean, despite being the abode of the ancestors (*pitṛs*), who in general inhabit a land of the blessed. There is also one hymn that asks Indra and Soma to pierce the evil-doers and cast them into an eternally dark pit from which they will never come forth (*ṚV* 7.104), but it is not certain whether this applies to humans or to evil spirits; in a later stage of the Vedic literature there is one passage that describes Yama as separating the upholders of truth from the speakers of falsehood (*Taittirīya Āraṇyaka* 6.5.13). By the time of the Brāhmaṇas, there is somewhat more definition, though still no single view. The main view is that of immortality in heaven (*svarga*), the abode of the gods, which is the goal of many of the sacrifices; in fact, the Mīmāṃsā system continued to accept these older views about the after-life long after they had been abandoned elsewhere. On occasion, however, ideas are expressed of how man dissolves into various natural phenomena, or the funeral fire is called the third birth of man, or some kind of continued existence through one's descendants seems to be envisaged. Although individual immortality is the main tendency, there also appears in the Brāhmaṇas the idea of repeated dying, the possibility that the future life may also have a limit (and thus immortality in its literal sense of freedom from death may not be achieved so easily).

The idea of rebirth as such appears first at the end of the Vedic period in the Upaniṣads but in the earliest accounts it is presented as an esoteric doctrine. Discussion of the idea of rebirth occurs first in an account found in two of the oldest Upaniṣads (*Bṛhadāraṇyaka Upaniṣad* 6.2; *Chāndogya Upaniṣad* 5.3–10) and is taught not by a member of the brāhman class but by a kṣatriya. The young brāhman Śvetaketu comes to a gathering of the princely Pañcālas and presents himself to one of them, Pravāhana Jaibali, assuming no doubt that as a brāhman he would be asked to perform a sacrifice for the prince or to instruct him, and would thus get a reward. But the prince asks Śvetaketu a series of five questions about the individual's fate at death, which he frankly admits that he cannot answer. His father too is unable to answer them on Śvetaketu's return and goes to the prince to ask for the answers. The prince is reluctant to reveal them, declaring that this knowledge had so far never been imparted to a brāhman, but then propounds in terms of fire as the underlying principle a theory of transmigration in which the conditions of rebirth are determined in the first account solely by one's knowledge, and which differentiates between the two paths travelled by the dead man, the path of the gods (*devayāna*), from which there is no return to earth, and the path of the fathers (*pitṛyāna*), from which follows rebirth. Those who reach the *pitṛyāna* follow a course that leads them to the moon, from which they return just as they ascended to attain another birth. In the second account the prince declares that *karma* is what controls one's rebirth, while a third version (*Kauṣītaki Upaniṣad* 1.2) simplifies the progression from death to rebirth and makes knowledge and action join to determine the conditions of rebirth. Very soon, however, rebirth had become the standard belief (accepted, for example, as axiomatic in both Buddhism and Jainism which originated not much later than the early Upaniṣads) and was linked with the doctrine of *karma* as the explanatory device by which the variety of rebirth is made intelligible. Another passage from the earliest Upaniṣad (*Bṛhadāraṇyaka Upaniṣad* 4.4.3ff) already specifies *karma* as the sole determinant of rebirth and knowledge as the source of one's release from it. It is interesting that the *Kaṭha Upaniṣad* has as the expounder of its ideas Yama, now Death itself, who answers a young brāhman's queries, the third of which is about man's destiny after death. Yama's reply is to expound the *ātman* which is not born and does not die, but is eternal and indestructible, since death is now seen as part of the life-cycle and deliverance is sought from the cycle of births and deaths, from *saṃsāra*. Kṛṣṇa in fact quotes from the *Kaṭha Upaniṣad* when he begins his sermon to Arjuna in the *Bhagavadgītā* by declaring that the *ātman*, being eternal and indestructible, does not die when the body is killed but transmigrates from body to body until it achieves final release: 'just as a man throws away worn out clothes and puts on new ones, so the embodied one abandons worn out bodies and acquires other new ones' (2.22).

The usual translation of *ātman* as 'self', with its implications of personality, is misleading here, while even the translation 'soul' is not entirely appropriate. The *ātman* is precisely that ultimate ground of the individual that is devoid of any of the accidents of the ego or the personality. Thus, in transmigration there is not normally any recollection of the events of past lives (even though one's present status is determined by the *karma* of past lives, by the results of one's actions) and it is the bare *ātman* consisting of consciousness and being that passes from one life to the next. The lack of continuity in experience between one life and the next does constitute a philosophical objection to the concept, since it is hard to regard as merited a status which one has no awareness of earning; in popular belief, exceptionally advanced individuals can remember past lives but this does not invalidate the general picture, which is very far from the romantic notions of the neo-Platonists reflected in Wordsworth's 'Ode on Intimations of Immortality from Recollections of Early Childhood'.[2] The *ātman* exists eternally and cannot be destroyed, because it is 'being' and whatever is existent cannot become non-existent, a view that denies all change in the *ātman*. Whatever the average Westerner thinks of as part of the individual in terms of personality and particularity is excluded from the *ātman* proper and belongs only to an empirical self (for which various terms are used, such as *jīva*, 'the living entity'; indeed, a frequent Hindu riposte to missionary activity has been to ask why Christianity fails to distinguish the *ātman* from the *jīva*). For example, the brief *Māṇḍūkya Upaniṣad* (building on an older analysis of the three states of the self, for example at *Bṛhadāraṇyaka Upaniṣad* 4.3) asserts that the individual has four progressively more basic states: the waking state, in which the self exists in the mundane world and is most influenced by externals; the dreaming state, in which it creates for itself its own interior world; the state of deep sleep, in which the individual overcomes the dichotomy of the world into conscious subject and external object; and the fourth state, which both sums up and transcends the other three and in which the seeker 'enters with his *ātman* into the *ātman*,' merging the immanent with the transcendent. Thus this fourth state is one of total oneness and tranquillity in which there is no place for the phenomenal world or the empirical ego. Although such a monistic goal might be seen as eliminating the loneliness of the individual by absorbing him completely into the whole, in reality it achieves the individual's release by totally eliminating the individual as such. This radical devaluation of personality may well be linked to the relative subordination of the individual to the family, the caste or some other grouping in the Hindu social system, just as the sometimes excessive emphasis on individualism in Western society can be traced to the influence of Greek philosophy, reinforced by Protestant theology.

This understanding of the nature of the *ātman* gives a characteristic flavour to the Hindu view of the world process, of *saṃsāra*. Hinduism talks in terms of *prakṛti* or nature rather than history, and the goal of religion is accordingly not the redemption of time so much as release from time as part of *saṃsāra*. The contemplation of an unending succession of lives is seen as an unattractive, indeed a repulsive, prospect, devaluing this life and providing the motivation to seek for an alternative, just as the contemplation of death puts a particular perspective on life for Christians. Release (*mokṣa*) is an escape from or a rising above *saṃsāra*, which comprises the whole of worldly existence, and *māyā*, which in the more philosophically expressed forms of Hinduism is not so much illusion as a delusory way of viewing reality. In any case, in the fully developed Hindu cosmology (detailed at length in the Purāṇas, though with many variations), the world perpetually undergoes a cycle of emanation from a state of non-differentiation through a series of ages to its dissolution back into the unevolved state, before the whole cycle starts all over again. Within this whole complex cosmology, with its enormous time-spans, the aspect of which there is greatest popular awareness is that of the four ages or *yugas* (which are strictly sub-units within larger periods of the emanation of the universe). These four ages of decreasing duration are marked by progressive moral and physical deterioration – the world is now in the middle of the last and worst of these ages, the Kaliyuga, popularly considered to have begun with Kṛṣṇa's death following the *Mahābhārata* war – which Viṣṇu's tenth *avatāra*, Kalkin, will according to some Purāṇas bring to an end by overthrowing the evil temporal powers of the time and inaugurating a new Kṛtayuga, the first and best of the four ages. In one common version, at the beginning of each new cycle Brahmā emerges on a lotus from Viṣṇu's navel and sets the evolutionary process in motion; each cycle lasts for a hundred years of Brahmā but one day and night of his existence lasts a thousand years of the gods, which in turn comprise twelve thousand human years. The inherent pessimism of this scheme (for even when there is a new beginning it is followed by inevitable decline) is not entirely foreign to Western thought, since it has considerable similarities to the scheme of the four ages in Greek and Roman mythology. It contrasts, however, both with the Christian outlook and with the unreflecting secular belief in the inevitability of progress which it has engendered and which is only now beginning to be questioned.

The understanding of the *ātman* as the eternal and unchanging substrate of human existence is linked in the Upaniṣads, where it first appears, with the concept of Brahman as the eternal and unchanging substrate of the universe. This leads ultimately in the Advaita Vedānta to the complete identification of the *ātman* with Brahman, realised fully in *mokṣa* and so to a total denial of any individuality to the *ātman* apart from Brahman. The goal of all religious endeavour is the intuitive realisation of this identity and thereby the merging of one's own *ātman* with Brahman. However, this is by no means the only view to be found within Hinduism, which contains quite a range of views, ranging from the popular notions which to a considerable extent ignore it to the theistic movements which, though much influenced by it, modify it considerably.

Since parts of the funeral ritual are drawn from the *Ṛgveda*, it is not particularly surprising that it is the Vedic view of an after-life which is implicit in it, coupled with popular beliefs about ghosts (*preta, bhūta*) and the like, although attempts have been made to bring these views into line with the concept of *saṃsāra*, the perpetual cycle of rebirth, which dominates the textually based tradition from the time of the Upaniṣads onwards. In fact not just the funeral ritual but all the *saṃskāras* lack any reference to the concepts of *saṃsāra* and *mokṣa* and are based on a different world-view that celebrates life and fertility and transports the dead to the world of the ancestors. It is indeed the need to have a son to perform the funeral and memorial rituals which has been one of the strongest incentives in the desire for sons, and so important are these ceremonies that the offering of the ball of rice, which is a main feature, gives its name to the rules of inheritance based on family relationship. The emphasis on periodic rituals, both annually and on family occasions such as weddings, suggests belief in the continued existence of the ancestors in their own separate world, since the logic of the ritual is that the dead person is in an after-state where these offerings can influence his well-being. This belief is also in conflict with the doctrine of *karma*.

In Vedic religion the symbolism of the sacrifice is strongly present in the funeral ritual; ashes are what all men become, for they are the remnants of one's sacred fires. In the act of cremation, the god of fire consumes, not a substitute for the sacrificer, but his body itself and by implication transports the individual to the region of the gods. In one Vedic prayer a dying person declares: 'Now my breath is the immortal wind, my body is ashes' (*Vājasaneyi Saṃhitā* 40.15). Ashes are the remains of the sacrifice and demonstrate that one's ritual duty has been fulfilled; they are the physical evidence of the purification, healing, and transformation which the sacrifice accomplishes. Ashes have indeed become a potent symbol within Hinduism, for they reflect the concept of life as a continuous sacrifice and so are regarded both as remnants of old existence and seeds of new creation. Ashes smeared on the *liṅga* of Śiva are mentioned already in the *Mahābhārata* and a body smeared with the ashes of the dead becomes a primary sign of that deity (and so of his renunciant devotee, the yogin), while another type of ash, particularly that of cowdung, became important to Vaiṣṇavas as well as Śaivas and its usual name designates it as a manifestation of power and expansion. We may contrast the attitude towards the body revealed in these practices with the way in which in mediæval European literature to be burned and have one's ashes scattered by the wind is seen as the ultimate horror. This is because it was associated with punishment for various specifically anti-religious crimes and presumably also because it involved the complete destruction and dispersal of the body, so that no funeral (i.e. burial) rites were possible and the spirit could not be laid to rest (as was certainly the case with the unburied Palinurus in Virgil's *Aeneid*). Cremation is indeed only reluctantly becoming acceptable to some Christians even now, because of the persistence of belief in the physical resurrection of the body.

In another alternative to the concept of *mokṣa*, death in battle was long seen as being rewarded by heaven (*svarga*), which is a place of endless material pleasures and happiness. One hymn of the *Ṛgveda* suggests that warriors dying in battle reap the same rewards as those who make gifts of a thousand cows in sacrifice (10.154.3, cf. *Atharvaveda* 18.2.17), while the *Mahābhārata* states that soldiers killed in battle become pure by the destruction of their sins, and the *Bhagavadgītā* (2.31–37) and the lawbooks declare explicitly that the reward of death in battle is heaven. Different deities had each their own heaven, although the world of Indra is the most frequently mentioned. In due course the concept of *svarga* was brought into line with the concept of *saṃsāra* by asserting that residence in it was not permanent (but lasted only as long as was earned by the good deeds or the sacrificial merit which had achieved it) and that it was therefore only one of the various forms of rebirth open to the individual; indeed, in the fully developed Hindu cosmology there are commonly six heavens above the earth (regarded as the lowest level of this group of seven), below which are seven levels of the nether world and a further seven of hells (that is, counterparts of the heavens where evil deeds would be punished until the next rebirth); some Purāṇas give lists of the various types of sinners in these hells together with their tortures. It is interesting to note that the Jesuit missionary, Roberto de Nobili (1577–1656), already had an understanding of this and so rejected the use of the term *svarga* for the Christian concept of heaven, both because it is a place of sensual pleasure and because it is linked with the continuing cycle of *karma* and *saṃsāra*; he preferred instead to use the term *mokṣa*, which he correctly saw as liberation. However, he was distinctly critical of the ideas of *sāyujya* and *sārūpya* (to be examined shortly), considering that they imply the individual's absorption by the deity and argued that this would mean that, instead of saving man, the deity destroys him, and that it would render the practice of *dharma* meaningless.

The *Bhagavadgītā* places great importance on one's thoughts at the point of death, suggesting that meditation on Kṛṣṇa at the time of death leads to union with him, while other thoughts lead to the appropriate destination (8.5–6) and certain sins lead to hell (1.42–44 and 16.21). Full consciousness at the moment of death is thus highly valued in the Hindu tradition, since it is crucial to one's destiny, and this is true even today. There is a marked emphasis on spiritual preparation for death (extending ideally over the whole of one's life), so that at the time of death the mind is fixed on the deity and his name is on one's lips; for someone already prepared spiritually and so detached from material things, there is less to fear in a sudden death. It is important to perform an act of penance and to put one's moral affairs in order before death. Such anticipation of death and even the willing seeking of it in certain circumstances make sense within the Hindu understanding of this life as just one of a lengthy series, although it is worth noting that the idea that the point of death is absolutely decisive for the individual's fate also developed in mediæval Christian theology and led to a noted emphasis on 'death-bed conversions' which to some extent has persisted into the evangelical tradition.

Fasting to death when afflicted by old age or disease as a deliberate and considered response to approaching death is especially characteristic of Jainism (where it is termed *sallekhanā*) but its equivalent is also found in Hinduism as *prāyopaveśana,* abstaining from food and sitting in a yogic posture to await death. The underlying principle in the Hindu context appears to be that the act of will inherent in it is a means of purification from the bad results of *karma* and so helps to prepare for death, although there may be traces of the idea of death as the final sacrifice. That this is not just a historical feature is shown by its occasional practice nowadays, for example by the Marathi patriot Vir Savarkar, who fasted to death in 1966 at the age of 83, and Vinoba Bhave (1895–1982), who undertook *prāyopaveśana* after a lifetime of celibacy and service to India both in the independence movement and in his concern for the landless expressed through his *bhūdān* movement.[3]

Whereas the oldest Upaniṣads (and the Advaita system based on them) see the goal of release, *mokṣa,* in terms of merging with Brahman, the Sāṅkhya and Yoga systems have as their aim the isolation of the individual selves, for which they employ the term *puruṣa,* from any contact with the world of matter or nature (*prakṛti*) composed of the three strands or *guṇas*. For these two schools there is neither an absolute nor a deity as the basis of the universe but rather an eternal dualism between spirit and matter, *puruṣa* and *prakṛti*. It is interesting to note that the Sāṅkhya system in particular adopts a quite distinctive teleology in that it regards the evolution of *prakṛti* as taking place for the sake of *puruṣa,* that is, in a manner which will facilitate the progress towards isolation of the *puruṣa* which is illusorily but firmly ensnared as a spectator of this world appearance; this is the doctrine of *puruṣārthatā*. An image used to illustrate this is that existence is a theatrical show where what takes place on the stage of life only acquires meaning through being observed and enjoyed by a spectator, who is so totally absorbed in the show that he identifies with it and enjoys it as his own; release occurs when the false identification ceases, insight arises and the spectator leaves the theatre, while the dancing-girl leaves the stage (cf. *Sāṅkhyakārikā* 59).

While the goal of release is central to the non-theistic aspects of Hinduism (with the exception for a long time of the conservative Mīmāṃsā system), there is a tendency within the *bhakti* movement in particular to shift the emphasis away from the idea of release in some distant future towards an immediate and direct relationship with the the deity. It may even be said that the very beginnings of this can be seen as early as the *Bhagavadgītā* with its stress on the happiness secured by detachment here and now, but this is only the start of a long process of development. Elsewhere in the *Mahābhārata*, in its didactic portions, the Sāṅkhya concepts are adapted to a more theistic outlook and, for example, in one passage (12.290) the self at liberation, after passing beyond the heavens and beyond the sphere of the three *guṇas*, reaches Nārāyaṇa and is carried on by him to the Supreme Self, of which it becomes the stainless dwelling-place. Subsequently, the *bhakti* movement has encouraged the idea that through devotion to the deity the devotee can pass into *mokṣa* at the end of this life or, as they more often express it, can achieve union with the deity in his heaven, while some *bhakti* poets even suggest that the experience of the deity's presence here and now is preferable to *mokṣa* or release.

The culmination of this trend in the *bhakti* literature is the treatment of the four types of liberation, *sālokya, sāmīpya, sārūpya* and *sāyujya* which are always thought of as stages in the experience of *bhakti*, the love of God. Viewing *mokṣa* positively as the state of union with the deity, *bhaktas* have used these terms to denote various levels within it: *sālokya* meaning 'being in the same sphere or world' as Īśvara, *sāmīpya* denoting 'proximity or vicinity (in space and time)' to the deity, *sārūpya* meaning 'sameness in form' or assimilation to the deity, and *sāyujya* expressing 'intimate union, communion' with the deity. Advaitins often interpret *sāyujya* in the sense of 'identification with, absorption into, the divine essence' but this is quite contrary to the spirit and intention of the *bhakti* movement. First the devotee is accepted into the sphere or world of Īśvara, then into nearness to him, and then becomes conformed to his essence and finally enters into union with him in love in the most intimate way, retaining however his own personality or individuality. Occasionally a fifth stage is added to the list, especially in the *Bhāgavata Purāṇa,* namely *sārṣṭi* which means 'enjoying the same powers as the deity'.

Rāmānuja is one of those who stress the continued individual existence of the devotee after release. He declares that the individual *ātman* returns at *mokṣa* to Nārāyaṇa to dwell in full communion with him but is still distinct. The *ātman* is always conscious of itself, though forming part of the deity, and so is both one with Nārāyaṇa and yet separate as the enjoyer of union with him. Against the Advaita Vedānta concept of total merging, Rāmānuja argues that a cessation of distinction would both be contrary to the evidence of our senses and destroy the point of religious activity.

Madhva applies to the spiritual world the concept of the capability of each soul which will be fully realised in liberation, introducing a principle of hierarchisation which is in marked contrast to the egalitarian trend of the *bhakti* movement generally. Selves belong to five graded categories from the gods down to men; even the gods are divided into castes. Even in *mokṣa* distinctions remain and those released have a purely spiritual or essential body corresponding to their capability, by which they can know the entirely spiritual form of Viṣṇu and attain the four types of association with him. Men are further divided into three kinds: those chosen for eventual liberation, those doomed to eternal damnation and those destined to perpetual rebirth. This concern by Madhva to individualise selves and to show that they have different destinies and especially his concept of eternal damnation have sometimes been seen as owed in part to Christian influences, perhaps through the Syrian Christians of Malabar; however, all of these features can be explained equally well from within the Indian context, in particular from Jainism.[4]

The early Śaiva sect of the Pāśupatas, originating probably in the second century, had a distinctive belief that, by purification from past *karma* and acquisition of good *karma,* they could build up a superhuman body which made them equal to Śiva. The ultimate goal of *mokṣa* was interpreted accordingly as not just release from suffering but freedom to act at will, meaning effectively omnipotence and the sharing of Śiva's nature. All Pāśupata texts emphasise this positive aspect, as they term it, of the goal of *mokṣa*. This basically tantric belief appears also later. The Nāths too, who are a tantric Śaiva sect active in North India between about the twelfth and fifteenth centuries, have as their aim the perfection of the body. What distinguishes Nāths from ordinary mortals is their power of control over death and decay. Whereas other contemporary groups saw release from the body as indispensable for final liberation, the Nāths sought *mokṣa* in a transformed or remade body, the perfect body. To judge by the mass of legend circulating about them, they were widely credited with various occult powers and total mastery over the body, so that death could be kept at bay.

Within the Judeo-Christian tradition there is a comparable evolution in ideas about the after-life to that in Hinduism. The Old Testament expresses a commitment to life as good, as the supreme good, and to God as the living God (Deuteronomy 5:26, 2 Kings 19:4, etc.). A long life represents the ideal (e.g. Genesis 15:15 and Job 42.16–17) and the certainty of numerous children is a blessing from God (e.g. Psalms 127–8). To that extent, to die after a long and full life was seen as natural and in the proper order of things (e.g. Genesis 46:30 and Job 5:26), as being indeed a good death, whereas a premature or violent death was seen as a threat or even a curse. Such an emphasis on the benefits of this life is very similar to the outlook of the Vedic poets and accompanies an equal vagueness about the after-life, seen essentially in negatives. When God's breath or spirit is withdrawn, men die and are excluded from the community of those who praise him, being reduced effectively to nothingness in at best a shadowy existence in the realm of the dead, Sheol.

In the New Testament views of the after-life are not entirely consistent. In Jesus's words to the repentant thief (Luke 23.43) there is a clear statement of immediate immortality and Stephen, as he is about to be stoned to death, sees 'the heavens opened and the Son of Man standing at the right hand of God' (Acts 7:56); more commonly reference is made to the sleep of the dead until the resurrection (e.g. 1 Thess. 4:13–17), but this has come to be reinterpreted in terms of Platonic and neo-Platonic ideas about personal immortality. The parable of Lazarus, which has him 'carried away by the angels to be with Abraham' while the rich man is in Hades (Luke 16:22–3), suggests an immediate translation to these contrasting states, and an immediate judgement has also been seen in the statement that 'it is our human lot to die once, with judgement to follow' (Hebrews 9:27). On the other hand, the emphasis is clearly on the future in Jesus's warnings about the end: 'when the Son of Man comes in his glory . . . He will separate people into two groups, as a shepherd separates the sheep from the goats' and those on his left 'will go to eternal punishment, but the righteous will enter eternal life' (Matt. 25:31–2, 46).

Many passages in the New Testament express the conviction that the believer already possesses eternal life in and through Christ even before his death, for the life of the world to come is a life lived in relation to God. Christ's first concern is with God and our relation to him and in general he discourages speculation about what the future life will be like, apart from the overriding fact that it will be lived with God. As the Epistles explain, eternal life is dependent on God, who alone possesses immortality (1 Tim. 6:16) and who enables believers 'to share in the very being of God' (2 Peter 1:4), a phrase which comes close to obliterating the distinction between God and the believer which the Bible usually passionately upholds for the same reasons as the *bhakti* tradition within Hinduism. Central to Christianity is the belief that Christ 'has broken the power of death and brought life and immortality to light through the gospel' (2 Tim. 1:10).

In his teaching about hell, Jesus used the traditional picture of Gehenna, which is based on the valley of Hinnom that served as Jerusalem's rubbish dump and incinerator; the image is therefore, not necessarily of the endless torture of the wicked, but rather of their degradation and destruction, as is implied by the exhortation: 'Do not fear those who kill the body, but cannot kill the soul. Fear him rather who is able to destroy both soul and body in hell' (Matt. 10:28, cf. Luke 12:5). While the first half of this verse clearly envisages the soul as the essential part of the individual which can survive and exist without the body, as in Greek thought, the second half of it, with its characteristically Judaic emphasis that God can destroy both body and soul, implies some kind of belief in a physical resurrection also.

Christ's main message, however, was about the coming of the Kingdom of God. Those who believed in him could enter or receive the Kingdom and in some sense 'the kingdom of God is among you' (Luke 17.21), for its coming was a present but hidden reality, while its fulfilment lay in the future. The expectations of the early church often linked the imminent coming of the kingdom with the resurrection of the dead (e.g. John 5:28–9, Phil: 3:20–21, 1 Thess. 4:15–17). St Paul comes increasingly to emphasise that the resurrected bodies of the dead will not be the same as those that have been buried and even those alive at the last will have their bodies changed into spiritual ones, for 'flesh and blood can never possess the kingdom of God' (1 Cor. 15:50, cf. 12–57); he quite deliberately contrasts the physical body which dies with the spiritual body which is raised (verse 44); he also transposes it all to a cosmic scale in asserting: 'As in Adam all die, so in Christ all will be brought to life' (verse 22) and in arguing that through Christ's death sin, as the cause of death, has been cancelled and the sting of death removed. In this passage Paul uses the image of the seed sown in the ground, which thus dies only to produce a new plant; elsewhere he uses the image of earthly and heavenly houses (2 Cor. 5:1–4). The emphasis on bodily resurrection can best be understood as an implicit counter to the older Jewish ideas of Sheol as a shadowy and insubstantial after-life; against that, it stressed the fullness and wholeness of life with God. It differed equally from the Greek philosophers in holding that life after death is wholly a gift of God. Despite Paul's efforts, the creeds formulated in the Western church have often taught the resurrection of the flesh in a literalist fashion (although the Nicene creed speaks simply of the resurrection of the dead) and it has been defended by some conservative theologians this century, but on the whole such notions have been abandoned in favour of the concept of personal immortality. Martin Luther, for example, in the end rejects the concept of the soul sleeping between death and final resurrection in favour of the view that the soul is awake and enjoys the company of God and the angels.

In early Christianity heaven is seen as the fulfilling state of bliss and reconciliation with God, assured through Christ, and also as the divine abode, from which Christ came and to which he ascended after his resurrection. The belief in the resurrection of the dead which is its concomitant is, however, in this earliest period quite distinct from the Greek concept of the immortality of the soul, best known from Plato and Aristotle; the reality of hell is equally clear as the destination of the unworthy. However, different views were being expressed at a relatively early period. Most notably, Origen (c.185–254), who was well read in classical philosophy, talks of pre-existent souls fallen into time being released by faith in Christ for immortality. This view does have the merit of logical consistency (compared with the view of immortality but not pre-existence) but it contrasts quite markedly with Paul's view of an imminent descent of Jesus Christ to lift up the living and the resurrected dead in glorified bodies to join him in his kingdom (1 Cor. 15.12–58, 1 Thess. 4.13–17). This view would also, incidentally, forestall Hindu objections about the goodness and justice of a God who creates new beings in such unequal situations as we see individuals being born into. Origen did indeed incorporate in his system a number of ideas which have remained outside the mainstream tradition, including not only this idea of man's earthly life as a time of purification and trial for those celestial spirits which had failed to choose decisively between good and evil, but also the view that Gehenna did not mean the eternal punishment of the wicked but punishment for however long was necessary to permit the restoration of all to the presence of God (thus his view of it was more like purgatory than hell). Gregory of Nyssa (c.330–395) was just as clear that this life is a discipline leading to virtue but that, if anyone is not yet fit by the time of death, the process will continue – however painfully – in the next world and so all will ultimately reach perfection; those who do not undergo purification by baptism will be purified by fire. Such universalist views were formally condemned at the Second Council of Constantinople in 553.

On the other hand, the view that the soul possesses some kind of immortality by nature became general within the Christian tradition, through the influence on patristic theology of the neo-Platonic emphasis on a soul-body dualism with its attendant attribution of immortality to the soul; indeed, the doctrine of the immortality of the soul was given the status of dogma by the Fifth Lateran Council in 1512. When Thomas Aquinas discusses 'man's last end', he does this both in terms of a goal or purpose and of an end in time. For him man's end in time is the unalterable destiny of his soul in death, understood in the light of the belief in personal immortality general among the Christians of his day, but he regards the soul as providing the body with its final goal through resurrection. Thus there arose the concept of an intermediate state through which the soul could be purified and so be able to experience the vision of God as the goal of its natural immortality. The Christian concept of immortality does not see it as a projection of temporal history but as resting on the continuity of God, who is beyond temporality; through the incarnation of

God within history in Jesus Christ, individuals are released from the inevitability of death in time to eternity.

The question of whether or not human nature possesses a kind of natural immortality came to be linked with the debate on Adam's nature before the Fall. Drawing on Paul's view that through one man sin entered the world and through sin death (Romans 5:12), Augustine put forward the view that, if the first men had not sinned, they would not have experienced any kind of death. In the Pelagian controversy, the local Council at Carthage in 418 declared an anathema against anyone who said that Adam was created mortal and so would have died whether or not he had sinned. Thus emerged the orthodox view that Adam was not mortal in the same sense as the rest of creation, that death is the consequence of sin, which broke the state of harmony with God, and thus that all people are now sinners by nature. Another patristic theologian, Irenaeus (c.130–200), who was a major opponent of Gnosticism, took the different view that Adam was originally created as an immature, mortal being with the possibility of becoming perfect; thus man is naturally imperfect and has to undergo moral development until finally he reaches the goal of perfection intended by God. On this view the fall of Adam is not some catastrophic reversal of God's plan, but rather an example of the immaturity from which he is gradually leading mankind to his proper end. In more modern times this type of approach has been adopted, for example, by Friedrich Schleiermacher (1768–1834), by F. D. Maurice (1805–72), who argued that God's nature was one of absolute and universal love and so rejected the idea of an eternity of torture, maintaining that in the New Testament 'eternity' had nothing to do with time, and recently by John Hick, who puts forward a third alternative in place of either bodily resurrection or reincarnation, that of a continuation of life after death in a series of lives lived in other worlds, which is in effect a synthesis of both positions.

In the Roman Catholic Church hell is considered to be the state of unending punishment for the unrepentant who die without the grace of God as given in the sacraments. Its formal position is that there is no salvation outside the church (*extra ecclesiam nulla salus*), and this was generally accepted at face value before this century; Pope Pius IX put it forcefully when he declared in 1854 that the Roman Catholic Church 'is the only ark of salvation and anyone who does not enter it will perish in the flood.'[5] In scholastic theology souls in hell are held to experience both exclusion from God's presence (*poena damni*) and the suffering of fire and other tortures (*poena sensus*). Orthodox teaching is also that hell is a destination of eternal fire and punishment awaiting the unredeemed, whereas heaven is the ultimate destiny of the redeemed; central to this is the emphasis on the resurrection of Jesus as assuring the resurrection of believers. Modern theology prefers to emphasise the point that hell is the logical consequence of finally rejecting God's grace, which inevitably produces that separation from God which is the essence of hell.

According to Roman Catholic teaching purgatory is the place of temporal punishment where those who have died in the grace of God have an opportunity for the expiation of venial sins and compensatory punishment for mortal sins; it is thus a transition state where souls which will ultimately be united with their resurrection bodies experience purification. Those in purgatory are not undergoing a further period of probation, for the judgement has been made at death (so it was held on the basis of Hebrews 9:27); they have already been saved but must undergo purification before entering heaven. Justification for the concept of proportional punishment can be found in the parable of the unfaithful steward (Luke 12:4–8; Matthew's version at 24:45–51 lacks the element of gradation). By about the fourth century Christianity had reached a stage where the aim of individual salvation had to be integrated with the concept of a divine purpose for mankind as a whole, from the Fall to the Second Coming, and thus was developed the concept of purgatory to fill the interval. Augustine, in his *De Civitate Dei*, was probably the first explicitly to define a doctrine of purgatory, asserting that not all who died in a state of grace were fit to go straight to heaven and that sins not purged in this life would have to be purged in the next. His contemporary, St Jerome (c.342–420), affirms that the images of unquenchable fire and undying worm drawn from the New Testament are to be taken as symbols of memory and conscience. Nonetheless, both hell and purgatory were pictured in crudely physical terms throughout the Middle Ages. Dante (1265–1321) in his *Divina Commedia* provides a detailed and imposing description of a journey through hell and purgatory to paradise; heavily indebted itself to Virgil (who is Dante's guide through the underworld), the poem is perhaps the source of many popular ideas on the subject in more modern times. As successively defined at the Councils of

Lyons (1274), Florence (1439) and Trent (1545–63), the concept of purgatory is of an intermediate state, which provides for the ultimate restoration of fellowship with God at the conclusion of the period of suffering. Linked with it is the practice of offering prayers and Masses for the dead, which would otherwise be meaningless. There have been attempts to reformulate the doctrine of purgatory in ways that make more sense to the modern world; for example, Karl Rahner (b. 1904) suggests that at death the soul does not leave the world but becomes 'pancosmic', so that it is more than ever aware of its surroundings and experiences therefore more acutely its own harmony or disharmony with the proper order of the world.

The Orthodox churches also attach importance to the practice of praying for the dead but are less explicit about their exact status. However, though influenced by the ideas of Origen, they have not on the whole formulated such clear-cut answers to the mystery of death as the Western church. Their basic conviction is that the cessation of physical existence merely ends one stage in human ascent towards God, and that the good and evil done on earth will continue to produce their effects long after the death of the individual, so that the final reckoning can be made only at the end of history. Relying on the revelation of God as love and on the all-sufficient sacrifice of Christ, they believe that no being that God has made for eternal life will fail in the end to find it. Thus, even the righteous do not achieve their full glory immediately after death, while those who have fallen short are given the chance to improve their position through the compassion of their friends. Accordingly the Orthodox Churches pray for all the departed, both saints and sinners, trusting in the efficacy of mutual love and forgiveness. They are reluctant to accept the Roman doctrine of purgatory as a place of pain and expiation, since they believe that God in his mercy washes away the transgressions of all who sincerely repent and have been reconciled to the Church.

The concept of purgatory was definitely rejected by the Reformers, who declared that souls are saved from sin by faith in Christ alone, and not by any works, and therefore go straight to heaven. They discarded such speculation regarding the state of the dead in the after-life as unbiblical and superstitious. Calvin, on the other hand, elaborated the doctrine of the 'double decree', arguing that, if some were predestined to salvation, then logically others were predestined to damnation. Some groups on the fringes of the Reformation, including some Anabaptists and the Socinians, believed that men were not naturally immortal and so the souls of the wicked perished with their bodies but those of the elect would sleep until they were restored to life at the final resurrection, while universalism was among the liberal ideas espoused in the late seventeenth century by the so-called Cambridge Platonists, a movement which emerged as a protest against Puritanism and its Calvinist tenets. In general, however, the Reformers were unequivocal about the certainty of damnation for the unbeliever.

The Protestant churches have accordingly often held a version of the Roman Catholic doctrine of *extra ecclesiam nulla salus* in asserting without qualification that there can be no salvation outside the bounds of Christianity. But there have long been those who refused to set limits on God's saving activity and so questioned the concept of predestination which goes back to Augustine and had been so strongly reaffirmed by Calvin, or who accepted the possibility of God working for the salvation of individuals outside the church, or who saw the Christian message in more general terms as applying to the whole of society rather than to the individual. John Wesley (1703–91) was strongly anti-Calvinist, holding that predestination made God out to be more unjust than the devil, and refused to believe that God consigned anyone to hell arbitrarily, arguing that, while hell is a reality for those who reject God, no one need go there; in 1778 he established the *Arminian Magazine* to put forward the view that God desires all men to be saved. The influential German theologian Albrecht Ritschl (1822–89) stressed the ethical content of Christianity and saw faith in the fatherly providence of God as the basis of the Christian world-view. Although he did not envisage God's kingdom as coming on earth, he believed that Christians could improve conditions in the world by their efforts for good. In his major work on the atonement (*Die christliche Lehre von der Rechtfertigung und Versöhnung*, published 1870–4) he insisted that it is in and through the community that justification is primarily achieved and he defended the Reformation concept of God as the moral power which satisfies the highest human interests; this emphasis on ethics and the community was accompanied by a corresponding repudiation of metaphysics and religious experience. With the development of the scientific world-view, especially since the middle of the nineteenth century, literal and spatial interpretations of heaven and hell have in any case increasingly been abandoned in favour of their definition as enjoyment of God's presence or separation from him. Karl Barth (1886–1968) has insisted that we are confronted with God in death and that retribution after death occurs in the context of Christ having taken this retribution on himself. God has already revealed his determination to punish sin through the death of his own son and thus it is God whom we have to fear rather than death, yet in that same act he has provided atonement for our sin. Barth therefore rejects the concept of eternal damnation and insists that the central Christian message is the election of all humanity in Christ.

The significance of heaven and hell as components of Christian faith is clearly seen in the portrayal of the completion of God's redemptive purpose in a new heaven and a new earth (Revelation 21) which ends the New Testament. Equally, it is here we find that emphasis on eschatology which has given rise to the apocalyptic and millennial strains which have been a continuing undercurrent in the history of Christianity. We may distinguish two strands, which for convenience I shall call the apocalyptic ('Apocalypse' is the Greek title of the Book of Revelation and similar works) and the millennial (so called from the thousand years by which the general resurrection is preceded in Revelation 20:4–6 by the resurrection of the martyrs). In the apocalyptic strand the expected event is seen largely as a doomsday or Day of Judgement, but in the millennial strand the emphasis is rather on the blessedness of the future state that is imminently expected. Millennial movements can be further divided into those which expect the millennium to precede and prepare the way for the Second Coming of Christ (or for an equivalent saviour) and those which believe that the Second Coming will inaugurate the millennium. Features that are generally common to both strands are belief that they will happen on earth, that they are imminent, that they will totally transform life on earth, and that they will be brought about by supernatural powers, whether God or his adversary. Some visions of the future combine elements of both, of course, envisaging doom and disaster for all non-believers and unalloyed happiness for the community of the faithful.

The situation of tension and persecution which seems to have been the background to St John the Divine's vision on Patmos (and, for example, to the apocryphal *Apocalypse of Peter*) disappeared with the recognition of the church by Constantine and so

Augustine has no place for millennialism in his world-view. Indeed, after Christianity became the official religion of the Roman Empire, the church tended to suppress millenarian beliefs. However, apocalyptic and millennial ideas have emerged at various periods thereafter. During the early Crusades, there were perhaps elements of the millennial in the people's expeditions, where the belief among the poor that they had a special role to play in freeing the Holy Land from the infidel can be seen as symbolic of the role of the elect in the millennium; insecurity among the poor and in particular famine in the areas from which these popular crusades originated may well have been a factor in encouraging such notions. Again, in various urban sects emerging in France and Italy in the twelfth century, gnostic influences linked with millennial ideas to produce the theme of man's perfectability.

Joachim de Fiore (c.1132–1202) provided the focus for one such movement. He seems to have envisaged history as divided into three periods, each belonging to one member of the Trinity: the first, the Age of the Father, was essentially that of the Old Testament dispensation and of the rule of law; the second, the Age of the Son, is that which is lived under grace but also is characterised by the rule of the clergy; and the third, the Age of the Spirit, would be lived in the liberty of the Spirit and would usher in the 'spiritual church'. His ideas were seized on and elaborated by the so-called Franciscan Spirituals, who interpreted them as predicting that the Spirituals would inaugurate this third age in 1260 and that it would be a millennium in which all men (including Jews, Muslims and other non-believers, now converted) would be united in prayer, contemplation and voluntary poverty. Condemnation by the ecclesiastical authorities followed and in turn the Spirituals began to see the church as the Whore of Babylon and the Pope as Antichrist and the Beast of the Apocalypse, even turning eventually to armed insurrection against the church around 1300 under one Fra Dolcino. Here the motive force was not one of protest against their own poor conditions (many of the Spirituals came from privileged backgrounds, though belonging to an order vowed to poverty) but rather of the imperfection and degeneracy of a church grown rich and so, as they saw it, untrue to their ideal of an all-embracing and poverty-loving church.

In other periods millennial movements have appeared alongside, and been at least loosely linked with, movements of social protest that were basically secular, for example John Ball and his followers during Wat Tyler's insurrection of 1381 (following which Ball was executed as a traitor), Thomas Müntzer (c.1490–1525) and his 'League of the Elect' in the German Peasants' Revolt of 1524–6, and the radical Anabaptists who established the 'New Jerusalem' at Münster in 1533–5. Women have generally formed a large proportion of the followers of millennial movements, and in the last couple of centuries a number of movements have been led by women. While this may well reflect the frequency of women as prophetesses and seers at all periods in religious history, a contributory factor may be the marginalisation of women as a group, providing a stimulus parallel to that which underlies a number of other millennial movements. One example is Joanna Southcott (1750–1814), who published her first book of prophecies in 1801 in Exeter, later moved to London, proclaimed herself the woman named in Revelation 12 and early in 1814 announced that a voice had proclaimed that she would soon give birth to the Shiloh announced in older translations of Genesis 49:10 (despite her age she began to show well-authenticated symptoms of pregnancy but died before the year was out). Others include Mother Ann Lee (d. 1875), the leader of the Shakers (formally 'The United Society of Believers in Christ's Second Appearing'), Ellen G. White, founder of the Seventh-day Adventists in the middle of last century, and Mary Campbell, the working-class girl from Port Glasgow who in the 1830s influenced Edward Irving (1792–1834) and the emerging millenarian Catholic Apostolic Church.[6] The members of this Catholic Apostolic Church were predominantly middle-class in background and certainly not an underprivileged group. On the other hand, Jehovah's Witnesses (who also show strong apocalyptic elements in their ideas) are on the whole drawn from traditionally underprivileged groups, though not exclusively so; the millennial aspect of their teachings is no doubt one factor in their success in Africa. Jehovah's Witnesses originated in America, in the teachings of Charles Taze Russell (1852–1916), and America has been the birthplace of a whole crop of millennial movements, perhaps surprisingly in view of the fundamental optimism of secular society there, for the predominant trend in American millenarianism has been pessimistic, even apocalyptic. Other millennial movements of American origin include the Millerites, the Mormons, the Christadelphians and, to a certain extent, the Disciples of Christ. There is also an apocalyptic element in much of the radical Christian fundamentalism typical of one strand in

American life, with its vision of the end of the age and consummation of the world in the fiery advent of Christ as Saviour to defeat the forces of Antichrist, sometimes identified with the current opponents of American global power. Indeed, the millennial scheme known as dispensationalism, linked particularly with J. N. Darby (1800–82), has through its presentation in the *Scofield Reference Bible*, first published in 1909 and widely popular among conservative evangelicals, gained a large measure of acceptance in such circles.

In general such apocalyptic and millennial concepts are lacking in Hinduism, largely no doubt because of the very different perspective imposed by the twin concepts of *saṃsāra* and *mokṣa*. However, they have not been entirely absent. One example has been mentioned in passing already (first at the beginning of Chapter 2): this is the figure of Kalkin who, as the future *avatāra* of Viṣṇu, will appear at the end of the present degenerate Kaliyuga to punish evil-doers and unbelievers and to reward the just. There is a definite this-worldly and political aspect to this expectation which to a certain extent makes it analogous to Christian or semi-Christian ideas, but the basic difference is that the new age of perfection which he inaugurates, the Kṛtayuga, is simply the first in the cycle of the ages and will be followed by inevitable decline back to the Kaliyuga again. Interestingly, the martial aspect to his appearance – he will appear as a warrior riding a white horse – is often thought to reflect a reaction to historical events, particularly in the invasions of Northwest India around the beginning of the Christian era (some texts say explicitly that he will come to destroy foreigners and heretics), which suggests that the emergence of such a figure was a reaction to a time of stress for the society. If so, there is an obvious parallel to some Jewish expectations at the same period for a Messiah who would drive out the Romans by force, expectations which Jesus disappointed. However, the amount of interest shown in Kalkin since that period has been minimal compared with, for example, Rāma or Kṛṣṇa.

There is perhaps a slight millennial tinge to Aurobindo Ghose's Integral Yoga and the same may possibly be said of a number of new movements that have emerged within Hinduism during the modern period, when the stress of coping with the impact of Westernisation and modernisation has been considerable. But it is difficult to point to any pronounced apocalyptic or millennial trend. One notable exception is the Brahmā-Kumārīs, founded by

Prajāpitā Brahmā, the name taken by a retired Sindhi gem dealer, Dada Lekh Raj (d. 1969); this movement is intended to prepare mankind for the imminent destruction of the world, envisaged both in traditional terms as a doomsday at the end of this Kaliyuga and in contemporary terms as the result of a nuclear holocaust. A mark of the degeneracy of the world by now is that only women are pure enough to propagate the movement's teachings. Both at its headquarters on Mt Ābu in Rajasthan and in other centres the movement has produced a number of 'mystically inspired' paintings of its basic teachings, one of which shows the *World Genealogical Tree*; this is based on the traditional ages of the cosmic cycle, though called the golden to the iron ages, and at the start of the copper age the tree puts out branches that comprise the religions and cultures of the world, including the Jewish, Buddhist, Hindu, Christian, Muslim, and others. Above the head of Prajāpitā Brahmā (identified with the creator deity Brahmā and also as the final fruit of the tree) are depicted a world globe wreathed in flame and two hideous animals, America and Russia, holding the weapons of war that have caused the conflagration. Given the different perspective of the Indian subcontinent, the similarities to the assumptions of some American fundamentalists are striking.

Another example, but even further removed from the mainstream of Hindu tradition, is to be found in recent developments in Transcendental Meditation; in this case the emphasis is millennial. In 1976 Maharishi Mahesh Yogi, the founder of Transcendental Meditation, announced the establishment of 'the World Government of the Age of Enlightenment with its sovereignty in the domain of consciousness', having inaugurated the dawn of the Age of Enlightenment the previous year. Through the 'Maharishi Effect' – 'the square root of one percent of a population practising the Transcendental Meditation and TM-Sidhi programme morning and evening together in one place is sufficient to neutralize negative tendencies and promote positive trends throughout the whole population' – crime, accidents and disease would be significantly reduced, the whole world would be set on a path of uplift and in due course the ideal society would be ushered in: utopia would arrive. The ultimate basis of such ideas is in a highly individual interpretation of traditional Yoga concepts, applied literally to external phenomena rather than to the self's inner development. However, as a movement with a Hindu background that has been propagated in the West, Transcendental Meditation belongs with a number of such movements to be looked at in the next chapter, where the history of the contact between Hinduism and Christianity will be taken up.

8

Contact, Conflict and Dialogue

The history of contact between Christianity and Hinduism is far longer than is often imagined. It is the firm belief of the Thomas Christians in South India that their church was founded by the Apostle Thomas, who was martyred in India around 72 A.D., although there is no direct confirmation of this tradition. There are in fact two quite separate traditions about St Thomas. In the South Indian version (attested from the sixth century onwards), the apostle went to the Cochin area in Kerala by sea in 52 A.D., founded churches both in Kerala and in Tamilnad, and died in Mylapore in 72 A.D., after some twenty years of missionary work. In the western tradition (for which the oldest record is the apocryphal *Acts of Thomas*, of which the Syriac version may belong to the third century), Thomas went across Persia towards India, converted an Indian king named Gūdnaphar or Gondophernes and later became a martyr in the neighbouring kingdom of king Mazda; there was indeed a king Gondophares or Guduphara ruling in northwestern India from 19 till at least 45–6 A.D.[1]

Nothing further is then known about Christianity in India until a group of Persian Christians, led by the merchant Thomas of Cana and bishop Joseph, fled to India in 345 to escape persecution. The members of this group still form a separate community and do not inter-marry with other 'St Thomas' Christians. Cosmas Indicopleustes, who visited the Malabar coast in 522, found long-established Christian communities of Persian background in south India and Sri Lanka (those in Sri Lanka subsequently died out but the Orthodox Church of Malabar survived as a small, closed community). Their Persian background may in fact provide the link between the two traditions about the Apostle Thomas, if we assume that they transferred their apostle with them to South India. These Indian Christians did not translate the scriptures or the liturgy but continued until modern times to use the Syriac versions.

The Portuguese discovered the existence of these Indian Christians after Vasco da Gama's landing near Calicut in 1498, when the community apparently consisted of some 30,000 families and was headed by a Metropolitan, assisted by three bishops, all from Mesopotamia and all Nestorians. The community sought protection by the Portuguese against the potential threat from Muslim incursions and at first were left to continue in their traditional ways; for example, St Francis Xavier (1506–52), who spent three years in South India, maintained friendly relations with them. However, by the end of the sixteenth century (at the synod of Diamper in 1599) they had been forced to accept papal supremacy, celibacy of the clergy and a much altered ritual. The last was accompanied by such widespread burning of the old service books and other documents that much of the earlier history of this church is lost. This imposed settlement caused much resentment and when the Dutch replaced the Portuguese in the area in the middle of the seventeenth century, one section took the opportunity to restore contacts with other Eastern Christians; however, the new Syrian bishop, Mar Gregorios, who arrived in 1665, in fact came from the Jacobite tradition (the Monophysite wing of the Syrian Church) not the Nestorian. Since then, this community has acknowledged the authority of the Syrian Patriarchs at Homs. On the other hand, another section remained in communion with Rome and, although its worship and teaching have been Latinised, it does retain certain distinctive features as the Malabar Uniat Church. Towards the end of the nineteenth century a reforming group among the Syrian Christians broke away to form the Mar Thoma Church in an effort to restore, as they saw it, the purity of faith and practice of the church; though largely following the liturgical pattern of the Syrian tradition, this church has revised it in order to remove intercessions to the saints or the Virgin Mary, prayers for the dead and any suggestion of the doctrine of transsubstantiation. The Mar Thoma Church can thus be regarded as in some sense both Orthodox and Reformed in character. A number of other denominations have also separated from the Jacobites.

In 1605 the Italian Jesuit, Roberto de Nobili (1577–1656), arrived in South India to work with the Portuguese missionaries but was disturbed to discover that they were only reaching the lower castes, since higher castes found Portuguese customs offensive and so would not even consider becoming Christians. He therefore decided to live like an Indian, adopting the style and dress of a *saṃnyāsin*, learning Tamil, Telugu and Sanskrit, and conversing with brāhmans. He worked in the city of Madurai (a noted Hindu temple city) and, while uncompromising on doctrinal matters, accepted that his high-caste converts could retain most of their social customs; this even went as far as the retention of the sacred thread, although a special thread blessed with Christian prayers was substituted for the original one, and of the hair-tuft characteristic of the twice-born, which he regarded as having purely social significance.[2] His methods inevitably aroused opposition at the time and, although Rome eventually signified its acceptance of his methods, in the apostolic constitution *Romanae sedis antistes* of 1623, this approach soon lapsed after his death. Though rejecting the idea that all religions are ways to salvation, while noting the views of Hindus on this point, de Nobili addressed seriously the issue of the salvation of non-Christians. He argues that God in his mercy will not condemn the good non-Christian who rejects erroneous ideas of God in his religion, considering God to be the first cause of the world, and acts morally for the sake of this one God; his merits will not win him salvation but God's saving grace can come to him.

Even before de Nobili, there had been the English Jesuit Thomas Stephens (or Stevens, 1549–1619) working from 1579 in Goa and publishing in 1616 a so-called *Christian Purāṇa*, an enormous poem in elegant Marathi intended to replace the Hindu Purāṇas for Christian converts. But Protestants were also active in missionary work from the seventeenth century, especially at first in South India. The Dutch Calvinist Abraham Roger (born early in the century), who served in Pulicat as chaplain to the small Dutch community, produced a vivid picture of Hinduism in South India at the time in his *De Open-Deure tot het verborgen Heydendom*, which first appeared in Dutch in 1651 and was translated into German in 1663 and French in 1670.

The next Protestant missionaries to arrive in India, in 1706, came to the Danish colony of Tranquebar in South India; they were Bartholomaeus Ziegenbalg and Heinrich Plütschau. Their strategy as Protestants was to enable Indians to become acquainted with the Bible and, to this end, Ziegenbalg (1682–1719) undertook the translation of the Bible into Tamil; steps were taken to train Indians for the ministry, with the first ordination taking place in 1733. Ziegenbalg also made a careful study of the beliefs of the South

Indians as part of his missionary preparations, although he was unable to find a publisher in Europe for his material.[3] Ziegenbalg is essentially the first example on the mission field of that pietist strand in Protestantism which in the late eighteenth and early nineteenth centuries was to be the main driving force behind the missionary movements; the pietist approach stressed that in matters of faith the vital principle is the believer's relationship to God, with a concomitant concern to save as many as possible from the corrupt world. The early missionaries therefore tended to condemn what they saw in the world around them, and much of the contemporary practice of Hinduism furnished them with some justification for such an attitude, while few Hindus and even fewer Western scholars at that period had any acquaintance with the oldest texts of Hinduism, which alone would have provided a different perspective. A later member of the Tranquebar mission, C. F. Schwartz, who was in India between 1750 and 1798, produced the first Tamil-English dictionaries and the first Tamil translation of the Bible.

William Carey (1761–1834) has often been described as the father of modern missions and it was largely through his efforts that the Baptist Missionary Society was founded in 1792. Together with Joshua Marshman (1768–1837) and William Ward he formed the pioneer group at Serampore, another Danish colony just north of Calcutta, to which they were obliged to go because the British East India Company banned missionaries on its territories as part of the Company's policy, maintained until 1813, of not interfering with the religious beliefs and practices of the people of India.[4] Carey and the other Serampore missionaries enlisted the help of many Hindu scholars in translating the Bible into the major Indian languages; a translation of the New Testament into Bengali was published in 1801 and within a few decades major parts of the Bible had been translated into the main languages of India. Such language activity led in due course to Carey being given some official recognition through his appointment to teach Bengali (and subsequently Sanskrit and Marathi) at the College of Fort William, the training establishment for new recruits from Britain to the Indian Civil Service. This translation activity also helped to stimulate many Indian languages (indeed, Carey has been called the father of modern Bengali prose) and laid the basis for a renaissance of regional cultures.

This approach was typical of one of the two types of missionary strategy which came to be adopted in early nineteenth-century Bengal, while the other is typified by Alexander Duff (1806–78), the first missionary of the Church of Scotland, who adopted a policy of starting from the top, which led to a different approach to evangelism by education through the English language.[5] The difference between the two strategies is basically that Serampore's was broad-based, while that of Alexander Duff was comparatively elitist, but this derives to quite an extent from the different social backgrounds of the missionaries concerned, which led to their different perceptions of the appropriate strategy in the Indian context. The main components of the Serampore strategy were preaching, mass education, and the production and distribution of vernacular literature. Public preaching was a frequent activity of Nonconformists in Britain, but when it was attempted in Bengal, relying either on interpreters or on the missionaries' imperfect Bengali, it was less effective. In education, the aim of the Serampore missionaries and of others who adopted this strategy was to reach large numbers rather than to achieve a high standard. Christianity, therefore, did not necessarily feature prominently in the curriculum and in some mission schools was not taught at all. The basically secular curriculum was a recognition that the schools depended on the co-operation of the pupils and their families, of the mostly Hindu teachers they employed, and of the Government, which often provided most of the funds.

The missionary strategy of Alexander Duff, who arrived in Calcutta in 1830, was in some respects a continuation of that exemplified by the Serampore missionaries, and in some respects its opposite, a fact of which he was well aware, as his defence of his policies shows. Like the Serampore missionaries and others before him, he set a high value on education as a means of preparing Hindus to receive Christianity. Instead of setting up a number of schools with native teachers in rural areas, though, he established just one in the capital, Calcutta, and the medium of instruction was English, for he was not attempting to produce a new literate class but to draw on one which already existed among the wealthy and influential Hindus who recognised the value of a liberal education. One manifestation of this is that the Bengali social reformer, Rām Mohan Roy, was associated with all Duff's educational activities. For Duff himself, however, not only would the Christian values embodied in English literature attract high-caste Hindus to Christ but the teaching of modern science would undermine their faith in their own religion. This 'cultural diffusion' approach has been significant in the subsequent history of India, for English education became the distinguishing mark of modern Indians and opened to them the whole of Western culture. Much of the expansion in English-language higher education in India in the second half of the nineteenth century was in institutions administered by missionary organisations; their impact in terms of conversions to Christianity was slight but they had a major impact in spreading an awareness of Christian values.

One of the main effects of missionary activity in India was, paradoxically enough, to help to bring about a renewal of Hinduism. Efforts at converting Hindus into Christians tended rather to convert traditional Hindus into reformed Hindus, since the challenge posed by the missionaries prompted the Hindu intelligentsia to seek out again the sources of their own traditions and to restructure their religion in the light of their new understanding of the past. The Brāhmo Samāj, established by Rām Mohan Roy (1772–1833), turned at first to the Upaniṣads, the Ārya Samāj of Dayānanda Sarasvatī (1824–83) harked back to the hymns of the Vedas, and Vivekānanda (1863–1902), the leading figure in the Rāmakrishna Mission, propounded a modernised version of the Advaita Vedānta. These and others then mounted a counter-attack on Christianity for what they saw as its deficiencies, while often claiming to provide a better assessment of Christ's message.

As early as 1820 Rām Mohan Roy compiled *The Precepts of Jesus*, in which he presented Jesus as essentially a moral teacher by bringing together ethical extracts from the New Testament. Already in that work he showed a distinct Unitarian influence and in the following year, along with Dwarkanath Tagore and the Rev. William Adam (a Baptist missionary turned Unitarian), he started the Calcutta Unitarian Committee, which made little progress, however, in its aim of bringing together Hindus and Christians on the basis of belief in the unity of God. Subsequently, many Hindus were willing to affirm their respect for, and even sometimes their allegiance to, the figure of Christ. For example, a later leader of the Brāhmo Samāj, Keshab Chandra Sen (1838–84), at one stage went as far as the acknowledgement of the truth of Christ's teaching and the formation of his Church of the New Dispensation, supposedly a synthesis of Hinduism, Islam and Christianity but with the last the main influence. He particularly came to the notice of the European public with his lecture at

Calcutta in 1866 on 'Jesus Christ, Europe and Asia', in which he dwelt on the moral excellence of Jesus's character and on his forgiveness and self-sacrifice and made the point that Jesus was an Oriental; this was the first of an annual series of lectures in which he developed his ideas on Jesus, the Resurrection and the Trinity (where he attempted to blend Trinitarian and Unitarian views).[6] In this lecture Sen spoke of Christ as 'the Son' and as 'an emanation from Divinity'. However, he also developed the idea that, just as there had been a Jewish Dispensation, a Christian Dispensation and a Vaiṣṇava Dispensation through Caitanya, so now there was a New Dispensation through Keshab Chandra Sen; some of his followers seem indeed to have paid him divine honours as the latest *avatāra*.

At much the same time the Theosophical Society, originally founded in 1875 in New York by Madame H. P. Blavatsky and Colonel Olcott, transferred its activities to India, where it turned into a warm admirer of Hinduism as not only the oldest religion but also as the source of all others. A later convert to Theosophy, Annie Besant, also became an enthusiast for Hinduism and had a significant role in alleviating the inadequacy, religious as well as political, which many Hindus felt at this period in the face of British domination. The Theosophical Society tended to be anti-Christian and equally was a major boost to Hindu morale.[7]

Vivekānanda was clearly impressed by the affluence and power of the West and in part his religious message sought to compensate for the feelings of inferiority which this produced in other Indians besides himself. His message was brilliantly conceived and effectively presented, to such a degree that it has indeed often become one of those unquestioned assumptions which underlie more conscious attitudes. Essentially it was the notion of the spiritual East and the material West, which had already been broached by Keshab Chandra Sen. Vivekānanda, however, went further by suggesting that Hinduism had more to offer than other religions; basing himself partly on his master Rāmakrishna's view that all religions were equally true and partly on Advaitin ideas internal to Hinduism, he utilised its attitude of inclusiveness to assert the superiority of Hinduism. At the World Parliament of Religions, held in Chicago in 1893, where he enjoyed considerable success, Vivekānanda spoke of himself as belonging to the 'most ancient order of monks in the world'[8] and of Hinduism as the 'mother of religions'. He claimed that the problem with the Church was that it spent too much of its time on its organisational structures and had institutionalised the Gospel, changing it from a liberating agent for the human spirit into a constricting one. He criticised the Christian preoccupation with sin, as he saw it, for being debilitating, rather as Nietzsche did. Vivekānanda saw the core of Christianity in the experience of Christ himself and of his disciples in meeting God, but argued that in the life of the Church this experience had subsequently degenerated into stultifying doctrine.

This myth of the material West and the spiritual East ignores important aspects of both cultures, the profound role of religion in shaping the modern West as much as the materialism often to be found within Indian life. Nevertheless, it answered a need of the moment, and it has proved attractive (though perhaps more often through other Hindu-based movements than through the Rāmakrishna Mission) to those in the West who have become dissatisfied with the more materialistic aspects of modern Western life; however, the very recent growth of the ecology movement is another response to or reaction against materialist values which seems likely to enjoy a wider popularity, and consequently a greater influence, than any of the religiously based reactions.

Dayānanda Sarasvatī, the founder of the Ārya Samāj, adopted quite a different tone towards Christianity from Vivekānanda and many other Hindu reformers, with their pretensions to universality; he was very much aware of the struggle between opposing religions and in the twelfth chapter of his *Satyārth Prakāś* (published in 1875) belligerently criticises Christianity, denigrating claims for the authority of the Bible and upholding the Vedas as the sole eternal revelation. One of his main concerns was to counter what appeared to him as a menacing stream of conversions to Christianity (and also to Islam), in particular among low-caste Hindus. Nevertheless, in establishing his Ārya Samāj, he adopted an organisational approach to religious and social reform which was in fact indebted to the West, though borrowed by him probably from the Brāhmo Samāj, whose members he also criticised as being ignorant of their own culture and traditions.

Religion is for Sarvepalli Radhakrishnan (1888–1975) an insight into the nature of reality and so a matter of direct experience, of a concern with the inner life. This insight into the inner self can be achieved by several routes, for Truth, which is essentially one, can be approached from several angles. Reacting sharply to his education at Madras Christian College, Radhakrishnan criticises

Christianity for its exclusivism, while claiming that in principle it is universal, but his views are clearly coloured by his own neo-Vedāntin approach. Basically for him Christianity, like all religions, is a universal faith, embodying as it does a quest for the Absolute culminating in a personal religious experience. It is significant that he has a high estimate of Gnosticism, which he rightly recognises as being syncretistic, this being for him its great virtue (which he ascribes to a lesser extent to early Christianity as a whole, seeing it as tolerant of ideas from other religions). On the other hand, Radhakrishnan regards the idea of a suffering God, 'the deity with a crown of thorns', as religiously unsatisfying. This is symptomatic of a basic difference between Hinduism and Christianity, for Radhakrishnan's view is based on the Hindu idea that man is naturally divine and that salvation or liberation consists in making man aware of his innate divinity and helping him to realise it, whereas the Christian view is that man is divine through God's gift of making him share the divine nature, and salvation is the restoration of this communion with God in and through Christ as man responds to God's grace. Essentially Radhakrishnan's view is that Vedānta represents the ultimate truth of religion, which can encompass the best of Christian belief and thus be universally valid. His tenure of the Spalding Chair of Eastern Religions and Ethics at the University of Oxford from 1936 to 1949 was undoubtedly significant in making Hindu-Christian dialogue an intellectual issue.

It is no longer valid in the contemporary situation to view the world exclusively from the angle of one's own culture. Equally it is no longer reasonable that the term theology should be restricted, as so often by implication it is, to Christian theology. Different religions will increasingly have to come to terms both with the existence of a plurality of religions and with the specific claims made by other religions. As we have seen, Hinduism was to a certain extent forced to do this during the colonial period, when the prestige position of Christianity in relation to the political powers tended, however, to provoke a rather defensive position (even if sometimes expressed in its apparent opposite, as in Vivekānanda's bold claims for Hinduism as the mother of religions). Christianity at that period generally adopted a corresponding attitude of superiority which dismissed the faith of Hindus as little more than superstition and it is only in very recent years that the increasing pluralism of our own society has encouraged a renewed concern with the issue of religious plurality.

Meanwhile, however, a considerable amount has happened within Christian theology which has altered the situation from inside as well as from the outside. By 1846, when he delivered his Boyle lectures, the radical Anglican theologian F. D. Maurice (1805–72) was examining how his belief in the universal revelation of divine order would affect the Christian understanding of non-Christian religions, arguing that Christ, as the root of humanity, had taken the nature of a man in general, not specifically of a European. All man's religion was evidence of God's work and one could truly speak of the Muslim, Hindu and Buddhist sides of Christianity and the lessons to be derived from those three religions. Later in the century this new awareness of other religions is seen in the work of Rowland Williams, Max Müller, Monier Williams and others. It is interesting to note that when Max Müller (1823–1900) and Monier Williams (1819–99) were competing for the Boden Chair of Sanskrit at Oxford in 1880 a major issue in the election (as it had been at the first election in 1832) was whether it was more important to find the best scholar or the individual most likely to further Christian missionary work in India; Max Müller was the candidate of the liberals and reformers and subsequently developed an interest in comparative religion, while the evangelical Monier Williams was favoured by the conservatives and his first public lecture after his election was on 'The Study of Sanskrit in Relation to Missionary Work in India'.

Ernst Troeltsch (1865–1923), noted for his examination of the place of religion in society, was concerned also to examine the place of Christianity in relation to other religions from his own standpoint of a modern historical approach. He rejects attempts to defend the truth of Christianity on the basis of miracles or by claims that it is the most perfect expression of religion. With regard to miracles, he points out that other religions besides Christianity lay claim to similar miracles; this is particularly relevant in the context of Hinduism where the standard reaction is not to question accounts of Christ performing miracles but to express surprise that they are so insignificant. With regard to Christianity as the most perfect expression of religion, Troeltsch argues that a study of the history of religions does not support such a view of Christianity as the culmination of an upward trend, for the study of history lends no support to the idea of a progressive development from lower to higher forms of religious life. It is impossible on historical grounds to see Christianity as the ultimate religion. He suggests that, alongside their individual features, there is an element of truth in all religions which can be recognised intuitively and which results from personal experience. The claim of Christianity to universal validity rests for him on its faith in revelation which differs in kind from that to be found elsewhere. Thus, although other religions are in a certain sense revelations of God, for Troeltsch Christianity remains the great revelation of God to men; while the prophets of other religions may also reveal the power of God, it is more profoundly revealed in Christianity than elsewhere. The particular historical character of Christianity which he emphasises is for him a major obstacle to claims for absolute validity. On the other hand, their own inner experience and conviction provides the warrant for its validity for Christians. Other religions rooted in different cultures may experience the divine in their own equally valid ways. This culturally relativist position clearly implies, as Troeltsch points out, that the concern of Christianity in relation to other major religions must be in increasing mutual understanding and not in seeking conversions, although he does suggest that there is still a place for missionaries to provide less developed cultures with something to replace the way of life which is liable to be threatened by contact with civilisation. Mutual understanding in the search for a common goal is then the right approach.

This growth of more liberal Christianity, and perhaps especially the 'quest for the historical Jesus', was a major factor in the development at the beginning of this century of a somewhat different attitude, further stimulated by the fact that Christians were beginning to know much more than their predecessors about other religions. The prime example of this new type of approach is J. N. Farquhar (1861–1929), who laid much stress on 'the religion of Jesus' as the most adequate statement of Christianity; this not only accorded with the current trends of liberal Christian thought but had already shown itself more effective than a more dogmatic approach in the Indian context. Farquhar pointed Hindus in the direction of the teaching of Jesus, presenting him as a teacher of moral principles and practices, and gave very little role to the church. In his major work, *The Crown of Hinduism* (first published in 1913), he argued for Christ as the 'crown' of Hinduism, since Christ alone crowns or fulfils the various longings revealed in the history of Hinduism, and endeavoured to demonstrate in a study of major aspects of Hinduism how they needed the figure of Christ to complete them and fit them for the future. This fulfilment theology, as it has been termed,[9] thus adopted a more sympathetic approach to other religions, while at the same time affirming the primacy of Christianity, in a way that is not so dissimilar from the way in which neo-Vedāntins from Vivekānanda onwards were placing their version of Hinduism at the top of a kind of evolutionary ladder of religious developments. It does, though, represent a sincere attempt to combine respect for other religions with belief in the uniqueness of Christ. Significantly, at the World Mission Conference of 1910 in Edinburgh one of its sections, commissioned to draw up an appropriate form of Christian apologetics towards other religions, sought the views of missionaries working among Hindus and discovered that their replies uniformly emphasised the need for a sympathetic attitude towards Hinduism and spoke of the harm done in the past by intolerant attitudes. To a large extent Farquhar was preaching to the converted so far as his missionary colleagues were concerned.

Though characteristic of Protestant theologians such a fulfilment approach was not exclusive to them. R. C. Zaehner (1913–74), a Roman Catholic convert, reveals in his work as a professional scholar of religion (holder of the Spalding chair of Eastern religions and ethics at Oxford from 1953 till his death) the influence of his personal beliefs, which basically consist of a fulfilment theology, especially in his later works which show the influence of Teilhard de Chardin's evolutionary thought. His Christian attitudes are also clearly apparent in his various publications on mysticism, where he distinguishes four contrasting types of mystical experience and implicitly assigns the highest value to theistic mysticism, regarding monistic mysticism, that is, in the Hindu context union with Brahman, as a lower level of salvation than theistic union.

A rather different perspective is apparent in the radical Protestant theological school, associated particularly with Karl Barth (1886–1968) and Emil Brunner (1889–1966), which stressed the radical dichotomy between God's revelation in Christ and any form of religious endeavour, even Christianity itself in so far as it was a manifestation of human effort rather than divine grace. In part, this dialectical theology was a reaction against the more liberal theological trends earlier this century and represents a reversal in the trend towards a more fruitful encounter between different religions, since it viewed other religions as no more than misguided efforts on man's part to raise himself religiously. Barth sees faith as man's response to God's self-revelation in his Word, which was incarnate in Christ and revealed in the Bible, and uses religion to denote what he sees as man's arrogant and futile endeavour to reach God by his own efforts; there can be no kind of continuity between natural theology and the revelation in Christ. Barth's use of the term proclamation (deriving from the Greek κήρυγμα with its image of the herald's sounding forth) serves to emphasise the unidirectional nature of the process. With such a dismissive attitude even towards institutional Christianity, there is little scope here for any encounter with non-Christian religions.

By contrast, much recent Roman Catholic theology (especially in the wake of the Second Vatican Council, 1962–65) has moved to a position in which Christ and Christianity are seen not so much as the fulfilment of other religions but rather as being universal in such a way as to include them. The Vatican Council itself went a long way in this direction. For example, the document *Lumen Gentium* issued in 1964, urging the faithful to follow the path of dialogue, states: 'Those also can achieve everlasting salvation who, through no fault of their own, do not know the Gospel of Christ or His Church, but who sincerely seek God and, moved by grace, strive in their actions to do his will as they know it through the dictates of conscience.' This is strikingly similar to the position of de Nobili some three and a half centuries earlier, while the advice in *Sacrosanctum Concilium*, that bishops should 'carefully and prudently consider which elements from the traditions and genius of individual peoples might appropriately be admitted into divine worship', accords well with his practice. Furthermore, the declaration *Nostra Aetate*, issued in 1965, acknowledged the duty of the Church to promote unity and fellowship among nations and peoples and declared that the Church does not reject anything that is true and holy in other religions, while reaffirming that the Church must proclaim Christ as the way, the truth and the life; this emphasis on the uniqueness of the Christian revelation is still clearer in another declaration of the same year, *Dei Verbum*.

One of the earliest examples of this shift was Raimundo Panikkar's *The Unknown Christ of Hinduism* published in 1964, which attempted to discern within Hinduism or more specifically within the Advaita Vedānta tradition (which in modern times has so often been taken as the sole representative of intellectual Hinduism), the hidden presence of Christ, though interpreted in a cosmic fashion which seems at times remote from Jesus of Nazareth. Panikkar claims that salvation in Christ is thus independent of the religion that an individual may profess and can come through the sacraments of that religion. If all things subsist in Christ, then it is Christ who inspires men everywhere to seek salvation; whatever truth there is in Hinduism derives from Christ and any true worship is directed towards him. More widely known, and even more controversial (indeed, officially condemned in *Mysterium Ecclesiae*, issued in 1973), has been the work of Hans Küng (b. 1928), who also in 1964 delivered a lecture on 'World Religions in God's Plan of Salvation' in which he made the point that other religions were also part of the history of salvation, while Karl Rahner (b. 1904) has gone a step further by talking about 'anonymous Christians' in relation to members of other religions. Küng questions whether it is any longer valid to maintain the doctrine of *extra ecclesiam nulla salus*. In his view, the Christian answer to the problem of religious pluralism lies in assigning non-Christian religions a positive place in the scheme of salvation. He points to some of the pronouncements coming from the Second Vatican Council in support of this more God-centred approach (as opposed to the traditional Roman Catholic church-centred view) which affirms that God revealed himself to man before his revelation in Christ and is capable of being known by all men. God provides the means for Christ to save men through other religions but as part of universal salvation history as distinct from special salvation; to that extent God sanctions other religions as an ordinary way to salvation (and it is proper to seek God within the religion that is available to the individual) but the extraordinary way of salvation still lies within the Church. This seems nonetheless to revert to a more church-centred stance.

The attitudes of Christian missionaries in India also developed over time. One of the more notable innovations (though in a sense only reverting to what Roberto de Nobili had attempted) has been the development of Christian Ashrams as an expression of Christian life and service. The first was the Khristukula Āśram (the Ashram of the Family of Christ) established in 1921 at Tiruppattur in Tamilnad, followed by the Christa Seva Sangha at Ahmadnagar in 1922, but subsequently a number have been formed. The French monk, Fr H. le Saux (1910–73), adopted the life of a hermit in the Himalayas for part of the year, took the name Swami Abhishiktananda, founded the Saccidānanda Āśrama in South India with Abbé Monchanin (1895–1957) and wrote extensively on the meeting of the Christian and Hindu contemplative traditions as the only possible focus for genuine dialogue; he asserts that in such a dialogue the Christian must be willing to open himself to the depths of Hindu spirituality and immerse himself in the Hindu world as lived by a Hindu, while recognising that on the whole Hindus do not feel the need for dialogue in this sense, considering that their own tradition already provides everything needed for the highest spiritual attainment. The English Benedictine, Bede Griffiths (b. 1906), shows a similar commitment to interpreting Christianity in terms of Advaita and to the indigenisation of Christian worship within the ashram setting; the Saccidānanda Āśrama, where he took over the leadership from Abhishiktananda, uses regularly in its worship the hymn to the Trinity as *saccidānanda* by Brahmabandhab Upadhyaya (1861–1907). In others, the emphasis on social service which is a frequent emphasis of the Christian Ashram movement could become totally dominant. Verrier Elwin (1902–1964) is an example of this. Starting as an Anglican missionary, he was a member of the Khrista Seva Sangh at Poona (1927–31) before embarking on the service in Central India over the next twenty years and more which led him increasingly into involvement with the Gond tribal people, both studying them anthropologically and acting as their champion against the outside world, but in the process becoming increasingly isolated from the church, which he eventually left.

Others, of course, continued to serve the Christian community in more traditional ways. One who also became a noted apologist for Christian missions and for the ecumenical movement was Stephen Neill (1900–84), who was Bishop of Tinnevelly from 1939 to 1945 and played a significant role in the preparations for the establishment of the Church of South India. One of the first bishops in the Church of South India was Lesslie Newbigin, who also played a major role on the wider ecumenical scene.

Indian Christians have also become prominent as theologians, not only in the areas noted at the end of the first chapter but also more widely. Some of the most prominent figures are A. J. Appasamy (1891–1975), K. M. Banerjee (1813–81), Paul Devanandan (1901–62), S. J. Samartha (b. 1920) and M. M. Thomas (b. 1916). Although Appasamy's theology generally followed Western patterns, he did also write *Christianity as Bhakti Marga* (published in 1927 and reflecting his upbringing in the Tamil Śaiva tradition) and compiled a selection of Hindu texts for Christian use called *Temple Bells* (published by the YMCA in 1930) to express his belief that the way for Christianity to make an impact on Hindus was to utilise the *bhakti* tradition. *Rethinking Christianity in India,* a collection of essays published in connection with the 1938 International Missionary Council held at the Madras Christian College, Tambaram, marked an important stage in the emergence of independent Indian Christian theology.

Another significant development was the growing impetus towards schemes of union among Protestant churches in India. After some twenty-eight years gestation, the Church of South India formally came into existence a month after the independent state of India, on 27 September 1947, bringing together all the major denominations except the Roman Catholics and the Lutherans. The Churches of the West have shown evidence of being impressed by the formation of the Church of South India but have shown little sign of being prepared to emulate it on the same scale. The reason for this no doubt lies in the difference of circumstances. Except where the challenge of new surroundings and an essentially secular environment, such as that which characterised the New Towns in Britain, has forced a reassessment of priorities – by local groups of Christians rather than the church as an institution – the established churches of the West are too entrenched in their existing structures readily to contemplate anything so radical. The Church of North India came into being along similar lines in 1970, through a union of Anglicans, Congregationalists and Presbyterians with parts of the Baptists, Disciples of Christ and Methodists (other parts continuing as independent bodies).

As the term is understood in the religious context, dialogue is a relatively new development so far as attempts to define and organise it are concerned. It should consist of more than just casual conversation and should involve the reaching out on a personal and more intimate level of one individual to another, rather than the confrontation of two rival systems, even if the dialogue is conducted on a group basis. Dialogue should be based on mutual respect, knowledge of both traditions and acceptance of their differences; as regards Hinduism and Christianity these differences will be internal as well as external, for both labels cover a wide variety of belief and practice. It has to be recognised that there is faith on both sides, however much either side might like to regard such faith as ignorance or unbelief on the part of the other. As has increasingly been recognised anyway, external criteria cannot offer any justification for monopolising faith for one religion, while internal criteria are not valid in relation to another religion. Dialogue therefore involves showing a real openness to believers in the other religion and making a real attempt to understand and to get an imaginative grasp of their feelings and beliefs. Indeed, it might be argued that each participant, being well grounded in his own convictions, will ideally display greater interest in discovering more fully the ideas and the perspectives characteristic of the other. This need not mean that either side cease to witness to what they believe – rather the reverse. Dialogue is also, however, a most demanding way of life; a striking testimony to this is the experience of Klaus Klostermaier in the heartland of Kṛṣṇa devotion, which he recounts in his *Hindu and Christian in Vrindaban*, published in 1969.[10]

Many Christians who have adopted a more traditionally biblical stance inevitably see any attempt at inter-religious dialogue as essentially missionary in aim and for them the ultimate purpose of any kind of dialogue remains the conversion of the other person; underlying this attitude are the twin assumptions that salvation is through Christ alone and that there is no saving merit at all in non-Christian belief systems. Following the Second Vatican Council, the Roman Catholic Church in India was freed from many of the restrictions which had been keeping it separate both from Hindu society and from other Christian churches. Once the Council had affirmed the principle of dialogue, a number of Catholics enthusiastically took up the process, especially on the level of spirituality. The traditional Roman Catholic doctrine that there is no salvation outside the church was understood as meaning rather that Christ and his Church are the channel of grace for all mankind; thus, this saving love need not be confined to formal Christians and non-Christian religions might be saving faiths for their adherents through the transcendent Christ. Some scope was also given for the indigenisation of worship but the response here has been less marked. Similarly, the Church of South India has recommended an attempt to express the universal Christian message in Indian cultural form and encouraged its members to celebrate the national Indian (in fact Hindu) festivals, but the response has been limited.

A number of movements deriving more or less directly from Hinduism have established themselves in the Western world: the International Society for Krishna Consciousness (ISKCON, more popularly known as the Hare Krishna movement), the Divine Light Mission, Ānanda Mārg, Transcendental Meditation, the followers of Rajneesh and so on. The arrival of these new religious movements is perhaps in part a symptom of the failure by Christianity to face up to the religious plurality of the modern world and its willingness to leave the problem of the encounter with other faiths to those on the mission field. Most of these movements, and also the older established Theosophical Society, basically belong to the monistic or non-theistic strands of Hindu thought, whereas the Hare Krishna movement has a firmly theistic background.

The Hare Krishna movement with its singing and dancing on the streets has undoubtedly been the most visible of these new movements. However, this is simply the transplantation to the West of patterns of worship long known in India. The movement is basically a branch of the form of Bengal Vaiṣṇavism established by Caitanya (1486–1533) and in most of its doctrines and its ritual is indeed impeccably orthodox by the standards of that *bhakti* tradition, a point that is endorsed by the extent to which ISKCON has been accepted as a spokesman for Hinduism by Hindus living in Britain. Its only radical departure from much older Hindu patterns has been its aim of recruiting Westerners into the movement, thus challenging the older concept of Hinduism as a non-proselytising religion, and the concomitant problem in terms of the caste identity of these recruits. The latter is in any case only a major problem in relation to Hindus in India, many of whom view with horror the claim by the movement to initiate certain of its followers as brāhmans, in effect as a kind of priesthood for the movement, when they have reached a sufficiently advanced level.

The movement was taken first to the United States by A. C. Bhaktivedanta Swami in 1965, a disciple of the leader of the Gaudiya Vaishnava Mission (established in 1886 as a vehicle for propagating belief in Caitanya), who first encouraged him to think of spreading the message of Kṛṣṇa beyond India. In 1968 three couples from his American converts moved to London and inaugurated the movement in Britain, one of their first aims being to make contact with the Beatles; the release a year later of the recording of the Hare Krishna *mantra* made with George Harrison's help really brought the movement to public notice, especially since its success coincided with Bhaktivedanta's first visit to Britain. Before his death in 1977, Bhaktivedanta Swami had made careful provision for the continuity of the movement, which reached its peak in Britain over the next few years. However, internal dissension in 1982 caused a considerable setback, from which the movement is gradually recovering. The nature of the recruitment by the movement in the West has meant that many of its new members have come from Christian or semi-Christian backgrounds and this may, indeed, be one aspect of its more missionary stance, if one presumes that such devotees' experience of Vaiṣṇavism has been coloured by beliefs and attitudes continued subconsciously from that background. On the whole, Bhaktivedanta himself showed a typically neo-Hindu attitude towards Christianity, regarding Christ as an *avatāra* of Kṛṣṇa and thus suggesting that through sincere worship of God Christians 'will one day become pure Vaiṣṇavas'. Paradoxically, perhaps, another feature of ISKCON has been its conservative and even reactionary character, which seems to have appealed to a number who were disenchanted with various aspects of the modern West, for the anti-scientific, anti-intellectual and fundamentalist elements in its message seem in some ways to be a return to the past.[11]

Other movements of Hindu origin that were exported to the West are of less interest, since they cannot be regarded to the same extent as ISKCON as belonging to the mainstream of Hindu belief and practice and lacked its staying power. The Divine Light Mission prominent in the early 1970s focused on the then teenaged *guru*, Maharaj Ji, as its leader in a movement which combined the more traditional aspects of some Kṛṣṇa sects – the authority figure of the *guru*, ecstatic and erotic devotion towards the deity, and the linking of the two – with a minimal doctrinal content and thus a pronounced appeal to the socially displaced young. The authoritarianism of the Ānanda Mārg (founded in 1955 by Anandamurti, the former Prabhat Ranjan Sarkar, who died in 1990 at the age of 69, and propagated internationally) is shown in the charge that the movement murdered followers who wished to leave the movement which led to its leader's conviction for murder in 1976; the movement is an uneasy blend of tantric Yoga with Marxist ideas. Transcendental Meditation, despite its efforts to present a purely secular and even scientific image as primarily a relaxation technique since its introduction to the West in 1958, is based on a rather literalist interpretation of Yoga concepts; its emphasis in its TM-Sidhi programme on such techniques as 'flying' is essentially the yogic *siddhi* of levitation seen as an end in itself. Its founder, Maharishi Mahesh Yogi, creator of the Science of Creative Intelligence and inaugurator in 1972 of the World Plan to solve all mankind's problems in this generation, enjoyed for a time a considerable vogue. However, since the establishment in January 1976 of the World Government of the Age of Enlightenment to usher in this ideal state, the ideas of the movement have ceased to attract as much serious attention as before. Bhagwan Shree Rajneesh (1932–90) attracted a considerable Western hippy following at his ashram in Poona during the 1970s with his message of yogic spirituality and the therapeutic value of free sexual expression; after the transfer of his activities in 1981 to Oregon following investigations of his financial affairs by the Indian tax authorities he never achieved quite the same measure of success and in due course he was deported from the United States after being found guilty of illegal immigration.

Most of these new religious movements are already in decline and are unlikely to be of long-term significance; ISKCON will probably continue to grow but then, as has been indicated, it does not really belong in the same category as the other movements. Of much greater significance is likely to be the arrival of Hindus in Britain – and in other European countries, the United States, Canada and Australia. There are records of pedlars from India being based in Birmingham since 1931 and there had been occasional students well before then but these were essentially transient. Slightly larger numbers of Hindus arrived to settle in Britain direct from India during the 1950s and 1960s, but the main inflow came from East Africa as a result of Africanisation policies there between 1965 and 1972, and especially the repressive measures introduced in Uganda by Idi Amin; more recently government immigration policy has greatly reduced the inflow from any source. Most of these East African Indians came originally from Gujarat and so about 70 per cent of the Hindu population in Britain is Gujarati, with 15 per cent coming from the Punjab and the rest from various other areas. Hindus have settled in most large towns but particularly in Wembley and Harrow within the London area, Leicester, Coventry, Birmingham and Bradford; there has been a tendency for particular caste groups to settle together and so, for example, Lohanas (a Gujarati trading caste) predominate in Leicester and Mochis (an artisan caste) in Leeds.[12]

Migration of Hindus to Europe has not been confined to Britain. There is also a substantial population in the Netherlands, which has largely originated from the indentured labourers recruited for Surinam from eastern Uttar Pradesh and Bihar between 1873 and 1916, many of whom used their Dutch citizenship and passports to settle in the Netherlands in the decade up to Surinam's independence in 1975. The largest concentrations of these immigrants are found in The Hague, Rotterdam and Amsterdam. In other parts of the world too, similar concentration is the norm; for example, in Canada, where the majority of Hindu immigrants have arrived since 1972, the largest numbers are found in the major industrial cities in Quebec, Ontario, Alberta and British Columbia.

The first Hindu temple in Britain was opened in 1969 at Leicester and the number has since grown to over a hundred. Some of these temples are large, some small, some in converted properties (on occasion former churches or chapels) and some in people's homes. While the majority are based on mainstream Hindu practice (*Sanātan mandirs* or temples), others represent different organisations (such as the Swaminarayan Hindu Mission, the Satya Sai Baba Fellowship or ISKCON). A number of temples are affiliated to the National Council of Hindu Temples, a co-ordinating body within Britain, and to the *Vishwa Hindu Parishad,* an international Hindu organisation which has links with the Bharatiya Janata Party.[13] In the West Indies, where Indian immigration came mainly in the nineteenth century in the form of indentured labour from Uttar Pradesh and Bihar (some being refugees from the 1857 uprising, others fleeing famine conditions), Hindu temples reflect in their actual form the innovation of congregational temple worship, which is exceptional in Hinduism within India but normal in the West Indies, no doubt under the influence of Christianity, from which new elements have been incorporated to add to the traditional components of temple worship. There are signs that the same development is beginning to occur in Britain.

Large numbers of Hindus in Britain attend these temples for annual festivals, such as *Dīvālī,* the festival of lights, *Holī,* the spring festival of which the best known feature is the throwing of coloured water or powder, *Janamāṣṭamī,* the celebration of Kṛṣṇa's birthday, and *Navarātri,* a typically Gujarati festival. Smaller numbers visit their local temple for regular services, for *pūjā* and *āratī,* in which the deities are honoured by offerings of flowers or food and by the waving of lamps. Most families conduct similar rituals in their own homes, where they generally have a small area for worship containing pictures and images of favourite deities, such as Kṛṣṇa, Rāma, Gaṇeśa and Ambamātā, and chosen *gurus*, such as Satya Sai Baba, and Pramukh Swami of the Swaminarayan Mission. However, the range of belief and practice among Hindus in Britain is extremely diverse, not only because Hinduism in general is so diverse but also because Hindus in Britain come from a variety of different geographical areas, social backgrounds and sectarian traditions. In actual fact, the consciousness of belonging to a particular sect or branch of the faith, rather than diminishing the awareness of belonging to that rather amorphous entity Hinduism, appears to increase it by making their religion more immediate and purposive for such Hindus. Membership of a specific sect or of a regional association provides a focus for individual self-identity.

The new situation facing such Hindu communities abroad has encouraged the growth of all sorts of associations to provide a focus for their social as much as their religious needs. Yet this situation is not so new, for the earliest was established over a century ago; the Edinburgh Indian Association, which appears to be the oldest, was established in 1883 mainly to meet the social and cultural needs of Indian students at Edinburgh University but, after a decline induced by the drop in their numbers, gained a new impetus in the 1970s from the settlement of Hindus locally and became a more broadly based organisation catering for their interests. While some of these associations were established formally as branches of Indian organisations (Arya Samaj centres or Vivekananda centres, for example, as religious bodies or the Bharatiya Vidya Bhavan primarily as a cultural one), many have been set up to answer the need felt by local communities to provide more systematic instruction in their religion to their children and so to compensate for the absence of exposure to the total culture which they would have had in India. As a consequence, the nature of Hinduism is inevitably beginning to change in Britain – and no doubt in other countries – as it becomes something consciously learnt about rather than absorbed naturally, with the concomitant shift from practice to doctrine.

What then is the future for the relationship between these two religions of Hinduism and Christianity that we have been studying, whether in Britain or elsewhere? In the 1970s there were many who saw the Christian churches declining into irrelevance and the vacuum, in so far as there was one, being filled by the various new religious movements, among which those based in one way or another on Hinduism were prominent, at least in the eyes of the media. Already the heyday of such movements in the West appears to be over and in this last decade of the twentieth century there are signs that Christianity is again beginning to be taken seriously (although the increasing polarisation between liberal and fundamentalist evangelical positions is not altogether healthy). Yet the situation is by no means the same as before. The presence of significant minorities belonging to other religions – not only Hindus, but also Muslims and Sikhs, not to mention numerically smaller groups – requires that in the resulting pluralist society the beliefs and feelings of all religions should be respected and that Christianity should no longer retain the privileged position which some would claim for it. In India, where the secularity of the state is under challenge from increasing communalism, religion has never ceased to be a major factor in the lives of the majority of the population but here too the situation is changing and the pace of change is likely to accelerate. Modernisation and industrialisation have still to make a significant impact on the life-style of many Indians but when they do they will cause radical changes in the patterns of behaviour which are so integrally linked with the religious aspects of Hinduism. Change is inevitable but, if there is one thing to be learnt from the study of religions, it is that they have been more adaptable and more durable than most of society's other institutions. The study of selected themes within this book illustrates both this adaptability and the internal variety of views to be found in both religions. These two features are indeed part of their strength and such richness of content can only be enhanced by the increased awareness of each other which will surely come from the increased proximity of their adherents, whether physically or by advances in communication. Both will learn about each other and must learn from each other in dialogue.

Notes

1: THE NATURE OF THE DIVINE

1. See *The Crucified God* (London, 1974) p. 277. Moltmann's perspective in this work is very much towards the future, to the 'Trinity in the glorification' in which the whole creation will participate in this End, and this glorification of God in the liberation of his creation is achieved by the inclusion of creation within the divine life.
2. The survey was done in 1981 and published in M. Abrams, D. Gerard and N. Timms (eds), *Values and Social Change in Britain*, (London, Macmillan, 1985), in association with the European Value Systems Study Group. I take the information from Kenneth Thompson, 'How Religious Are The British?', in Terence Thomas (ed.) *The British, Their Religious Beliefs and Practices 1800–1986* (London, Routledge, 1988) p. 231, who adds: 'Furthermore, little more than a quarter of the population accept absolute, as opposed to relative, guidelines concerning good and evil, and only a quarter accept the full range of Christian beliefs when these are taken to include both hell and the devil.'
3. There are of course a good many other passages where a threefold formula is found, from the angel's words to Mary (Luke 1:35) to Jesus's commission to his disciples: 'Go therefore to all nations and make them my disciples; baptize them in the name of the Father and the Son and the Holy Spirit (Matthew 28:19); others are John 20:21–2, 1 Cor. 12:4–6, 2 Cor. 13:14. Examination of the precise significance of these passages for the understanding of the Trinity in the New Testament is beyond the scope of this work. They are cited simply to establish that some doctrine of the Trinity is already found there, even if the focus is on the position of the Christian in relation to God rather than on the elaboration of the doctrine as such.
4. This type of modalist approach, which leads to an overemphasis on the unity of the Godhead by treating the three persons as interchangeable facets of a single, basically undifferentiated deity, was indeed propounded by Sabellius in the third century.
5. No other creed achieved as wide a measure of acceptance as this Nicene Creed. Even the so-called Apostles' Creed, retained by many Protestant churches, in its present form is a later formulation of the eighth century and so is a Western creed, never formally accepted by the Orthodox Church.
6. This way of looking at the world as containing good and evil as

objective and cosmic forces does indeed resemble the explicit dualism in the religion propounded by Zoroaster, and elements of that dualistic outlook do seem to have infiltrated Christianity at times, along with certain other ideas from the same source.

7. It is interesting to note that the early missionary, Roberto de Nobili (on whom more will be said later, especially in Chapter 8) tried first of all to use the Vedas as the basis for constructing a Christian-oriented natural theology in the same sort of way that Thomas Aquinas had used Aristotle but later, and with more success, simply adopted Thomas's 'five ways' as a common foundation with theistic Hindus on which to erect a Christian superstructure.

8. The Mīmāṃsā system (to be discussed further in Chapter 3) is a school of exegesis of the Vedas which adopts distinctive views that they are eternal and uncreated – with their inerrancy uncompromised by any author, whether human or divine – and develops principles of interpretation for those texts.

9. I am indebted for the ideas expressed in this and the preceding paragraph to George Chemparathy, *An Indian Rational Theology* (Leiden, 1972) and especially to John Clayton, 'Religions, Reasons and Gods' (*Religious Studies* 23, 1987, pp. 1–17) and 'Piety and the Proofs' (*Religious Studies* 26, 1990, pp. 19–42). It is incidentally worth noting that such philosophical debate centred around the concept of Īśvara, making the same assumption as Western philosophy of religion that there is only one deity. On the other hand, the emphasis on the self-validating nature of these means of knowledge means that, rather than being concerned with issues of verification as in Western philosophy of religion, Hindu philosophical systems tend to be concerned with theories of error.

10. In fact a more cogent parallel to the concept of Brahman as *saccidānanda* in Western thought is to be found in neo-Platonism as found in the writings of Plotinus in the third century. Here the divine existence took a threefold form: the One which was beyond being and naming, the νοῦς or Mind, and the Soul or World-Soul, each of the latter two forms (ὑπόστασεις) drawing its power from the one above. There are also traces of such ideas in Pythagoreanism. In both instances there is at least a possibility of some influence from Indian thought.

11. The *Bhagavadgītā* is one of the most popular of Hindu religious texts, though not strictly scriptural, since it is incorporated within the great epic, the *Mahābhārata*, as the sermon preached by Kṛṣṇa to Arjuna just before the great battle; further discussion will be found at the beginning of Chapter 2.

2: DIVINE INTERACTION WITH MANKIND

1. The term *dharma* is not in fact precisely equivalent to 'religion', for which Hinduism has no specific term, since it does not separate off religious activity from the rest of life in the same way that the

Romans (from whom the term religion comes) once did or the modern West again does; if necessary, contemporary Hindus will designate their own religious and social complex as *sanātana dharma*, 'the eternal tradition'.

2. This point has been brought out by Madeleine Biardeau in 'Études de mythologie hindoue, I. Cosmogonies purāṇiques' *Bulletin de l'École Française d'Extrême Orient* 63 (1978) pp. 87–238.
3. An account of the rituals performed in connection with images will be given in Chapter 4.
4. In particular Psalm 22 is used, but also Psalms 41 and 69 and Zechariah 9–13.
5. Earlier, Origen (c.185–254, also teaching at Alexandria), though recognising that the Son had been generated in and from eternity, had concluded from the Son's submission to the Father in his earthly life and work that submission was basic to his personhood and thus that the Son was eternally subordinate to the Father, arguing that whatever attributes were predicated of the Father must be predicated of the Son, as image of the Father, in a lesser and relative manner.
6. See in particular his *East and West in Religion*, London, 1933, pp. 59ff.
7. This is not quite exclusively an Indian view. Aldous Huxley (in *The Perennial Philosophy*, 1946, pp. 60ff.) criticises the error of Christianity, as he terms it, in believing in only one *avatāra*, on the grounds that it is too pre-occupied with history and so with the uniqueness of the Incarnation.
8. Some account of de Nobili's missionary activity in South India is included below in Chapter 8.
9. In the verse Kṛṣṇa declares: 'Though myself unborn, with an unchanging self, the lord of creatures, I establish myself in my own nature and come into being through my own creativity (*māyā*)'. The ambiguity lies in the term *māyā* which can also be translated as 'magical power, illusion' and would be so understood in the Advaita Vedānta tradition, whose greatest figure Śaṅkara glosses this verse thus: 'I seem to be embodied and to be born, through my own *māyā* but not in reality, only conventionally.'
10. See in particular his *God and the Universe of Faiths*, London, 1973. An Advaitin might still reasonably object to the theistic bias of his formulation. A thoughtful critique of Hick's views will be found in J. J. Lipner, 'Does Copernicus Help? Reflections for a Christian Theology of Religions', *Religious Studies* 13, 1977, pp. 243–58.
11. Before we too readily castigate the psychology underlying such notions about demons and other powers, we should perhaps reflect that modern concepts such as the id and superego of Freudian psychology are no more amenable to ordinary sense perception; they are essentially constructs, the value of which is to provide a model to apply in understanding the world around us and their relationship to reality is not susceptible to scientific testing.

3: AUTHORITY AND MEDIATION

1. On the phenomenon of fundamentalism as a reaction to modernisation and secularism I am indebted to E. J. Sharpe, *Understanding Religion*, London 1983, pp. 120–2, and to Caplan's own contribution to Lionel Caplan, ed., *Studies in Religious Fundamentalism*, London 1987.
2. Nonetheless, with the decided pragmatism that the Mīmāṃsā system also reveals, it accepts the principle that when two commands contradict each other there is an option to follow either. The standard example concerns the kinds of grain used in a rite; some texts enjoin rice and others barley (cf. Śabara on *Mīmāṃsāsūtra* 12.3.15), and so Mīmāṃsā allowed the use of either rice or barley. However, the system developed the theory of the eight faults of an option and avoided options whenever possible.
3. As Radhika Herzberger has neatly put it (*Bhartṛhari and the Buddhists*, D. Reidel, Dordrecht, 1986, p. xix): 'Not to make the founder appear incompetent (Uddyotakara's oft repeated phrase: *akuśalaḥ sūtrakāraḥ syāt*) becomes a guiding principle of many a philosophical commentary of the period.'
4. Practice on the relationship between confirmation and the first Eucharist has varied. The Catechism of the Council of Trent (issued in 1566) laid down seven to twelve as the proper age for confirmation, preferably twelve. Subsequently, children tended to be admitted to their first communion some years before their confirmation. Since 1971, however, the normal order has been declared as being confirmation and then the Eucharist.
5. Despite the difference in practice and particularly age at which it is administered, the Eastern chrismation is accepted as valid confirmation by the Roman Catholic Church.
6. Outside India funeral practices may well have to be modified to take account of local factors. For example in Trinidad, where cremation was illegal until 1936, local Hindus have buried their dead and have taken over the practice of honouring the dead on Halloween, in their case by lighting little clay lamps on the graves. In Britain and elsewhere, the fact that death so commonly occurs in hospital often forces modifications in the rituals around the point of death, with an inevitable concentration of most of the ritual element into the brief period when the body is brought back to the house on its way to the crematorium.

4: DEVOTIONALISM AND PERSONAL PIETY

1. See the beginning of Chapter 8 for a survey of the early history of Christianity in India.
2. More will be said in Chapter 5 on the *saṃnyāsin* as an ascetic and in Chapter 6 on the relationship of this stage of life to the other three.

3. See Chapter 3.
4. *Young India*, 10 June 1926. Although Gandhi was certainly influenced by Western ideas, in particular by the writings of Tolstoy, the frequency of his allusions to prayer in *Young India* is striking.
5. Among the most important rituals are the funeral rites and the memorial ceremonies which follow at periodic intervals, some of which are intended for the benefit of the ancestors, regarded as being in some kind of after-life. This point will be examined in more detail in Chapter 7.
6. The cumbersomeness of such cars undoubtedly on occasion led to accidents in which those hauling a car were crushed by it. Since the annual car festival at the Jagannāth temple at Puri is still one of the most famous of such festivals and certainly was during British rule in India, it led to the term juggernaut (from the Anglo-Indian pronunciation of the deity's name) entering the English language to denote an unwieldly monster.
7. Strictly this is not the eleventh day but the eleventh *tithi*, for the traditional Indian calendar divides the lunar month into thirty *tithis*, which are thus slightly shorter than the solar day to which they are adjusted by complex calculations.
8. In fact pilgrimage in India may well be older still. Certainly, the tradition of pilgrimage to sites associated with the Buddha is found at a very early period, with the emperor Aśoka, for example, recording his visit to the Buddha's birthplace, probably in 248 B.C.
9. Though absent on the whole from Hinduism, this concept of a treasury of merit (established by Christ through the infinite merit of his sacrifice on the cross and added to by the merits of Mary and the saints) and the transfer of merit to devotees is not entirely foreign to the Indian context, since the transfer of merit from Bodhisattvas (who have gained an inexhaustible treasury by their total altruism) to their worshippers forms an important strand in Mahāyāna Buddhism.

5: MEDITATION AND ASCETICISM

1. For a discussion of the way that yogic practice is used for a variety of purposes and at varying levels of importance, see E. J. Lott, *Vision, Tradition, Interpretation: Theology, Religion and the Study of Religion* (Berlin, 1988), pp. 94–96.
2. These lifestyles will be treated more fully in Chapter 6, as part of the system of *varṇāśramadharma*.
3. However, it may be noted that Origen was a firm proponent of a life of prayer, celibacy and austerity, while his doctrine of the fall of the soul and its gradual return to God through asceticism and teaching proved influential in Christian monasticism to the extent that he has been called the 'father of monastic theology'. In any case, the impulse to monasticism and asceticism can plausibly be traced in part to the influence of such Jewish communities as the

Essenes or the practices of John the Baptist, as well as to some facets of St Paul's writings.

4. This summary of Eastern monasticism is mainly based on Nicolas Zernov, *Eastern Christendom: A Study of the Origin and Development of the Eastern Orthodox Church* (London, 1961), pp. 77–80.
5. Incidentally, the problems of succession posed by the charismatic leadership of the founders of monastic orders are again being illustrated in this order, with Mother Teresa recently (September 1990), despite her desire to resign for health reasons, being re-elected as head because the members failed to agree on any successor. The dress of the sisters – a modification of the usual attire of lower-class women in Calcutta – also illustrates the way in which the initial identification of such orders with the poor has been expressed in their dress.
6. These two groups were explicitly compared by Deirdre Green in 'Living between the Worlds: *Bhakti* Poetry and the Carmelite Mystics' in *The Yogi and the Mystic*, ed. Karel Werner (London, 1989), pp. 121–39.
7. I am indebted for the substance of this paragraph to material from my wife, Mary Brockington's study on the motif of the Separating Sword, now in preparation.

6: SOCIAL VALUES AND MORALITY

1. This constitutes, therefore, an exception to the striking statement, made on the basis of the centrality of the Eucharist in Christianity by James Mackey (*Jesus, the Man and the Myth*, p. 149): 'The meal is, of course, ready-made for religious ritual, since it is such a natural sacrament. No other ritual could half as effectively convey to human beings the experience of God as the author of life. There has not been a religion in the history of human kind, nor will there be, to the ritual of which the meal is not of central importance.' Indeed, the development by Sikhism of the institution of communal dining as a deliberate counter to Hindu restrictions on commensality shows how far the reverse is true for Hinduism.
2. The Ravidāsīs belong mainly to the *camār* caste of leather-workers. A similar community is that of the Bālmīkis, who are both a caste (the Punjabi sweeper caste, the *cūhṛās*) and a religious movement, named after Vālmīki, the traditional composer of the *Rāmāyaṇa*, which is installed as the sacred scripture in their places of worship; they show an interesting blend of Hindu and Sikh practices. Problems of acceptability by the rest of the Hindu community are not confined to India. Untouchables who have migrated to Britain are liable to find that other Hindus discriminate against them to such an extent that they feel obliged to establish their own separate community centres or temples, as has been done by Ravidāsīs in Derby, for example, and by Bālmīkis in Coventry, Bedford, Southall and Birmingham.

3. Menstruation seems to have been regarded as more than just pollution, probably because of ideas that after conception the menstrual blood goes to nourish the foetus; these ideas also perhaps underlie the view that the father of a daughter who has reached puberty is guilty of abortion at each menstruation until she marries, and the equivalent view that the husband has a duty of intercourse with his wife at each fertile period. But there are variant views; for example, *Baudhāyana Gṛhyasūtra* 2.2.4 suggests that the temporary impurity of menstruation purifies the woman.
4. For the *satī* to be able to remove impurity properly, she had to be as pure as possible and so the texts prohibit menstruating women or those still impure from childbirth from becoming a *satī*, while she had to have a ritual bath and dress in new clothes to ensure her purity before ascending the pyre. For different reasons, a pregnant wife was barred from becoming a *satī* – in her case because of the inviolability of the unborn child. Incidentally, there are indications that the practice of burning all of a man's personal possessions with him was a widespread Indo-European practice, which Hinduism has retained for the widow alone, thus emphasising her chattel status.
5. For further information, see Burton Stein, 'Social Mobility and Medieval South Indian Hindu Sects' in *Social Mobility in the Caste System in India*, ed. by James Silverberg (1968), pp. 78–94.
6. Probably the oldest presentation of this idea of the three debts is that in *Taittirīya Saṃhitā* 6.3.10.5; it is not, of course, linked there in any way with the concept of the *āśramas*, which only emerges in the period of the post-Vedic Dharmasūtras (roughly the sixth to fourth centuries B.C.).

7: TELEOLOGY: MEANING AND ENDS

1. The term eschatology, literally 'talking about the last things', has in Christian theology traditionally been used to denote examination of the final destiny both of the individual soul and more often of mankind in general. In this sense, its use can readily be extended to Hinduism. Rudolf Bultmann (1884–1976) developed its use to refer to the moment of decision at the start of Christian faith, when an individual puts his trust in God rather than in the things of the world, and to every subsequent occasion on which the individual has to choose decisively between this world and the 'beyond'.
2. The concept of a cycle of rebirth finds a place in Greek thought in Orphism and neo-Platonism (in the latter case, possibly as a result of Indian ideas mediated through Alexandria) and from time to time has surfaced elsewhere within Western thought, for example with the Kabala and with the Doukhobors (a Russian Christian sect originating in the eighteenth century and holding a number of heretical views).
3. A distinction should be drawn between this and fasting to death

as a means of political blackmail, employed for example in the Quit India campaign and imitated sporadically since, notably but briefly by the IRA; such fasting has the advantage that it is slow and so achieves maximum publicity, maximum opportunity for a concession from the authorities and ample time for the faster to change his mind. As a means of protest suicide it is now being replaced in India by brāhman students setting themselves on fire in the manner of Jan Palach in Czechoslovakia or of Buddhist monks in Southeast Asia, as a protest against the dilution of their caste privileges involved in extension of the quota of job reservations for Scheduled Castes.

4. On the other hand, elements in the legends which later clustered round Madhva may well have been borrowed from the Gospels: as a boy he successfully disputed with learned brāhmans in a temple; when he undertook asceticism a voice from heaven proclaimed his greatness; he fed multitudes with handfuls of food; he walked on water and stilled the raging ocean with a glance.
5. Since the Second Vatican Council in particular, however, there have been considerable shifts of attitude towards greater inclusiveness, which will be examined in more detail in Chapter 8.
6. More recently still, for example, but in an African context which may have influenced its form, there is the so-called 'Alice' movement during the 1950s in Zambia (then Northern Rhodesia).

8: CONTACT, CONFLICT AND DIALOGUE

1. For information on the Apostle Thomas and India, see J. F. Fleet, 'St. Thomas and Gondophernes', *Journal of the Royal Asiatic Society* 1905, pp. 223–6, J. N. Farquhar, 'The Apostle Thomas in North India', *Bulletin of the John Rylands Library* 10.1 (Jan. 1926), P. J. Thomas, 'The South Indian Tradition of the Apostle Thomas', *Journal of the Royal Asiatic Society, Centenary Supplement*, 1924, pp. 203–23, and Susan Visvanathan, 'Reconstructions of the past among the Syrian Christians of Kerala', *Contributions to Indian Sociology, New Series*, 20, 1986, pp. 241–60.
2. The hair-tuft is left uncut when the rest of the head is shaved at initiation (so nowadays restricted to traditional brāhmans, but in de Nobili's time adopted by the first three *varṇas*); it is, therefore, in appearance a mirror-image of the tonsure in Roman Catholic monastic orders but has much the same significance. De Nobili was careful to appeal to authority for his policy of adaptation, citing in particular *Decretalia Gregorii IX*, which instructs clerics to adapt to the customs of the people to whom they are preaching.
3. It was eventually published, over a century and a half later in 1867 at Madras, as *Genealogie der Malabarischen Götter* (and an English translation was published a couple of years later). The Danish mission authorities' reaction to such activities was that it was his task to propagate Christianity in India and not Hinduism in Europe.

4. William Ward was responsible for one of the first published studies of Hinduism in *A View of the History, Literature, and Religion of the Hindoos* (Serampore: Mission Press, 1811; 4 vols) which, while expressing some admiration for the philosophical and devotional aspects of Hinduism, adopts a broadly condemnatory approach in line with his evangelical outlook.
5. For an analysis of these two types of strategy and the Hindu reaction, see D. H. Killingley, 'The Hindu Response to Christian Missions in Nineteenth-Century Bengal' in *Changing South Asia: Religion and Society* (London, 1984), pp. 113–24.
6. Between 1866 and 1872, during the earlier part of this series of lectures, Sen was greatly taken with the Unitarian social gospel, which he saw something of at first hand during a visit to Britain in 1870, but completely abandoned after about 1876.
7. It also played a role in encouraging interest in Hinduism in the West; for example, Mme Blavatsky had considerable influence on W. B. Yeats. In a similar fashion, the Vedānta Society, which Vivekānanda established in New York in 1894, proved attractive to writers such as Aldous Huxley and Christopher Isherwood.
8. This claim was in fact erroneous, as Vivekānanda ought really to have known. Presumably he was claiming continuity with the Daśnāmī order reputedly founded by Śaṅkara (traditionally 788–820), since there is no older monastic tradition within Hinduism, although the practice of individual asceticism is of course much older, going back at least to the Upaniṣads. Within India, though, the Buddhist monastic order, the *saṅgha*, was established by the Buddha in the fifth century B.C., while the Jain monastic tradition claims similarly to go back to Mahāvīra at the same period. Even in the Christian tradition, the Orthodox monastic tradition looks back to its ordering by St Basil in the middle of the fourth century. However, this claim is all of a piece with Vivekānanda's general tactic of utilising the lack of precise historical dating for so much of Indian culture to claim greater antiquity and thus originality for everything Hindu.
9. The concept originated with F. D. Maurice but was developed by Farquhar. Farquhar asserted that this was the attitude of Jesus himself to other religions, for each contains a partial revelation of God's will but each is incomplete, and He comes to fulfil them all. More realistically, one might point to an inclusive attitude (such as is characteristic of neo-Hinduism) in Paul's reference to the 'unknown god' of the Athenians and his claim that without knowing it they already worship the God whom he proclaims to them (Acts 17:22–28), a claim that de Nobili explicitly referred to.
10. This is the English translation (SCM Press, London, 1969) of the German *Christ und Hindu in Vrindaban* (Hegner, Köln, 1968).
11. Klaus Klostermaier has put this trenchantly when he states that in some respects ISKCON 'resembles a nineteenth-century British puritanical pietistic movement much more than a typical Hindu

religious movement.' ('Will India's Past be America's Future?', *Journal of Asian and African Studies* 15 (1980) pp. 94–103 (p. 100)).

12. The material on temples and ritual in Britain in this and two subsequent paragraphs is closely based on Kim Knott, 'Other Major Religious Traditions', in *The British: their religious beliefs and practices, 1800–1986*, ed. Terence Thomas (London, 1988), pp. 133–157 (especially pp. 141–2), which provides a convenient summary of her previous publications on the subject.
13. This right-wing Hindu party is achieving considerable publicity in 1990 for its intransigence over insisting on the erection at Ayodhya of the Rāmjanmabhūmi temple to mark the presumed birthplace of Rāma in place of the Bāburi Masjid (the mosque which replaced the earlier Hindu temple in 1528–9); its attitudes to Muslims over this have led to great communal unrest in India and demonstrate that the common stereotype of Hindu tolerance is by no means the whole picture.

Bibliography

The purpose of this bibliography is twofold: to indicate those works, in addition to those cited in footnotes, on which the material of this book is based and to suggest suitable books in which the interested reader may wish to pursue the subject further. Preference has been given to books, as more accessible to most readers, but a few articles are included.

Abhishiktananda [Henri le Saux], *Saccidānanda: a Christian approach to advaitic experience* (Delhi, I.S.P.C.K., 1974).

Anderson, Ray S., *Theology, Death and Dying* (Oxford, Basil Blackwell, 1986).

Arokiasamy, Soosai, *Dharma, Hindu and Christian, according to Roberto de Nobili* (Rome: Editrice Pontificia, 1986).

Babb, Lawrence A., *The Divine Hierarchy: Popular Hinduism in Central India* (New York: Columbia University Press, 1975).

Baird, Robert D. (ed.), *Religion in Modern India*, 2nd edn (New Delhi: Manohar, 1989).

Bebbington, D. W., *The Nonconformist Conscience: Chapel and Politics, 1870–1914* (London: Allen & Unwin, 1982).

Berkouwer, G. C., *The Sacraments* (Grand Rapids, Michigan: Eerdmans, 1969).

Bhardwaj, S. M., *Hindu Places of Pilgrimage in India* (London: University of California Press, 1973).

Bolle, Kees W., *The Persistence of Religion: an essay on Tantrism and Sri Aurobindo's philosophy* (Leiden: E. J. Brill, 1965).

Bowes, Pratima, *The Hindu Religious Tradition, a philosophical approach* (London: Routledge & Kegan Paul, 1978).

Bowker, John, *Problems of Suffering in Religions of the World* (Cambridge: Cambridge University Press, 1970).

Brockington, J. L., *The Sacred Thread: Hinduism in its continuity and diversity* (Edinburgh: Edinburgh University Press, 1981).

Brown, Cheever MacKenzie, *God as mother: a feminine theology of India* (Hartford, Vermont: Claude Stark, 1974).

Brown, W. Norman, *Man in the Universe* (Berkeley: California University Press, 1966).

Burghart, Richard, *Hinduism in Great Britain: The Perpetuation of Religion in an Alien Cultural Milieu* (London: Tavistock Publications, 1987).

Burghart, Richard, and Audrey Cantlie, *Indian Religion* (London: Curzon Press, 1985).

Caplan, Lionel (ed.), *Studies in Religious Fundamentalism* (London: Macmillan, 1987).

Carman, J. B., *The Theology of Rāmānuja* (New Haven: Yale University Press, 1974).

Clothey, Fred W. (ed.), *Images of man: religion and historical process in South Asia* (Madras: New Era, 1982).
Coward, Harold G., Julius J. Lipner, Katherine K. Young, *Hindu Ethics: Purity, Abortion, and Euthanasia* (Albany: SUNY, 1989).
Coward, Harold (ed.), *Hindu-Christian Dialogue: Perspectives and Encounters* (Maryknoll, New York: Orbis Books, 1990).
Cronin, Vincent, *A Pearl to India: The Life of Roberto de Nobili* (London: Rupert Hart-Davis, 1959).
Davies, J. G., *Pilgrimage Yesterday and Today: Why? Where? How?* (London: SCM Press, 1988).
Davies, J. G. (ed.), *A New Dictionary of Liturgy and Worship* (London: SCM Press, 1986).
Deutsch, Eliot, *Advaita Vedānta: a philosophical reconstruction* (Honolulu: East-West Center Press, 1969).
Dhavamony, Mariasusai, *The Love of God according to Śaiva Siddhānta* (Oxford: Clarendon Press, 1971).
———, *Classical Hinduism* (Rome: Università Gregoriana Editrice, 1982).
Dimmit, Cornelia, and J. A. B. van Buitenen, *Classical Hindu Mythology, a reader in the Sanskrit Purāṇas* (Philadelphia: Temple University Press, 1978).
Edwards, David L., *The Last Things Now* (London: SCM Press, 1969).
Eliade, Mircea, *Yoga, Immortality and Freedom*, 2nd edn (London: Routledge & Kegan Paul, 1969).
Fitzgerald, Timothy, 'Hinduism and the "World Religion" Fallacy', *Religion* 20 (1990) pp. 101–18.
Gold, Daniel, *The Lord as Guru: Hindi Sants in North Indian Tradition* (New York: Oxford University Press, 1987).
Griffiths, Bede, *Return to the Centre* (London: Collins, 1976).
Gupta, Sanjukta, D. J. Hoens and T. Goudriaan, *Hindu Tantrism* (Leiden: E. J. Brill, 1979).
Hardy, Friedhelm, *Viraha-bhakti: The early history of Kṛṣṇa devotion in South India* (Delhi: Oxford University Press, 1983).
Hawley, John Stratton, and Mark Juergensmeyer (tr.), *Songs of the Saints of India* (New York: Oxford University Press, 1988).
Hawley, John Stratton, and Donna Marie Wulff, *The Divine Consort: Rādhā and the goddesses of India* (Berkeley: Graduate Theological Union, 1982).
Hein, Norvin, *The Miracle Plays of Mathurā* (New Haven: Yale University Press, 1972).
Hick, John F., *Christianity and Other Religions* (Glasgow: Collins, 1980).
Hiltebeitel, Alf, 'Toward a Coherent Study of Hinduism', *Religious Studies Review* 9 (1983), pp. 206–11.
Jordens, J. T. F., *Dayānanda Sarasvatī: His Life and Ideas* (Delhi, Oxford University Press, 1978).
Kinsley, David R., *The Sword and the Flute: Kālī and Kṛṣṇa* (Berkeley: California University Press, 1975).
———, *Hindu goddesses: Visions of the Divine Feminine in the Hindu Religious Tradition* (Berkeley: University of California Press, 1986).
Klostermaier, Klaus, *Hindu and Christian in Vrindaban* (London: SCM Press, 1969).

——, *Mythologies and Philosophies of Salvation in the Theistic Traditions of India* (Waterloo, Ontario: Wilfred Laurier University Press, 1984).

Kopf, David, *The Brahmo Samaj and the Shaping of the Modern Indian Mind* (Princeton: Princeton University Press, 1978).

Küng, Hans, *Christianity and the World Religions: paths of dialogue with Islam, Hinduism and Buddhism* (London: Collins, 1987).

Laird, M. A., *Missionaries and Education in Bengal, 1793–1837* (Oxford: Clarendon Press, 1972).

Lipner, Julius J., *The Face of Truth: A Study of Meaning and Metaphysics in the Vedāntic Theology of Rāmānuja* (London: Macmillan, 1986).

Lott, Eric J., *Vedantic Approaches to God* (London: Macmillan, 1980).

——, 'The Conceptual Dimensions of Bhakti in the Rāmānuja Tradition', *Scottish Journal of Religious Studies* 2 (1981) pp. 97–114.

Mackey, James P., *Jesus, the Man and the Myth: A Contemporary Christology* (London: SCM Press, 1979).

McKenzie, John L., *The Roman Catholic Church* (London: Weidenfeld and Nicolson, 1969).

Morinis, E. Alan, *Pilgrimage in the Hindu Tradition: A case study of West Bengal* (Delhi: Oxford University Press, 1984).

Narayanan, Vasudha, *The Way and the Goal: Expressions of Devotion in the Early Śrīvaiṣṇava Tradition* (Washington D.C.: Institute for Vaishnava Studies, 1987).

Neill, Stephen Charles, *Christian Faith and Other Faiths*, 2nd edn (London: Oxford University Press, 1970).

——, *Bhakti, Hindu and Christian* (Madras: Christian Literature Society, 1974).

——, *A History of Christianity in India*, 2 vols (Cambridge: Cambridge University Press, 1984–5).

Nicholls, David, *Deity and Domination: Images of God and the State in the Nineteenth and Twentieth Centuries* (London: Routledge, 1989).

O'Flaherty, Wendy Doniger, *Asceticism and Eroticism in the Mythology of Śiva* (London: Oxford University Press, 1973).

——, *The Origins of Evil in Hindu Mythology* (Berkeley: University of California Press, 1976).

Panikkar, Raimundo, *The Unknown Christ of Hinduism* (London: Darton, Longman & Todd, 1964).

——, *The Trinity and World Religions: Icon-Person-Mystery* (Madras: Christian Literature Society, 1970).

——, *The Vedic Experience: Mantramañjarī* (London: Darton, Longman & Todd, 1977).

——, *Myth, Faith and Hermeneutics: Cross-Cultural Studies* (New York: Paulist Press, 1979).

Parrinder, Geoffrey, *Avatar and Incarnation* (London: Faber and Faber, 1970).

——, *The Indestructible Soul: The Nature of Man and Life after Death in Indian Thought* (London: Allen & Unwin, 1973).

——, *Mysticism in the World's Religions* (London: Sheldon Press, 1976).

Paternoster, Michael, *Thou Art There Also: God, Death, and Hell* (London: S.P.C.K., 1967).

Potter, Karl H. (ed.), *Encyclopaedia of Indian Philosophies* (Delhi, Motilal Banarsidass, 1970-).
Radhakrishnan, Sarvepalli, and C. A. Moore, *A Source Book in Indian Philosophy* (Princeton: Princeton University Press, 1957).
Ramanujan, A. K. (tr.), *Speaking of Śiva* (Harmondsworth: Penguin Books, 1973).
Renou, Louis, *Religions of Ancient India* (London: Athlone Press, 1953).
Richards, Glyn, *Towards a Theology of Religions* (London: Routledge, 1989).
Richards, Glyn (ed.), *A Source-book of modern Hinduism* (London: Curzon Press, 1985).
Robinson, John A. T., *Truth is Two-Eyed* (London: SCM Press, 1979).
Schreiner, Peter, 'Roman Catholic Theology and Non-Christian Religion', *Journal of Ecumenical Studies*, 6 (1969), pp. 376–99.
Sharma, Arvind, *Neo-Hindu Views of Christianity* (Leiden: Brill, 1988).
Sharpe, Eric J., *Comparative Religion: A History* (London: Duckworth, 1975).
——, *Faith meets Faith: some Christian attitudes to Hinduism in the nineteenth and twentieth centuries* (London: SCM Press, 1977).
Singer, Milton (ed.), *Krishna: myths, rites and attitudes* (Hawaii: East-West Center Press, 1966).
Smart, R. Ninian, *Doctrine and Argument in Indian Philosophy* (London: Allen & Unwin, 1964).
——, *The Yogi and the Devotee: the interplay between the Upanishads and Catholic theology* (London: Allen & Unwin, 1968).
Sutherland, Stewart, Leslie Houlden, Peter Clarke and Friedhelm Hardy (eds), *The World's Religions* (London: Routledge, 1988).
Thomas, M. M., *The Acknowledged Christ of the Indian Renaissance* (London: SCM Press, 1969).
Thomas, Terence (ed.), *The British: Their Religious Beliefs and Practices, 1800–1986* (London: Routledge, 1988).
Tiwari, Kapil N. (ed.), *Suffering: Indian Perspectives* (Delhi: Motilal Banarsidass, 1986).
Toon, Peter, and James D. Spiceland (eds), *One God in Trinity* (London: Samuel Bagster, 1980).
Werner, Karel, *Yoga and Indian Philosophy* (Delhi: Motilal Banarsidass, 1977).
Werner, Karel (ed.), *The Yogi and the Devotee: Studies in Indian and Comparative Mysticism* (London: Curzon Press, 1989).
Whale, J. S., *The Protestant Tradition* (Cambridge: Cambridge University Press, 1955).
Whaling, Frank, *Christian Theology and World Religions: A Global Approach* (Basingstoke: Marshall Pickering, 1986).
Whaling, Frank (ed.), *The World's Religious Traditions: Current Perspectives in Religious Studies* (Edinburgh: T. & T. Clark, 1984).
Wynne, Edward A., *Traditional Catholic Religious Orders: Living in Community* (New Brunswick: Transaction Books, 1988).
Young, Richard Fox, *Resistant Hinduism: Sanskrit sources on anti-Christian Apologetics in early nineteenth-century India* (Vienna: Institut für Indologie, 1981).
Zaehner, R. C., *Hinduism* (London: Oxford University Press, 1962).

Zaehner, R. C. (ed.), *Hindu Scriptures* (London: J. M. Dent, 1966).
Zernov, Nicolas, *Eastern Christendom: A Study of the Origin and Development of the Eastern Orthodox Church* (London: Weidenfeld and Nicolson, 1961).

Index